"Rarely do experts on calling urge people t̲ is shaped by race, gender, class, and much more. In honest, profound, and biblically informed prose, Susan Maros opens up a whole new horizon on calling, revealing its complexity and brilliantly translating complicated concepts into everyday language so that all of us can grapple with vocation in more culturally sensitive and faithful ways. An invaluable addition to literature on calling!"

Bonnie J. Miller-McLemore, E. Rhodes and Leona B. Carpenter Chair and Professor of Religion, Psychology, and Culture, emerita, Vanderbilt University, and coeditor of *Calling All Years Good: Christian Vocation Throughout Life's Seasons*

"Before the end of the introduction you will discover why Dr. Susan Maros is one of Fuller Seminary's most respected and popular professors. By the end of the book, you will realize that almost all your assumptions about how God calls a person will be challenged. Filled with biblical reflections that will cause you to reconsider what you think you know, and stories and studies that will encourage you to rethink what you believe to be settled about the way vocation is formed, this book disturbs and deconstructs, and then provides wisdom and a way for reconstructing perhaps the most personal moments in a Christian's life. I heartily recommend it."

Tod Bolsinger, Fuller Seminary and the De Pree Center for Leadership, author of *Canoeing the Mountains*

"How we talk about things matters, and how we address the subject of calling and vocation matters in its proper context. This work by Susan Maros is a much-needed text to help us understand how social location informs and shapes our understanding and experience of what calling and vocation actually mean. This meaning making allows the reader to step out of their own social location and create connection to a greater community seeking to honor the God who calls in their lives and their work. This is a formational text for scholars, practitioners, pastors, and workers in the global field."

Joy E. A. Qualls, associate dean of the Division of Communication at Biola University

"In *Calling in Context* Susan Maros counters the popular notion of vocation as an individual's calling discovered outside of time and place with a fresh, communal understanding that is grounded in God's action in the world and discerned in the midst of personal intersections and diverse experiences. Claiming vocational discernment is contextual and lifelong, Maros seeks to deepen awareness and awakening unconscious assumptions by inviting readers into a reflective process. Well written with personal stories, rich connections to Scripture, and challenging reflection questions, this book is a great resource for Christian leaders as it recognizes the importance of social location and directly addresses the impact racial-ethnic-cultural identity, socioeconomic status, sex/gender, power, and privilege play in vocation."

Terri Martinson Elton, professor of leadership at Luther Seminary

"Creatively critical, *Calling in Context* fills a much-needed space in the literature on Christian vocation, engaging ways in which gender, racial and ethnic identity, economic status, and social class shape people's vocational possibilities and practices of discernment. The book challenges individualist and idealist assumptions present in dominant North American understandings of vocation, inviting readers into richer conversation and vocational practice that is more attuned to the variety of ways in which vocation is experienced globally, more faithful to the range of biblical narratives of vocation, and more attentive to God's interaction with human beings over time."

Jane Lancaster Patterson, professor emerita of New Testament at Seminary of the Southwest, Austin, Texas, and director of the Communities of Calling Initiative at the Collegeville Institute

SUSAN L. MAROS

CALLING

IN

CONTEXT

SOCIAL LOCATION AND
VOCATIONAL FORMATION

Academic
An imprint of InterVarsity Press
Downers Grove, Illinois

InterVarsity Press
P.O. Box 1400, Downers Grove, IL 60515-1426
ivpress.com
email@ivpress.com

InterVarsity Press® is the book-publishing division of InterVarsity Christian Fellowship/USA®, a movement
of students and faculty active on campus at hundreds of universities, colleges, and schools of nursing in the
United States of America, and a member movement of the International Fellowship of Evangelical Students.
For information about local and regional activities, visit intervarsity.org.

Scripture quotations, unless otherwise noted, are from the New Revised Standard Version Bible, copyright
© 1989 National Council of the Churches of Christ in the United States of America. Used by permission.
All rights reserved worldwide.

While any stories in this book are true, some names and identifying information may have been changed
to protect the privacy of individuals.

Figure 1: Geordie Bosanko, Mercator Projection image, https://commons.wikimedia.org/wiki/File:Mercator
_Projection.svg (Creative Commons License CC BY-SA 3.0, https://creativecommons.org/licenses/by-sa/3.0)
Figure 2: Mike Linksvayer, Peters Project, black.png image, https://commons.wikimedia.org/wiki/File:Peters
_projection,_black.png, public domain.
Figure 3: CaseyPenk, Vardion, blank map world south up.png image, https://commons.wikimedia.org/wiki
/File:Blank-map-world-south-up.png, public domain.

Cover design and image composite: David Fassett
Interior design: Jeanna Wiggins
Images: path through trees © mel-nik / iStock / Getty Images Plus
        blueprint pattern © Yobro10 / iStock / Getty Images Plus

ISBN 978-1-5140-0144-8 (print)
ISBN 978-1-5140-0145-5 (digital)

Printed in the United States of America ♾

Library of Congress Cataloging-in-Publication Data
Names: Maros, Susan Lynn, 1966- author.
Title: Calling in context : social location and vocational formation /
    Susan L. Maros.
Description: Downers Grove, IL : IVP Academic, [2022] | Includes
    bibliographical references and index.
Identifiers: LCCN 2021047366 (print) | LCCN 2021047367 (ebook) | ISBN
    9781514001448 (print) | ISBN 9781514001455 (digital)
Subjects: LCSH: Vocation—Christianity. | Christianity—United States.
Classification: LCC BV4740 .M245 2022 (print) | LCC BV4740 (ebook) | DDC
    248.4—dc23/eng/20211001
LC record available at https://lccn.loc.gov/2021047366
LC ebook record available at https://lccn.loc.gov/2021047367

P	25	24	23	22	21	20	19	18	17	16	15	14	13	12	11	10	9	8	7	6	5	4	3	2	1
Y	38	37	36	35	34	33	32	31	30	29	28	27	26	25	24	23	22								

To my students—my faithful teachers

CONTENTS

ACKNOWLEDGMENTS

Writing this book was often a solitary process but one that could not have happened without the support and engagement of many people. My academic community has been an important space for me to process my thinking and continue learning. Thanks to my colleagues in the Office of Vocation and Formation, particularly Brenda Bertrand, Harmony Halley, Tracey Stringer, and Julie Tai, each of whom gave me important feedback in the initial stages of writing. Thanks also to faculty colleagues Scott Cormode, Erin Dufault Hunter, and Brad Strawn, who read drafts at various stages and gave constructive feedback and encouragement. My appreciation to students who interacted with drafts of this book, particularly the participants in Practices of Vocational Formation, a number of who had the courage to critique the professor's writing.

To my Facebook reading group—Elisa Blethen, Shelly Burkhalter, Heather Card, Christa Lopez, and Gretchen Salbaach—knowing I owed you chapters helped me persist through some hard writing days. Special thanks to Birgit Herppich, companion in writing since my PhD studies, who read the *whole* of the book, some chapters multiple times. I value your companionship on this journey.

Pastor Marcos and Dr. Andrea Canales, Pastor Rosa Ramirez, and the church family of La Fuente Ministries provided a faith community in which to continue to listen to the stories of people from backgrounds similar to and different from my own. You nourish my soul as we together listen to the story of God in the Bible and discern how God is inviting us to participate with the Spirit's work in the world.

Thanks to my editor, Jon Boyd, the anonymous peer reviewers, and the editorial staff of IVP. Your critiques and questions made this a stronger book.

To my family, who like other authors' families, bear most of the cost of long hours of writing and constant references to the material, thank you for sharing this journey with me and keeping my feet on the ground. Particular thank you to my folks, Roger and Esther Schrage, for support and multiple readings; to our emerging adults, Joshua and Ashe, for keeping my feet on the ground; and to my husband, Edward, for being my companion on the journey and my soft place to land.

And, finally, thanks to all the people who have shared their stories with me over the years with special thanks to Phil Allen, Jean Burch, Kutter Calloway, Daniel Cheung, Joyce del Rosario, Rob Dixon, David Douglas, Tony Dunn, Laura Gordon, Christa Lopez, Inés Velásquez-McBryde, Jude Tiersma Watson, and Cassie Williams-Dymers who generously gave permission for their stories, told in their own words, to be included in this book.

INTRODUCTION

*For we are God's handiwork, created in Christ Jesus to do good
works, which God prepared in advance for us to do.*

EPHESIANS 2:10 NIV

"WE ARE GOD'S MASTERPIECE," begins Ephesians 2:10 in the New
Living Translation. God is a master artisan; human beings, collectively
and individually, are an expression of God's creative power. Who we are
is being formed by God across a lifetime of experience. What we do, how
we perceive and engage with God's activity in the world, flows out of who
we are and who God is making us to be. When we seek to identify our
callings, we are, at a fundamental level, seeking to understand God's
transformational work in our lives—to recognize who we are created to
be and discern the Spirit's invitation to participation in God's work in
the world.

A primary assumption I bring to the writing of this book is that God
is dynamically engaged in the universe God created, constantly forming,
shaping, healing, and transforming lives—yours, and the lives of the
people around you. Simply put, the Spirit is always fundamentally present
and active. Sometimes we recognize this activity and cooperate with it;
other times we cannot recognize that it is God's activity, or we recognize
it but either don't understand it or resist the transformation. This book

is, in a sense, an invitation to reflection; my hope is that you will come to identify the fingerprints of the Artist in your life—both by renewing a recognition you have already experienced and seeing God's activity in ways you'd not noticed before.

My own sense of calling centers around engagement with developing leaders, especially interacting with women and men in a way that facilitates their capacity to discern God's work in their lives and respond. For the last twenty-five years, higher education has been a significant location of that work. From time to time, I have had a student comment, "You are clearly called to be a professor." I would say my call is to the formation of God's people; being a professor has been a main role through which I live out that calling.

One of the joys of my life is to see my students grow and flourish in their unique callings. I feel deeply honored when my engagement in their lives has been helpful for their formation. This is my hope and my intention at all times. I am human, however, and still under development. Sometimes the impact of my work is different from my intention. Let me tell you the story of one such instance and then tell you why this experience, and others like it, has led to writing this book.

ARIANA'S STORY

I can still picture Ariana's face and where she sat in the classroom.[1] This young Latina undergraduate was the kind of student who brings out the best in a teacher—bright-eyed, eager to learn, intelligent, and inquiring. I was glad, then, when she joined a ministry I was part of and I had the opportunity to get to know her better as we labored side by side. I thought very highly of Ariana, both as a developing Christian leader and as an emerging academic. I hoped I was interacting with her in a way that helped her develop into the person God had created her to be. I wanted to see Ariana flourish in her calling.

---

[1]My thanks to Ariana Salazar for her willingness to allow me to tell something of her story from the perspective of my encounter with her.

Ariana graduated from my institution and headed across the country to a prestigious graduate program. I was so proud of her. The administration of our school was proud too. I heard our dean say, on more than one occasion, "Our graduates are accepted into such-and-such a school." Her hard work and gifts brought luster to our community.

While Ariana was in graduate school, she became involved with other people of color at the institution. I listened, from a distance, as she articulated a sense of her distinctive racial-ethnic-cultural identity.[2] She used her gifts as an orator to advocate for equity and inclusion. I saw Ariana's flame burn brightly and I rejoiced.

I continued to follow Ariana's development over the subsequent years. She finished her master's and then went on to pursue a PhD at yet another prestigious institution. She took up a position at a well-known organization. I continued to feel delighted at her academic and professional development. Here was the bright, dynamic, passionate young woman maturing into a bright, dynamic, passionate professional woman.

During this time, I encountered a piece of spoken-word poetry Ariana had posted online. In this piece, she reflected on her life and her experiences as a woman of color. Although she didn't name names, Ariana's description of our shared context was clear. She talked about the racial and gender hierarchy that demonstrated preference for the White male students. She lamented the power religious indoctrination had in teaching her to hate ethnic identity. She concluded her reflection on her experience in our shared space by saying, "I got broken there."[3]

My intention had been to help Ariana develop into the person God had called her to be. Ariana's spoken-word piece told me she experienced me, along with my colleagues, as diminishing and denigrating her identity and her sense of calling. Watching the spoken-word poem for the first time broke my heart.

---

[2]For a comment on the use of *racial-ethnic-cultural identity* terms, see "Race and Ethnicity: A Brief Overview" in chapter four.

[3]Ariana Salazar-Newton, "Processing My Past: A Poem by Ariana Salazar-Newton," January 1, 2015, YouTube video, 11:52, https://youtu.be/an6GH6tftjc.

As I look back on this experience, I find my reaction instructive. I felt wounded because I thought so highly of Ariana and celebrated her every accomplishment. I assumed her experience of me would reflect my intentions toward her. My hurt, at least initially, was less about realizing the ways in which my colleagues and I had collectively facilitated a wounding context and more about my personal sense of offense. It took time for me to process the shift in perspective provoked by a new understanding of Ariana's experience.

Sometime after watching her spoken-word piece, I sat on an airplane on the way back from a leadership conference reading Michael Emerson and Christian Smith's seminal book, *Divided by Faith*.[4] As they unfolded for me the difference in perspectives between White and Black evangelical Christians around issues of race,[5] I saw myself with new eyes. I realized that I had adopted and practiced well-intentioned, White, evangelical, individualistic views of race and class. In the voices of the White Christians in the book, I heard my own voice with new clarity.

The Holy Spirit used Emerson and Smith to speak deep, deep conviction in my soul. I sat in my seat at 35,000 feet with tears streaming down my face. I thought of Ariana and all the other students of color who had come through my classroom. How many people had felt unseen, unheard, disregarded, and disrespected? How many others had I been complicit in hurting like Ariana? God only knows.

In the years prior to watching Ariana's spoken-word piece, I was passionately convinced that each person is God's masterpiece, uniquely formed for a distinctive place of participation in God's work in the world. I still believe this. Indeed, this conviction is at the foundation of this book. However, at the time Ariana was my student, my understanding of that distinctiveness reflected my background and

---

[4]Michael O. Emerson and Christian Smith, *Divided by Faith: Evangelical Religion and the Problem of Race in America* (New York: Oxford University Press, 2000).
[5]Emerson and Smith focus particularly on the Black/White binary in the United States in this text. In other books, they each address different aspects of racialized experience in the United States. See, for example, Michael O. Emerson, Jenifer L. Bratter, and Sergio R. Chávez, eds., *(Un)Making Race and Ethnicity: A Reader* (New York: Oxford University Press, 2017).

experience. I assumed all people are made in the image of God and gave very little thought to how social identities are part of God's unique formation of each person. Ariana's poem was a God-ordained invitation to deeper transformation.

NAMING MY "COME FROM"

When I write about calling, I do so from the perspective of a particular context and a distinctive set of experiences. I write as a White, US-American, cisgender, middle-class, highly educated woman from a conservative evangelical Christian background.

> ### ▶ NAVIGATION POINT
> **US-American**
>
> I use the term *US-American* throughout this book to clearly identify when I am talking about citizens of the United States. The more common, popular term, *America,* is the name of two continents—North America and South America. Technically, everyone in the Americas—Canadians and Mexicans, Brazilians and Costa Ricans, Guatemalans and El Salvadorians, and so forth—is American.
>
> I specify US-American as an identifier and the United States as a context because this is a significant part of my social location and the social location of many of my students and colleagues. I also endeavor to avoid expressing experiences from this context as if they are normative for people from other parts of the world.

I name something of my social location to acknowledge that I have a specific "come from" that influences what I see as important and how I present what I see. Working in academia, I've been shaped by a social context that assumes objectivity is not only desirable but actually attainable. Personal stories are frowned on as being too subjective; some scholars go so far as to refer to personal stories as "me-search" instead of research.[6] I have come to realize, though, that objectivity is ultimately

---

[6]Thanks to Ariana Salazar for the suggestion of this phrasing in our personal communication.

humanly impossible. I always have a perspective; every person has a perspective from which they see the world. The point is not to try to rid myself of the particularities of my perspective but to be conscious of and name those particularities.

I find missiologist Paul Hiebert's framing of what he referred to as the "naïve realist" and the "critical realist" to be helpful.[7] The naive realist sees reality as $r = R$, believing that "what I see as reality *is* reality. The two are identical." The critical realist sees reality as $r \sim R$, believing that "my reality is one perspective on reality. I see a part. I do not see the whole of reality." Note that the critical realist's position is different from a complete relativist, who would say, "There is no reality, only perception." I approach the subject of calling and of the impact of social location on our vocational formation as a critical realist, assuming there is both Reality and my sense of reality. I recognize I have perspectives that have been formed by my life experience that differ from other people's perspectives.

My thinking about the impact of social location on vocational formation began in the context of my work as an educator. I noticed the effects of theological environments first. As I sought to facilitate students' discernment and articulation of their sense of God's call on their lives, I became aware that many of my Pentecostal and charismatic students seemed to expect calling to be a vivid experience of direct communication from God. They didn't share the theological assumptions of authors writing about calling who came from more Reformed perspectives emphasizing God's quiet, sovereign, providential work.

My efforts to understand my students' particular concerns and experiences led me to work on a PhD, researching how people process their sense of calling. I was privileged to do this work in a multinational cohort. Early on in my studies a Malaysian colleague, Siew Pik Lim, having patiently listened to me grapple with a literature review on vocation, commented to me, "I don't like to read vocational books written

---

[7]Paul G. Hiebert, *Anthropological Reflections on Missiological Issues* (Grand Rapids, MI: Baker Books, 1994), 19-34. See also Hiebert's seminal article "Critical Contextualization," *International Bulletin of Missionary Research* 11, no. 3 (1987): 104-12.

in the United States; they're too American." This offhanded comment surprised and unsettled me. "Too American?" *Isn't calling universal?* I wondered. *Doesn't this concept apply to all people everywhere? Aren't authors writing from a biblical/theological perspective and, therefore, writing about something that applies to everyone?*

I began listening carefully to calling stories from people who come from a variety of nations. That listening provoked me to attend to my US-American students with fresh ears as well, and to think about their diversity. They come from all over the United States, bringing their regional differences with them into the classroom. They come from a wide range of theological traditions, with differing perspectives shaped by those traditions. I also began to think deeply about race and ethnicity. As I listened and read, I began to see how the racialized experience of life in the United States shapes our assumptions about calling and experiences with vocational formation.

It is my deep desire to facilitate the telling of and the attending to stories of our experiences with God. As I come to understand my own identity as situated in a specific context, I am better able to articulate my story. As I come to understand my identity grounded in a particular social location, I am better able to hear the distinctives of the stories of brothers and sisters I'm in conversation with, both those who have similar identities to my own and those who tell their stories from a situated experience different from my own. As I hear the stories of people not like me and appreciate the work of God in their lives, seeing the image of God expressed in them and through them in ways marked by the Spirit, I live into the vision of Revelation 7:9: a church made up of people from every tribe and tongue and nation—and men and women and every socioeconomic status—standing before the throne of God.

INVITATION TO A REFLECTIVE JOURNEY

I assume if you are reading this book that it is because, in some way, you are asking the question, "What is my calling?" You may be interested for yourself, seeking to discern your place of participation in

God's work in the world. You may also be interested for people with whom you work, seeking to help individuals in the process of discernment and formation.

I write from a distinctively White, US-American, evangelical perspective. Even as my perspective has shifted because of the interactions I have had with people who experience the world differently from me, I still demonstrate the formation of my background. I hope by naming my "come from," and encouraging you to think about yours, to set a large table at which people from diverse contexts and backgrounds can listen to the stories of their sisters and brothers in Christ, articulate their own stories, and have their stories heard and honored.

To my White readers, particularly those who, like me, come from conservative, evangelical backgrounds: you may find some elements of this work challenging. One of the reasons I share as much of my own story as I do is to express my sense of being a fellow sojourner. I too am in the process of lifelong formation. My prayer is that you will perceive the invitation of the Spirit to step into a new awareness of God's diverse, creative work.

To my BIPOC readers: students, friends, and colleagues of color have taught me that their own identity development is complex and dynamic with distinctive blessings and challenges. Much of what I explain in this text, particularly around social location, may be familiar to you from your lived experience. My hope is that these explanations will offer terminology that will assist you in having more fruitful discussions with people in your social context. I also hope that you will be welcomed to tell your story and that your story will be heard on its own terms.

> **NAVIGATION POINT**
White, Black, and BIPOC

Throughout this text, I use the term *White* to identify persons who, like me, are of northern European descent. In general, I use *Black* as the identifier for persons of African descent unless they use a different term for themselves or their social group. I use the term *Black, Indigenous, person of color (BIPOC)* or *person of color* to generally reference individuals who do not identify as White.

I recognize that self-referential terms shift with time. I also recognize that no racial-ethnic-cultural group is monolithic in terms of their preferred self-referencing identifier. I have endeavored to retain the terms used by authors and by the individuals who have shared their calling stories.

The metaphor of life as a journey is a concept with deep biblical roots. We are walking in the footsteps of Abraham, who was called by God in Ur of the Chaldeans to get up and go to a land he would be shown. We walk alongside Moses as he wandered the back side of the desert, keeping a motley group of former slaves alive on the way to the Promised Land. We walk behind Joshua, who called the priests to put their feet in the floodwaters of the Jordan and the army to walk around a city in silence. We walk with Esther in fear and trembling as she stood before a king who had sentenced her people to death. We walk with Saul on his way to Damascus, certain of his righteous anger. Over and over, God told people to go to places, meet people, and do impossible, even ridiculous, things. Over and over, God's people encountered God on the road.

In this book, I offer a space to reflect on the journey with an invitation to take a good look at the contexts you have experienced thus far in your life. I do so with these two deep convictions: that God has been walking with you, utilizing your context to shape you, for the entirety of your life, and that, in pausing to reflect, you will see God's fingerprints on your life with greater clarity.

I bring a set of theological convictions to this conversation. These principles undergird every part of this book. I offer them here for your consideration and to identify a common point of departure for our journey.

> ➤ God is at work in the world.

> ➤ God invites us, as children of God and co-heirs with Christ, to participate with God's work in the world.

➤ God calls us as communities of people; God calls us as individuals within those communities.

➤ The distinctive characteristics of our communities are based in God's creative work; these particularities are part of the foundational formation of our lives through the work of the Spirit.

➤ As followers of Jesus, we seek to discern God's transforming work in our own lives and in our communities.

➤ Storytelling is an essential part of how we articulate our understanding of the nature of our unique individual and communal responses to God's calling.

The first section of the book lays out a theoretical framework that demonstrates how vocational narratives are shaped by the contexts in which we are embedded. These three chapters are about naming some common assumptions that shape how we think about calling. The second section explores three areas of social location—racial-ethnic-cultural identity, socioeconomic status or class, and gender—considering how our identities influence the identification and development of calling. The third section suggests themes that offer a context for intercultural and intersectional conversations about calling. Throughout this book, I include calling stories that have been contributed by students, friends, and colleagues. My intention is to offer their stories told in their own words as a model of a key spiritual practice: listening. Each chapter also includes a Bible study and questions for reflection. My hope is that these exercises might be useful for thinking deeply into God's work in your life.

Welcome, fellow sojourner. Let us walk for a while on this road together.

PART 1

MAPS, THEORETICAL FRAMEWORKS, AND "YOU ARE HERE"

When we navigate a city using a digital map on our phones or when we use a posted map in a large space such as a shopping mall, we need to have a sense of where we are before we can figure out how to navigate to where we need to go. We know to look for the "you are here" marker on the mall diagram or for that blue dot on our digital maps. This first section of the book seeks to orient us to the "you are here" of our vocational development at this moment in time.

> **NAVIGATION POINT**
> **Calling, Vocation, and Vocational Formation**

I use the terms *calling* and *vocation* somewhat interchangeably in this text. The popular understanding of *vocation* tends to focus on a career or occupation. However, the word comes from the Latin word *vocare*, which means "to call." Theologically, calling and vocation are synonyms. I use the phrase "vocational formation" to reference the process of being equipped and sustained in a lifetime journey of faithful participation in God's work in the world.

In this section, I lay out foundational concepts, exploring some common elements in how Christians in the United States think about calling and the process of vocational formation. The first chapter introduces a key idea for the text—social location—and a central metaphor: maps. The second chapter investigates elements of biblical content related to calling, considering how our cultural maps affect how we approach the Bible and what we see in the calling stories we most commonly reference. The third chapter explores the nature of vocational formation as a lifelong process by reflecting on useful perspectives from developmental psychology.

All of this work is intended to help us name our current locations, both literally in terms of the communities and social groups where we live and figuratively in terms of where we are in the process of discerning and developing in our callings. God is already present and already at work in our lives. My prayer is that you will reflect on this content in such a way that you are able to perceive with greater clarity the presence of God in your circumstances.

"WHAT IS MY CALLING?" AND OTHER PROBLEMATIC MAPS

The place God calls you to is the place where your deep
gladness and the world's deep hunger meet.

FREDERICK BUECHNER, *WISHFUL THINKING*

"YES, BUT WHAT IS MY CALLING?"

Dante was a man in his early thirties working as a counselor in a program for at-risk youth. Many nights he could be found out on the streets, engaging the teens he encountered with a winsome evangelistic presence. Dante had a deep love for God and for people, particularly young people on the margins of society. His passion was evident and he clearly demonstrated giftedness and skill in this work. Yet Dante wondered about his calling.

Dante's question "What is my calling?" came in the context of an intense classroom discussion about the ways God works through life experiences to shape a person's sense of calling. The discussion followed an assignment—an exercise intended to help a person think through their life experiences and what those experiences suggest about God's purposes in their lives.[1] Dante had a long list of experiences in which he saw

---

[1]The "Destiny Log" exercise was from the work of J. Robert (Bobby) Clinton, longtime professor of leadership at Fuller Theological Seminary. See the "destiny processing" content in J. Robert

God at work in his life. Many of them were part of the series of experiences that led Dante to the ministry he was currently engaged in and to the decision to return to school for further training. Yet somehow this was not enough for Dante to feel he "knew" his calling. "I'm encouraged to see, in writing, all the events and ways in which God has been active," Dante said. "But I still want to know: What is my calling?"

What was the gap for Dante? Given that he was already engaged in ministry and that he was able to name experiences that demonstrated God's leading to that place, why did Dante still wonder about his calling? Why were the experiences Dante identified insufficient to create a narrative of calling?

Dante was one of the many emerging and developing Christian leaders I worked with in a quarter-century as a professor in undergraduate and graduate education. My focus has been the formation of individual leaders: helping women and men discern God's distinctive formation in their lives and the particular place of invitation to participation in God's work in the world. Some of these emerging leaders were traditional college students in the early stages of figuring out what they wanted to do with their lives. Many were adult learners with significant life experience. For some of these individuals, assignments like the one Dante engaged in helped them identify and articulate their sense of call. For many others, though, the response was like Dante's: "That was an encouraging exercise. But what is my calling?"

Over the years, I watched people go from book to book, workshop to seminar, counseling session to prayer session, class to class, seeking to know their calling. The search is often full of anxiety. I see many people struggle and question themselves, even when they, like Dante, are already meaningfully engaged in some area of work or ministry. They seek to have some clear method, some strategy for being assured that they know their calling. They fear missing God. They fear choosing wrongly. They fear making decisions that will result in a wasted life. They fear purposelessness.

Clinton, *Leadership Emergence Theory: A Self-Study Manual for Analyzing the Development of a Christian Leader* (Altadena, CA: Barnabas Publishers, 1989).

FRAMING LENSES OF VOCATION

A number of unspoken assumptions undergird the question, "What is my calling?" These assumptions have to do with who God is, who we are as God's people, and how God relates to us and to the world. They also have to do with what constitutes a Christian sense of calling and whether or not calling and vocation are the same thing or two different but related things.

The challenge with engaging assumptions is that assumptions are largely unconscious. We don't know what we assume. Until some experience comes along to show otherwise, we usually don't even know that we have assumptions. Or we may know, in principle, that we have assumptions but we cannot name them. They are like the 90 percent of the iceberg that lies underwater, present but hidden from our sight.

In the early 1990s, I was on the staff of a training program with a mission organization. We hosted groups of participants from multiple countries who were living, working, and studying together for six months at a time. During the first week, while everyone was still excited about meeting new people from all over the world, we divided the participants into small, diverse groups and gave them a task to do together. The assignment was to name whether, in their church context and in their broader social context, each item on a list of activities was considered an acceptable behavior or not. We told the groups that the purpose of the discussion was not to debate the rightness of the activity; it was simply to name how their church or their community viewed that activity.

One activity on our list inevitably generated a lot of conversation: hunting. The US-Americans in the group often seemed puzzled as to why we included hunting on the list. They thought it was a random activity to mention. The Europeans in the group often expressed surprise that their US-American colleagues didn't immediately see how "wrong" it is to kill animals for sport. It became clear that the US-Americans had one set of assumptions and the Europeans another, and both had cultural and theological values that shaped their assumptions. The goal of the exercise was to bring the assumptions to the surface and make them discussable.

From that point we were able to introduce a mantra that became very important in later stages of the development of the group: "different, but not wrong."

"Different, but not wrong" applies to the discussion of vocation as well. I, as an educator and scholar, hold a set of assumptions about calling. You, as the reader, hold a set of assumptions too. Some of our assumptions are shared and others are different. My purpose in this book is not to attempt to replace your "wrong" assumptions with my "right" assumptions. Instead, my purpose is to offer reflections and a set of skills that foster our capacity to be aware of and examine our assumptions about vocation. The issue is less about what assumptions are "wrong" or "right" and more about considering what assumptions are helpful for pursuing a life of faithful engagement with God's work in the world and what assumptions hinder that engagement.

We turn now to a central metaphor of this book: maps. Looking at maps can illustrate the power of assumptions as well as help us take a first pass at what "different, but not wrong" and "helpful versus hindering" mean for thinking about calling.

WORLD MAPS: AN ANALOGY

I love maps. On family road trips when I was a child, I would sit in the car with the road atlas, tracing the route of our journey, watching the landmarks go by. As an adult, I became interested in world maps and have collected world maps from different countries during my travels. Let me share several of my favorite maps with you.

The world map in figure 1 utilizes the Mercator projection, a cylindrical projection developed by Flemish cartographer and father of modern mapmaking, Gerardus Mercator (1512–1595), in the mid-sixteenth century.[2] Mercator was a maker of scientific instruments and terrestrial and celestial globes who became interested in problems experienced by European marine navigators. Mariners could find themselves

---

[2]For more on Mercator's life and faith, see Ann Heinrichs, *Gerardus Mercator: Father of Modern Mapmaking* (Minneapolis, MN: Compass Point Books, 2007).

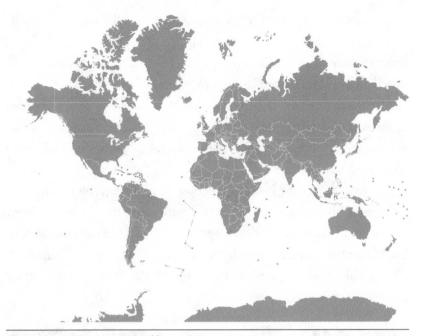

Figure 1. Mercator projection world map

hundreds of miles off course because a constant direction at sea did not match a straight line on their charts. Mercator's solution was to devise a map designed around longitudinal (north-south) lines, increasing the latitude (east-west) lines in such a way that a constant direction at sea could be recorded as a straight line on the map. Together with the development of the magnetic compass and the use of the northern pole star, Polaris, this Mercator's projection became the standard map used by northern European seafaring navigators. This map was adopted as a standard world map and used commonly in many contexts, including US-American school rooms, through the twentieth century.

Notice that the midpoint—top to bottom—on this map goes straight through northern Europe. The equator—the actual, physical midpoint on the globe—is located almost three-quarters down the image, making the northern hemisphere more than twice as large as the southern hemisphere. One of the ways to see the distortion of land masses caused by this choice is to compare Greenland and Australia. Greenland is the large mass at the top center-left of the map. Australia is the largest landmass on the bottom-right. In this projection, Greenland looks like it is several times the size of Australia, whereas in reality, Greenland is more than three and a half times *smaller* than Australia.

Also notice the size of Europe on the Mercator projection compared to the size of Africa. Measuring north to south, they appear to be approximately the same length. Now take a look at Europe and Africa on the map in figure 2.

Figure 2 utilizes the Peters projection. Arno Peters (1916–2002) was a German historian who, concerned with what he saw as the Eurocentric bias of common world maps, developed a new equal-area map, likely based on an earlier map by Scottish clergyman, James Gall (1808–1895).[3] This equal-area projection depicts the landmasses in their correct relative sizes.

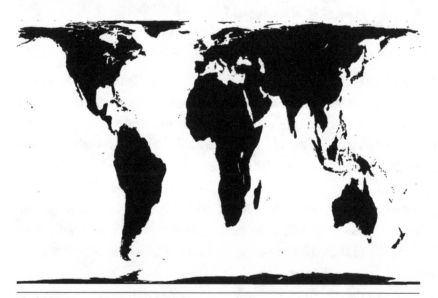

Figure 2. Peters projection world map

---

[3]There was some controversy as to the origins and design of Peters's map. For a summary of this debate among cartographers, see Jeremy Crampton, "Cartography's Defining Moment: The Peters Projection Controversy, 1974–1990," *Cartographica: The International Journal for Geographic Information and Geovisualization* 31, no. 4 (1994): 16-32.

One comment I hear about this map is "It's stretched out." The Peters projection retains accurate relative area of landmasses, correcting the distortion of the Mercator projection in that regard, but doing so by introducing a distortion in the *shape* of those masses. For many of us, used to seeing the world from the perspective of a Mercator projection map, this distortion is very noticeable. Meanwhile, we don't notice the distortion of the Mercator projection because that map has been the familiar and normative projection for much of our lives.

Notice how much larger Africa is on the Peters projection map compared to Europe. One response I've often heard when showing this map is the question, "Is Africa really that big?" The unspoken assumption for some US-Americans is that Africa is, perhaps, the size of the United States. In reality, Africa is large enough to fit the United States, China, India, Mexico, and many European countries combined inside it. Notice, too, the location of the equator on this map. Whereas in the Mercator project map, the equator is far down on the image, the Peters projection puts the equator at the vertical center. The "northern hemisphere bias" of the Mercator projection is one reason why the Peters projection has gradually been replacing the Mercator projection as a world map, supported and promoted by a variety of educational and religious organizations concerned with the implications of map design on how developing nations are viewed.[4]

Continuing to keep in mind the idea of a map in our heads, consider figure 3. Sometimes when I show people this map, they spontaneously comment, "It's upside-down!" To this I respond with, "Says who?" The tradition of having north at the top of maps was a development of northern European cartographers, such as Gerardus Mercator, who created maps for use by northern European ship navigators. The use of the magnetic compass and the northern pole star, Polaris, for navigation made the orientation of north at the top a sensible adaptation. (Many earlier European maps put the East at the top.) We continue to put north

---

[4]For a discussion of the impact of the adoption of particular world maps, see chapter four in Hannah Higgins, *The Grid Book* (Boston: MIT Press, 2009).

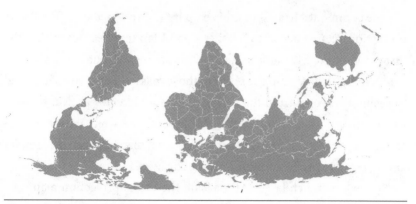

Figure 3. South-up world map

at the top of our North American world maps because that's the convention we are used to. It is an embodiment of our assumption that north
is "up" and south is "down."

Take a look at figure 3 again. Can you find Spain? When I've shown
people a map like this and asked them to find a particular country, often
they will tilt their head upside-down so they can look at the map in a familiar orientation. It is hard to recognize the world on this map because it
is so different from the world map most of us carry around in our heads.

So, here's the question: Which of these maps is accurate? Think about that
for a moment. The answer is all of them and none of them. All of them are
"accurate" for some purpose. The Mercator projection is accurate for navigators on sailing ships who need to determine their longitude. The Peters
projection is accurate in the relative area of land mass. The south-up map is
an accurate depiction of the globe with south as the top orientation.

At the same time, all of these maps are also inaccurate. Each one of
them distorts the world in some way. Taking a three-dimensional, round
planet and making it into a two-dimensional flat map inevitably results
in deforming the land masses. Every world mapmaker has to deal with
this problem. But there's a purpose to the problem. Carrying a globe
around would be awkward and impractical; the flat map is a useful, por-
table tool even while it misrepresents reality.

One challenge with how we use maps is that we become used to the distortion of our most familiar map and think of that map as an accurate representation of reality. The physical artifact of a map on the wall is an expression of a mental map we carry in our heads. Sometimes the negative consequences of the assumptions of our mental maps of the world are minimal; at other times, they are quite significant. Take, for example, one place where I saw the Mercator projection map in use: in the conference room of a church. In this instance, the particular version of the map used the Mercator projection and put the Americas in the center.[5] There were pins on the map, indicating the locations of the church's short-term mission teams. The mental model this physical map supports is that the United States is the center of the world. The map is both a product of a particular view of mission and an artifact whose presence forms and perpetuates that view in successive generations of church members, even if the church has a theology that says something different.

FROM MENTAL MAPS TO COGNITIVE SCHEMA

Physical world maps with all of their complexity and diversity are a metaphor for mental "maps" that we carry in our minds. Just as physical world maps are shorthand depictions of something larger and more complex—the planet—so too are our mental maps cognitive shorthand for something larger and more complex: experienced reality. Just as the world maps are both accurate and inaccurate, so too are our mental maps. The mental maps we develop are necessary and helpful to navigate life. At the same time, they oversimplify a complex reality and have distortions embedded in them.

Cognitive schema. Leadership theorist Peter Senge writes about "mental models" as cognitive maps that help us navigate a complex world. They are "deeply held internal images of how the world works, images

---

[5]If you google "Rand McNally cosmopolitan world map Mercator projection," you will find an image of the map as I saw it. A copy of this "so awful, it is beautiful" map is one of the most treasured items in my collection.

that limit us to familiar ways of thinking and acting."[6] They contain "the images, assumptions, and stories which we carry in our minds of ourselves, other people, institutions, and every aspect of the world."[7]

Cognitive scientists refer to these mental structures as "cognitive schemas." Cognitive schemas are "learned, internalized patterns of thought-feeling that mediate both the interpretation of ongoing experience and the reconstruction of memories."[8] A key point here is the phrase "thought-feeling." North Atlantic cultures tend to define cognition purely in terms of abstract conceptualization, enacting a false dichotomy between so-called rational thought and so-called irrational emotion. In reality, the limbic system in the human brain is the center of emotion, so that all human thought is both conceptual and emotional. Cognitive schemas are patterns of thought-feeling: conceptualizations imbued with emotional significance.

Each one of us has cognitive schemas related to vocation: what vocation is, what constitutes a person "having a calling," and so forth. These schemas influence what we think of as a calling. They also influence how we interpret our life experiences related to vocational formation. Importantly, our cognitive schemas about calling carry with them a great deal of emotional significance. Indeed, the concern about "missing" God's purpose and the anxiety many people express about making a wrong choice point to the deep meaning and importance calling has. To simply address calling as a conceptual construct and ignore that it has deep, emotional components is to attend to only a part of the significance of vocational formation.

About salience: schema as interpretive lenses. Cognitive schemas are necessary for navigating life. Mental maps are shortcuts for dealing with the complexity that is a daily part of our experience. They are "salience enhancing templates"[9] that focus our attention on some content as important and ignore other content as irrelevant.

---

[6]Peter Senge, *The Fifth Discipline*, updated and rev. ed. (New York: Currency, 2006), 163.
[7]Peter Senge, *The Fifth Discipline Fieldbook* (New York: Currency, 1994), 235.
[8]Claudia Strauss, "Models and Motives," in *Human Motives and Cultural Models*, ed. Roy G. D'Andrade and Claudia Strauss (New York: Cambridge University Press, 1992), 3.
[9]Bradd Shore, *Culture in Mind: Cognition, Culture, and the Problem of Meaning* (New York: Oxford University Press, 1996), 315.

Our brains filter and process information at a level below our consciousness. We need our brains to do this work for us. If we had to be aware of every bit of information at every moment of every day, we would have a hard time functioning. We rely on our brains to process incoming sensory data and make determinations about what needs attention and what does not.

Sensory data can be overwhelming. If you have ever traveled outside of your home country, you may be familiar with the sensation of being overwhelmed by the sights, sounds, and smells of a new place. The exhaustion we ascribe to jet lag is certainly related to a disrupted circadian rhythm, but it is also sensory overload. The newness of the experience and lack of familiarity overwhelms our brain's capacity to filter out some sensory input. Indeed, in a new space, we lack filters that will help us by sorting through all the incoming stimulus, ignoring what is unimportant and highlighting to us information to which we need to give attention. Our mental maps don't fit the new context.

We may feel a similar sense of overload in situations like intercultural interactions. Working with people from different countries involves communication containing complex combinations of information such as words and their meanings, tone of voice, or expressions, many of which are different from our own even when we're using a common language. Our brains have developed shorthand ways of processing the information we take in and making sense of it. Intercultural interactions are uniquely tiring because the kinds of mental shorthand we've developed in our context doesn't fit the intercultural context, so every interaction requires a lot of effort.

When we process our calling, we use mental maps that filter the information we receive through a variety of experiences. Over time, we develop a conceptual framework of what we understand calling to be, who is called to what, and how. We may be conscious of some aspects of this framework, able, for example, to articulate something of a theology of calling, while at the same time being largely unaware of the way our cultural models have influenced the development of that theology. What we pay attention to in a particular experience is dependent on what we assume calling to be. Similarly, we ignore data that doesn't fit our mental map of calling. Simply put, our cognitive schema of calling suggests to us what experiences to pay attention to and what to disregard.

Distortions in our mental maps. Like physical maps of the world, our mental maps are an approximation of reality. World maps take a round thing, the globe, and make it flat for the purpose of navigation; our mental models take a complex thing, life, and make it "flat" for the purposes of navigating experience. The problem with our mental maps of vocation is similar to the problems with world maps: we need our mental maps to function, but sometimes the very maps that should help us end up distorting our perception of reality.

In this book, I will offer a number of reflections for you. The purpose is not so much to identify what is "wrong" with your mental map as it is to facilitate your capacity to become aware of your assumptions and possible distortions about the nature of calling and about your experience with vocational formation. Some of those distortions have been helpful to you, like the distortions of the Mercator projection were helpful to ships' navigators. Other distortions may lead you to think some aspect of calling is larger or more prominent than it really is or to miss recognizing something as God's work in our lives. The point is to have the ability to reflect and, in reflection, to see with greater clarity. With this aim in mind, we turn to a foundational concept of this book: context.

THE POWER OF CONTEXT

When I am talking about context, I am thinking of the various social, cultural, organizational, and family groups that are the environment in which we live out our lives day to day. Social location is a sociological concept that highlights how a person's various group identities have an effect on that person's experiences. Dimensions of social location include a person's ethnicity, race, social class, gender, age, ability, religion, sexual orientation, and geographical location. Our social locations establish our "come from"—the perspective from which we look at the world.

Going back to the maps, consider the social location elements present in Gerardus Mercator, the cartographer who created the Mercator projection. As a Flemish maker of maps and globes, he was geographically positioned to be interested in how the world looked from a northern European perspective. That his map gave preference to northern Europe is understandable considering his geographical and cultural location.

I named my "come from" in the introduction, and I will continue to name the particularities of my experience, to acknowledge what is distinctive about my experience and the experience of people who share aspects of my social location. I don't expect my colleagues in Malaysia or Australia or Peru to see things the same way I do. Likewise, I know there are regional differences within the United States; my years residing in the Los Angeles area have shaped how I look at the world, and that may be different from how someone in, say, Seattle or Atlanta or rural Nebraska may view the world. In this text I focus on racial-ethnic-cultural identity, socioeconomic status, and gender but we could also explore ability /disability or age or religion as distinctive social locations that influence our vocational formation. This book is the beginning of reflections, not a sum total of all that could be considered.

Consider my student Dante's social location and its impact on how he thought about his calling. Dante had the beginnings of a sense of purpose in that he cared deeply about troubled teenagers. He assumed this was "just because" those teens reminded him of his own troubled youth growing up in the church and rebelling as a teenager. He didn't see this life experience as part of God's shaping, in part because he was formed by a calling narrative that emphasized being a "good church kid" as a qualification for calling. Dante was also a gifted, natural evangelist. Because that role came easily to him, he assumed it comes easily to other people.

Meanwhile, Dante's church experience—both as a child and as an adult—shaped his expectations about what calling looks like. His work on the streets did not fit the "norm" of what a minister looked like in his church, so he had a hard time seeing what he did as a calling. Further, in

Dante's church, a person was expected to have a clear "calling story" in which they could articulate a deep sense of knowing that God had assigned them a particular task. Dante could point to different choices and events that led to his current work but didn't feel like he'd heard directly from God. Because of the expectations of his tradition, he did not see the quiet, providential work of God in his life as a legitimate basis for a calling story. Additionally, Dante had chosen to return to Bible school for a formal degree. In his tradition, Bible schools and seminaries were viewed with suspicion. The assumption was that what a person needs to know to minister well cannot be learned in a classroom. Dante had heard his pastor joke about seminaries being "cemeteries" of faith.

My assumptions, the assumptions of the author of the class exercise, and Dante's assumptions all played a role in the gap between Dante's lived experience and his capacity to articulate a clear sense of calling. Each one of our mental maps of calling was both accurate in some ways and distorted in others. Dante's mental map of calling hindered him from being able to recognize all of what God had done and was doing, even though the Spirit was actively shaping him for participation in God's work in the world and Dante was faithfully responding to the work of God in his life. The issue was not the doing; it was the perceiving.

SO, "WHAT IS MY CALLING?"

When it comes to processing vocational formation, our mental models determine what we pay attention to and what we ignore about our context and life experiences, and they shape what we will experience, how we will interpret those experiences, and how we'll respond moving forward. In other words, those mental maps are shaped by our experiences in context and then, in turn, they shape our interpretations of new experiences. We live at the intersections of our various social identities and the impact of those identities on our life experiences.

The task of this book is to guide you in the process of taking a fresh look at your understanding of calling both as a concept and as a lived reality. Because mental maps are unconscious, we need something to bring them to the surface where we can consider them. The content of this text, the stories and examples, and the questions for reflection are all intended to facilitate that process. You may see parts of your mental maps that you decide are faithful representations of the world. There may be other parts that you decide you want to edit or even discard. The point is to make mindful and self-reflective choices. The ultimate purpose of this exploration is to be able to perceive God's work in the world and God's invitation to participate in that work with greater clarity and accuracy.

QUESTIONS FOR REFLECTION AND DISCUSSION

1. Notice your reactions to this chapter. Does this chapter fit your expectations for what a book about calling should address?

2. Where does this chapter conflict with your expectations about what a book about calling should cover? How comfortable or uncomfortable are you with having your expectations go unmet?

3. Think of an example of a person you would say clearly has a calling. What are the characteristics or qualities of this person that indicate to you they are called? How does this reflection help you begin to name your assumptions about the nature of vocation?

EXPLORING A BIBLICAL NARRATIVE: PETER

1. Read Acts 10:9-33.

2. Think about Peter's reaction to the vision. What values, beliefs, and behaviors does the vision engage? What values does the vision challenge?

3. Consider: Why would God give Peter such a vision? Why was it necessary? What was at stake in this story?

4. Imagine: What would have happened if God had not intervened and challenged Peter's mental map? What do you imagine might have happened for Cornelius and his household if Peter had been unwilling to adapt his assumptions?

SUGGESTIONS FOR FURTHER READING

Kaiser, Ward L., and Denis Wood. *Seeing Through Maps: The Power of Images to Shape Our World View*. Amherst, MA: ODT Inc., 2001.

For a presentation of the changing art and science of world maps (from a Western perspective), see Stoner, Julie, Rodney Hardy, and Craig Bryant. "Maps That Changed Our World: World Maps at the Library of Congress." Library of Congress, March 15, 2021, www.loc.gov/ghe/cascade/index.html?appid=ddf9824ff56b4fb6a0f3e11515716738.

2

IN SEARCH OF A BIBLICAL MAP

*It is not the church that has a mission of salvation
to fulfill in the world; it is the mission of the Son and
the Spirit through the Father that includes the church.*

JÜRGEN MOLTMANN,
THE CHURCH IN THE POWER OF THE SPIRIT

*But you are a chosen people, a royal priesthood, a holy nation,
God's special possession, that you may declare the praises of him
who called you out of darkness into his wonderful light.*

1 PETER 2:9 NIV

KATE LINGERED AFTER CLASS and then approached me a bit hesi-
tantly, saying, "Can I ask you a question?" She paused to gather her
thoughts and continued. "We're talking about vocation formation in this
course. You've had us read different authors with different perspectives
and I'm learning a lot! But I'm wondering: when are you going to tell us
the biblical model of calling?"

Consider what Kate's question suggested about her mental maps regarding vocation and regarding the Bible. Kate grew up in a church tradition that taught her the Bible is a blueprint for godly living, and the
benchmark against which other knowledge is measured; learning from

books is good but learning from the Bible is best. She was taught to study the text to understand how God works in the world. Kate assumed there is a single, authoritative biblical model to be discerned. She also assumed that if she understood the biblical model, then she could apply that model as a road map for identifying her own calling.

Kate is not alone in her desire for biblical guidance in understanding her calling. She longed for someone to show her an authoritative and trustworthy road map. Even people who don't share Kate's view of Christian Scriptures as establishing normative models for life yearn for some reliable guidance as they seek to live faithfully to God.

In chapter one, I suggested that all of us have mental maps that guide our engagement with the world, and that our maps can be helpful for interpreting our experiences as well as distort our interpretations. We also have mental maps that affect how we approach the Bible, including theological assumptions about what the Bible is, how to read it, and how to engage with Scripture as a guide to life.

> **NAVIGATION POINT**
Authority of Scripture

I come from a conservative, evangelical faith background. This context and my experiences in it have shaped my approach to the Bible. I see the Christian Scriptures as the God-breathed record (2 Timothy 3:16 NIV) of God's interaction with human beings and human cultures. Attending to what the Spirit is saying and doing in my community, I believe, needs to be influenced by and shaped by attention to how the Spirit has been at work in the people of God in the record we hold in our hands.

Missiologist Chuck Van Engen has commented about mission with words that I believe can be said about calling: "With notable exceptions, [biblical scholars'] analysis of Scripture has seldom asked the missiological questions regarding God's intentions and purpose. On the other hand, the activist practitioners of mission have too readily superimposed their particular agendas on Scripture, or ignored the Bible altogether."[1] In

---

[1]Charles E. Van Engen, *Mission on the Way: Issues in Mission Theology* (Grand Rapids, MI: Baker Books, 1996), 36.

addressing calling, I seek to take context and action seriously while continuing to attend to the Spirit's revelation in Scripture. I value the Bible as an authoritative guide for life and mission.

This chapter focuses on elements of our mental maps of calling that influence how we read the Bible, particularly the stories of women and men of faith. We'll consider how those maps shape what we see and don't see as we examine Scripture on the subject of calling. The aim is not to suggest a single, universal framework for understanding vocation as if there is one and only one "biblical" model. Instead, I offer an approach to engagement with biblical/theological content that takes seriously God's work in distinct cultural and social contexts. The Bible records God's self-revelation to people in different cultures and through multiple languages. God called nations and individuals. God spoke to women and men, to rich and poor, to the elite and the marginalized. The Bible has multiple models of calling; what we tend to search out and see is that one model that best fits the assumptions of our particular faith community. Let us explore together some of those assumptions, considering biblical calling narratives and their implications for us and our communities of faith.

EXPLORING BIBLICAL CALLINGS

When I ask people to list names of individuals in the Bible they see as examples of people who are called by God, those lists almost always include Moses, Paul, and David. Frequently, lists also include Abraham and the disciples.[2] Jeremiah and Isaiah may appear farther down on some lists. There are a number of other people in Scripture who are far less likely to be named as examples of "called people." Was Nehemiah called

---

[2] A free list exercise was part of my doctoral research with a group of Pentecostal adults in the United States. This group collectively most frequently listed Moses, Paul, David, Abraham, and the disciples as examples of called people in the Bible. I later replicated this methodology in Malaysia with a group of Pentecostal adults and discovered the same top five individuals mentioned in that context as well. As I continued to use this exercise with a people from a variety of national and denominational backgrounds, I saw there seemed to be a group of biblical stories consistently identified as exemplars.

by God to do what he did? Were Philip and Stephen called by God? Timothy? Saul? Aaron? Would a list include Miriam, Hannah, Esther, Ruth, and Mary? How about Huldah, Priscilla, Junia, and Lydia?

The people we name as models of a "called person" in Scripture depends on the mental map of calling we carry in our subconscious. Those people in the Bible we think of first when asked for examples of calling are the people who most closely match our mental map. Those who don't fit the map are much farther down on the list, if they appear at all.[3]

Many of the people I have worked with come from conservative theological environments where they have been taught to value the Bible as authoritative. They, like Kate, frequently articulate a desire to understand "the biblical model of calling." This is a different way of asking, "What is my calling?" The assumption is that if a biblical model is identified, since the Bible is authoritative, then that model is the authoritative guide. Stories in the Bible are seen as exemplars of how we should (and should not) live. How God worked in the lives of people through the thousands of years and multiple cultural contexts covered by the span of the Bible is assumed to be the way God works to call people today. The fundamental belief is that, if we understand "the biblical model," then we will be able to discern God's calling in our own lives.

What is not included in this set of assumptions, but is a key principle of this book, is that we read the Bible through lenses of experience. People identify "timeless truths" from the perspective of their particular context. Each of us ignores some texts and focuses on others as essential. Our culturally conditioned mental models form interpretive lenses that help us understand who God is and what the Spirit calls us to as God's children. Those same mental models also form blinders that keep us from paying attention to other elements of God's revelation.

---

[3]For more on how schemas are demonstrated by the creation of lists, see H. Russell Bernard, *Social Research Methods: Qualitative and Quantitative Approaches* (Thousand Oaks, CA: SAGE Publications, Inc., 2000), 264-67. For background on the development of cognitive anthropological approaches, see Roy D'Andrade, *The Development of Cognitive Anthropology* (New York: Cambridge University Press, 1995). Note particularly chap. 6, "The Growth of Schema Theory."

To illustrate this point, consider some common elements of a cultural model of calling in the United States. This is not to suggest that US-Americans have a monopoly on thinking about calling. My phrasing here reflects the awareness that how people in the United States (in all our diversity) think theologically about calling is distinct and different from how people in other countries think theologically about calling. While I work with international colleagues and students who contribute a great deal to challenging my context-shaped assumptions, I recognize I am located in the United States and thus write as a person who has been shaped by the perspectives and values of this context.

In my research, I identified five key characteristics that seem to recur in multiple theological environments. Four of these elements are seen as essential to identifying the presence of a calling: God as the caller, the task or role as the calling, the individual as the one who is called, and the centrality of knowing. In general, if any one of these elements is missing from a person's story, they and others around them are likely to question their identity as a called person. Once these four elements are known to be present, however, the fifth element is sought as support: confirmation.[4] This confirmation can take various forms. In some traditions, the endorsement of the individual's pastor is essential, while in other traditions individuals seek the affirmation of the faith community of which they are a part. In some contexts, the community looks to see whether a person persists in their calling for a long period of time, particularly persevering in the face of hardship. Such perseverance is seen to be confirmation that they were indeed called as they claimed. Another point of confirmation cited is that of "fruitfulness" in ministry, particularly in terms of measurable outcomes such as the size of the church or the number of converts. The variety of types of confirmation mentioned by my research participants suggests that it isn't the specific form the confirmation takes that is essential, it is having confirmation in some form that is part of the model.

---

[4]Susan L. Maros, "Knowing My Call: A Cultural Model of the Experience of Call in a Pentecostal/Charismatic Context" (PhD diss., Fuller Theological Seminary, 2014).

Consider this model at work in the story of David. In 1 Samuel 16, God sends Samuel to Jesse, saying, "I have seen for myself a king" among Jesse's sons.[5] David is God's choice; Samuel's role is to discern which of Jesse's sons God has chosen and to anoint him as king. In other words, God picks the king and Samuel gives the person the news that God has chosen him. Samuel's anointing of David is a marker of that calling. All four essential elements of the cultural map of calling I identified are present in this story: God is the caller, kingship is the calling, David is the individual called, and David knows he is called because Samuel conveys the message from God to him. David's calling is then confirmed by the ways in which God is with David through David's early "ministry" as a commander under King Saul and David's persistent faithfulness in the face of Saul's mistreatment.

We could engage this same exercise for any number of people whose stories are recorded in the Bible. God calls Moses at the burning bush to confront Pharaoh to set Israel free. God is the caller, Moses is the called one, setting Israel free is the calling, and the entirety of the discussion in Exodus 3:1–4:17 is all about Moses coming to "know" he is assigned the task and empowered for it. God gives the confirmation: "This shall be the sign for you that it is I who sent you: when you have brought the people out of Egypt, you shall worship God on this mountain" (Exodus 3:12).

Turning to the New Testament, we have Peter, a fisherman on the Sea of Galilee, who encounters Jesus. Jesus' call to Peter is, "Follow me, and I will make you fish for people" (Matthew 4:19). Peter immediately leaves his nets and boat to follow Jesus. Sometime later, after a night of prayer, Jesus appoints Peter and eleven others to be apostles (Luke 6:12-19) and then sends the Twelve out with a specific task: preach the good news and demonstrate the power of God (Matthew 10:1-3; Mark 3:13-15). Jesus is

---

[5]My translation of 1 Samuel 16:1 is influenced by the literal meaning of the Hebrew *raah*, "to see" and the significance of seeing in 1 Samuel 16:1-13. For a discussion of this dynamic in the passage, see Ralph W. Klein, *1 Samuel*, Word Biblical Commentary, vol. 10 (Waco, TX: Word Publishers, 1983), 159-61.

the caller, Peter and the other disciples are the called, "follow me" is the calling, and they all know because Jesus spoke to them directly.

Jesus calls Paul, then still called Saul, when he is on the road to Damascus. Jesus' instruction to Saul is "Get up and enter the city, and you will be told what you are to do" (Acts 9:6). God sends Ananias to Saul to pray for Saul's healing and to give him God's assignment, explaining: "Go, for he is an instrument whom I have chosen to bring my name before Gentiles and kings and before the people of Israel" (Acts 9:15).[6] This story of Ananias is an example of "double confirmation,"[7] similar to David's experience: God is at work in the called one's heart and then someone who didn't previously have engagement with them comes to deliver a word that confirms for them what God is saying and doing.

The temptation at this point is to see this recurring pattern as the evidence that there is, indeed, a single "biblical map" and that these stories demonstrate the elements of that map. We expect that a pattern should exist, so, upon finding a pattern that fits our expectations, we move on without considering whether this is a case of confirmation bias. This leads us to ignore biblical narratives that do not fit this model and, therefore, to miss the wisdom present there for our own vocational journeys.

Moreover, we have a cultural mental map of what a biblical calling looks like that influences how we read the biblical texts. This cultural map provides what I earlier referred to as a "salience enhancing template," determining what we pay attention to and what we ignore. We may pay attention to stories of God speaking to individuals, for example, and ignore narratives that do not include direct communication. We pay particular attention to stories that focus on an individual receiving a specific assignment, generally ignoring collective callings to families and groups. Our desire to "know" our callings influence our preference for biblical

---

[6]Paul's testimony of this event later in Acts 22 indicates Ananias delivered the charge as well as prayed for his healing. In Acts 26 before King Agrippa, Paul leaves out Ananias as the agent and just narrates the content of message.

[7]For more on double confirmation, see J. Robert Clinton, *The Making of a Leader: Recognizing the Lessons and Stages of Leadership Development* (Colorado Springs: NavPress, 2012), 115-17.

narratives, which we interpret as cases of a person coming to a clear understanding of their vocation. We see the data that fits the model. Meanwhile, we ignore the information in these stories—not to mention whole other individual stories—that doesn't fit the model.

To illustrate this point, let us consider King Saul from the perspective of the cultural model of calling. The people have asked for a king "like other nations" (1 Samuel 8:5). God chooses a man from the tribe of Benjamin: Saul. God first indicates this choice to Samuel by the word that the young man who comes looking for his father's lost donkeys is the person God has chosen (1 Samuel 9:15-16). When Saul arrives, Samuel draws him aside to convey the message that he is to be king and to anoint Saul. This choice is later demonstrated to the community by the casting of lots (1 Samuel 10:20-21).

This story too has all the markers of the cultural map of calling: God picks Saul for a specific task and Saul knows God has picked him through his encounter with Samuel; Saul's calling is confirmed through the casting of lots. In fact, King Saul's calling story is directly parallel to King David's calling story. Each of them is chosen by God to be king. Each of them is anointed by Samuel. Yet, when we think of examples of called people in Scripture, David is often named and Saul usually is not. We ignore King Saul as a model of calling and thus disregard anything his story has to say to us about the nature of God's activity in calling people to participate in God's work in the world.

A similar case can be made when comparing Peter and Judas. Both men were among the larger group of disciples that followed Jesus. Both men were among the Twelve that Jesus specifically prayed about and identified as apostles. Each man was picked by God for that particular role and called out of the group in a way that allowed him to know that he was called as an apostle by Jesus. Yet, we don't tend to see Judas as an example of a called person.

Bringing up Saul and Judas as biblical examples of called people provokes a variety of reactions. Saul repeatedly disobeyed God and was ultimately rejected as king (see 1 Samuel 15:23). How could he be an example of calling? Judas walked with Jesus and saw his ministry firsthand for years. Then he betrayed Jesus and committed suicide when he realized the consequences of his actions (see Matthew 27:3-5). How could he be an example of calling? Some people will suggest that Saul and Judas are examples of people who fail the confirmation element of the model of calling; they are not faithful, persistent, and fruitful and, therefore, cannot be considered to be called. But does their lack of faithfulness mean God did not call them?

Exploring Saul and Judas as called people highlights the complexities of God's sovereignty and human agency. What was the role of human choice in the life of these two biblical characters? Did God choose Saul to be a failed king? Sometimes Saul's story is interpreted in this way: God wanted to teach Israel a lesson so God first called a "bad king," Saul, so the people would recognize and appreciate the "good king," David, when he arrived. This interpretation ignores Saul's agency; it robs him of the responsibility to respond faithfully to God, making him a puppet of a deity making a point.

We can think about Judas in a similar manner. Was Judas called to betray Jesus and die? One of my research participants asked the question, "Since someone had to betray Jesus, did God pick Judas for the job?" Again, this interpretation removes Judas' human agency. It also raises hard and fearful questions: if God picked Judas to fail, was that a one-time choice or does God still pick some people to fail? What if God picks *me* to fail?

Alternatively, some people interpret these stories as cautionary tales: the threat of failure and rejection hangs over our heads. We must be absolutely obedient or we might, like Saul, be rejected by God. We must be absolutely faithful and correct in our behavior or we might, like Judas, cause the destruction of all we've worked for. One way to avoid the difficulties inherent in these questions is to erase Saul and Judas from consideration as called people. If we don't think about their calling, we don't have to grapple with the challenging parts of their stories.

This is one of the reasons why *the* biblical model of calling doesn't exist. The record in Scripture of God's interactions with God's people across time is complex. The search for simple mile markers that can be guides to our own lives encourages us to ignore that complexity. However, ignoring complexity in Scripture leads us to ignore complexity in our own lives. When people ask me to identify "the biblical model of calling," they are often unconsciously asking for certainty and security. We perceive uncertainty to be antithetical to faith. We want to *know* our calling, to feel safe and secure that God is in charge and at work, that our lives have purpose and meaning.

BIBLICAL PERSPECTIVES ON CALLING

Consider that the elements of the common cultural model of calling—God as caller, a person as called, a task as the calling, and knowing as the central factor—are valid but only up to a point. Perhaps our emphasis on individually wanting to know our particular assignment leads us to ignore other biblical content that has direct implications for how we think about calling.

A significant element of my own mental map of the Bible is that the text records God's self-revelation to particular people in particular places across the span of more than two thousand years. The God of the Bible is active and present. God engages with people personally and directly. God spoke languages people could understand; God continues to speak so that we can understand. God uses cultural idioms and practices that are already present in the context that God engages in. While we are separated by thousands of years and many miles from the cultures and contexts of the Bible, the dynamics we see in Scripture of the ways God engaged people in those contexts give insight into how God engages people in our twenty-first-century contexts.

There is biblical material about calling that we tend to overlook as our cultural model of calling forms blinders for our reading of the text. Two points are particularly significant for the process of considering how our social locations, particularly in the United States, have been used by God to shape us for participation in God's work in the world. The first is the communal nature of calling that we miss because of our emphasis on the individual. The second is the biblical evidence of God working within human cultures.

Called to be the people of God. In the Old Testament, Israel is called into being to be the people of God for the sake of demonstrating God's character and purpose to the world. This global intention is evident in God's call to Abraham:[8] "I will bless those who bless you, and the one who curses you I will curse; and in you all the families of the earth shall be blessed" (Genesis 12:3). Missiologist Arthur F. Glasser observes, "Abraham's election and God's covenant with him represents the first expression of God's redemptive concern for all nations."[9] God restates this same promise of global blessing to Isaac: "I will fulfill the oath that I swore to your father Abraham . . . and all the nations of the earth shall gain blessing for themselves through your offspring" (Genesis 26:3-4).

When the Israelites come to Sinai, God says to them, "Now therefore, if you obey my voice and keep my covenant, you shall be my treasured possession out of all the peoples. Indeed, the whole earth is mine, but you shall be for me a priestly kingdom and a holy nation" (Exodus 19:5-6). Repeatedly in the giving of the law, God charges Israel: "Be holy for I am holy" (Leviticus 11:44; 19:22; see also Numbers 15:40-41). In Leviticus 20:26 we see a broader statement: "You shall be holy to me; for I the Lord am holy, and I have separated you from the other peoples to be mine." For what reason had God set Israel apart? They were constituted as the people who would represent God to the nations and bring the nations to God.

Later in their history, as the people of God struggle to be faithful in the midst of an empire, God says this through the writer of Isaiah: "I am the Lord, I have called you in righteousness, / I have taken you by the hand and kept you; / I have given you as a covenant to the people, a light

---

[8]The change of name from Abram to Abraham is important for the narrative of this man's life and calling formation. However, for the sake of simplicity and clarity, I will use Abraham.

[9]Arthur F. Glasser, *Announcing the Kingdom: The Story of God's Mission in the Bible* (Grand Rapids, MI: Baker Academic, 2003), 57. For a discussion of blessing in Genesis and Abraham's call from a missiological perspective, see Sarita D. Gallagher, "Genesis: Declaration of God's Blessing," chap. 2 in *Abrahamic Blessing: A Missiological Narrative of Revival in Papua New Guinea*, American Society of Missiology Monograph Series, vol. 21 (Eugene, OR: Pickwick Publications, 2014).

to the nations" (Isaiah 42:6). God's intention in calling Israel into being was never solely for Israel as a nation. There was nothing special, nothing majestic, nothing important about this people. In fact, the barrenness of Abraham and Sarah and the recurring instances of barrenness in their descendants gave reason for God to not choose this family. Israel was always to be a "peculiar people" (1 Peter 2:9 KJV) for the sake of demonstrating God's presence to the world. Similarly, God chooses people today not because they have something God lacks but rather to be in relationship with God and to demonstrate God's character to the world as a result.

When twenty-first-century Christians steeped in individualism read the Old Testament, we often miss the importance of the collective nature of the identity of the people of God. As children of the Reformation in the West, we default to thinking of the law as a bad thing that has been superseded by the gospel. But many of the laws were about identity: how to live in a way that demonstrates you are a member of God's people. Many of the stories of God's people, particularly during the Babylonian exile, are about how they are the people of God in the midst of a context that is hostile to that identity.

The New Testament church was an extension of the Old Testament collectivist understanding of vocation. They did life together as an expression of their identity as Jesus-followers (Acts 2:44-47). They cared for widows (Acts 6:1-6; 1 Timothy 5:3-8) and engaged in disaster relief (Acts 11:27-29). These acts of social justice were a part of the community's life together in addition to regular prayer (Acts 3:1; 10:9; 13:3) and teaching (Acts 2:42; 5:21; 18:11).[10]

---

[10]For an excellent reflection on collectivist and individualist perspectives on Scripture contrasting a US-American approach to perspectives from other parts of the world, see Richard James, *Misreading Scripture with Individualist Eyes: Patronage, Honor, and Shame in the Biblical World* (Downers Grove, IL: IVP Academic, 2020). For reflections on Scripture expressing the experience and concerns of distinctive communities in the United States, see Karen González, *The God Who Sees: Immigrants, the Bible, and the Journey to Belong* (Harrisonburg, VA: Herald Press, 2019), and Esau McCaulley, *Reading While Black: African American Biblical Interpretation as an Exercise in Hope* (Downers Grove, IL: IVP Academic, 2020). See also Vincent L. Wimbush, ed., *Misreading America: Scriptures and Difference* (New York: Oxford University Press, 2013).

The context of any individual sense of calling is the call to be a member of the body of Christ, the collective identity of the people of God who have been called out of darkness and into the light (1 Peter 2:9). For many Christians in the United States, however, this call out of darkness and into the light is limited to individual salvation. We believe something like, "God calls me personally out of my individual darkness" with no reference to either the families and groups we come from or the community God calls us to enter. There is little sense of the significance of our callings as they relate to our belonging.

Some Christian vocational literature talks about calling "for the common good," and this is certainly a place to start. Amy Sherman focuses on the *tsaddiqim* (Hebrew for "the righteous") as "the people who follow God's heart and ways and who see everything they have as gifts from God to be stewarded for his purposes."[11] The *tsaddiqim* "steward everything—their money, vocational position and expertise, assets, resources, opportunities, education, relationships, social position, entrée, and networks—for the *common* good, for the advancing of God's justice and shalom."[12] This is vocation expressed *for* the collective. Notice, though, that the vocation is not seen as *from* the collective or *with* the collective.

Let's consider a few more examples from Scripture. The parable of the talents in Matthew 25 appears in a section of Jesus' teaching about the end times. As Jesus is giving warnings—"Keep awake therefore, for you know neither the day nor the hour" (Matthew 25:13)—and descriptions— "the kingdom of heaven will be like this . . ." (Matthew 25:1)—he tells the story of the king who entrusts wealth to his servants. The faith community that fostered my early spiritual development tends to read this parable individualistically: some people have five talents, some three, and some only one. Using *only* as a descriptor for one talent ignores the fact that a talent was worth 6,000 denarii, or 6,000 days' wages for a

---

[11]Amy L. Sherman, *Kingdom Calling: Vocational Stewardship for the Common Good* (Downers Grove, IL: InterVarsity Press, 2011), 16.

[12]Sherman, *Kingdom Calling*, 17, emphasis in the original.

common laborer.[13] This was substantial wealth, not minimal sustenance. Regarding this parable, Stanley Hauerwas comments, "No parable has been more misused. . . . Jesus is not using this parable to recommend that we should work hard, make all we can, to give all we can. Rather, the parable is a clear judgment against those who think they deserve what they have earned, as well as those who do not know how precious is the gift they have been given."[14] When we read the parable and interpret it as the king exacting individual judgment on the individual productivity of each person—in other words, when we see the king's judgment as being about profit and increase—we are reading the parable through the lenses of a Western, capitalistic, individualistic cultural map.[15]

We typically read the next parable—the parable of the sheep and goats—through these same individualistic lenses as well. We interpret the sheep and goats as individual people being judged for their individual actions to individual people. Generally, commentators look at this parable as a parable about the universality of Jesus' kingship and "caring for the least of these" as the basis of judgment, not attending at all to the significance of the presence of the nations standing in judgment.[16] I raise this question about the passage: Matthew 25:32 says "All the *nations* will be gathered." This is all of the *ethnē* of the world. What if the sheep and the goats are not individual people but the *ethnē* themselves being sorted based on how we collectively treat the "least of these"? Father Greg Boyle quotes Mother Teresa diagnosing the world's ills in this way: "We've just 'forgotten that we belong to each other.'"[17] What if there is some element

---

[13]Donald A. Hagner, *Matthew 14–28*, Word Biblical Commentary, vol. 33b (Dallas, TX: Word Books Publishers, 1995), 734. There is some dispute among scholars as to the exact value of a talent, but the point of a talent representing significant wealth is consistent through the various valuations.

[14]Stanley Hauerwas, *Matthew* (Grand Rapids, MI: Brazos Press, 2006), 378.

[15]For an example of a reading of this parable from a different cultural context, see Lung-pun Common Chan, "Reading the Matthean Apocalypse (Matthew 24–25) in the Glocalization Context of Hong Kong's Bourgeois Society and Middle-Class Churches," in *Matthew*, ed. Nicole Wilkinson and James Grimshaw (Minneapolis: Fortress Press, 2013), 175-88.

[16]For example, see Hagner, *Matthew 14–28*, 742-43. See also Jeannine K. Brown and Kyle A Roberts, *Matthew* (Grand Rapids, MI: Eerdmans, 2018), 187-88.

[17]Gregory Boyle, *Tattoos on the Heart: The Power of Boundless Compassion* (New York: Free Press, 2010), 187.

of our shared calling that is God's concern that we care for the "least of these" because we collectively belong to one another and to God?

The community is the context of the calling of individual people. When God appoints someone to a task, it is always with the well-being of the community in mind, and it is always in line with God's broader intentions for the world. And when God appoints an individual, that individual's calling is always in relation to the calling of their community.

With this in mind, we now turn our attention back to some specific examples of people God called in Scripture, but with new questions to consider:

> ➤ What was the context in which they were called?
> ➤ How did God speak to them in the midst of their context?
> ➤ How did God use their context as a means of preparing them for God's purposes?

Calling in cultural context. Abraham is one of the heroes of faith in Scripture. His life is a model of a called person that shapes our mental maps of what calling looks like and how we should respond to God. The narrative is generally summarized in this way: Abraham was faithful and God made him into a great nation, giving his offspring the Promised Land. However, many parts of Abraham's story are glossed over and even ignored as irrelevant to understanding the nature of God's calling to Abraham and as a pattern for understanding our own callings.

In Genesis 12, God calls Abraham to go from his country to a land that God would show him. God promises to make Abraham a great nation, to bless him, and, through blessing him, make him a blessing to the world. As a reader in the twenty-first century, we start the story already knowing thousands of years of the outcomes of the tale. Still, at that very moment, all Abraham knew was to get up and go. Even when Abraham arrived in Shechem and heard from God that this was the land God would give to him and his descendants (Genesis 12:6-7), Abraham still moved, first to a spot between Bethel and Ai, then toward the Negeb, and finally to Egypt because there was famine in the land (Genesis 12:8-10).

Abraham responded to God's call to get up and go, God identified the land of Abraham's inheritance, yet Abraham continued to wander without a settled home.[18]

The writer of Hebrews references this point, saying, "By faith [Abraham] stayed for a time in the land he had been promised, as in a foreign land, living in tents, as did Isaac and Jacob, who were heirs with him of the same promise. For he looked forward to the city that has foundations, whose architect and builder is God" (Hebrews 11:9-10). If Abraham's story reflected a US-American perspective on calling, Abraham would have immediately settled down, built a home and a city. God's word that this was the land God had given would be expected to result in immediate occupation. Abraham's wandering and waiting is contrary to our popular notions of what calling looks like.

Another element of Abraham's story that is generally overlooked is the long-term and progressively developing nature of his understanding of his calling. When Abraham left Haran, he only knew to leave his country. Even upon arriving in Canaan, there was more Abraham did not know. How would he have a son? How would he have descendants? It took decades of life for Abraham to understand more of God's call and promise. It took decades, and an attempt to fulfill God's promise through Hagar, for Abraham to see something of that promise fulfilled in the birth of Isaac. We tend to despair of God's work in our lives if we don't see fulfillment in months or years, let alone decades.

Furthermore, much of God's promise to Abraham was not lived out in Abraham's lifetime. Abraham died seeing only part of God's promise to him fulfilled. Hebrews 11:13 explains, "All of these died in faith without having received the promises, but from a distance they saw and greeted them." We acknowledge this reality for Abraham and the others men- tioned in Hebrews 11 but fail to see that it could apply to our own lives. We expect calling and concrete results, not calling and wandering and

---

[18]For an interesting reflection on Abraham as immigrant and alien, and the implications for all of Abraham's children, see Miguel A. De La Torre, *Genesis* (Louisville, KY: Westminster John Knox, 2011), 139-42.

partial fulfillment. This vocation of living faithfully and only seeing part of your calling fulfilled is not often preached and affirmed in our churches.

The covenant enactment recorded in Genesis 15 is also an aspect of Abraham's story that we tend to overlook, and it's a prime example of God using existing cultural constructs to communicate God's purposes. For the twenty-first-century reader, the ritual God directed Abraham to execute—cutting animals in two and laying the halves on the ground— sounds strange and even barbaric. For Abraham, though, this would have been a familiar practice. Archaeological evidence demonstrates that similar enactments were a regular part of covenant-making in the ancient Near East.[19] God used a familiar cultural practice to communicate something important about Abraham's calling. God still uses existing cultural practices to communicate something significant to a human person in a way that person can comprehend.

At the burning bush, God instructed Moses to remove his shoes because the place he was standing was holy ground (Exodus 3:5). This action of going barefoot seems to have been a cultural sign of respect according to Near Eastern practice.[20] As such, Moses would have immediately comprehended the symbolic significance and meaning of God's direction.[21] Meanwhile, in our present-day cultural contexts, we do not interpret this passage as God establishing shoelessness as a norm for people encountering God and receiving God's assignment to a task because being barefoot does not have the same cultural connotation. By overlooking the cultural practice, though, we can miss the significance of the action and fail to recognize when there is a parallel action of honor and awe-filled respect in our own encounters with God.

As we established earlier, Moses is often held up as an exemplar of calling, and his encounter with God at the burning bush (Exodus 3) an

---

[19]For a discussion of treaty practices in the ancient Near East, see David J. Bederman, "Making Faith: Treaty Practices Amongst Ancient People," chap. 5 in *International Law in Antiquity* (New York: Cambridge University Press, 2001).

[20]Carol L. Meyers, *Exodus* (New York: Cambridge University Press, 2005), 53.

[21]Joshua had a similar experience in which he had an encounter with God at a crucial turning point in his life and was told to remove his sandals "for the place where you stand is holy" (Joshua 5:15).

exemplary event.[22] Depending on a person's theological tradition, this kind of awe-inspiring, direct encounter with God is the expected norm for an authentic call.[23] The emphasis is on the individual hearing directly from God and God directing a person to a particular task, just as happened for Moses. Yet, like Abraham, much of his story is glossed over or considered irrelevant to thinking about vocation in favor of focusing only on those elements that are part of our common mental map of calling. We typically ignore the eighty years that preceded this event, for example, deeming the leadership and character formation that took place in these years as irrelevant to calling, yet this was the cultural context in which God shaped and prepared Moses for the work that was ahead of him.

Another facet of the story we tend to ignore is its focus on Israel as a people. God was the one who "hears and remembers and sees and knows"[24] and was going to act on behalf of the people. Moses understanding what he was tasked to do was in service to this larger act of God. While we tend to focus on the story of Moses' encounter with God as an example of an individual calling, the biblical narrative is far more focused on God's concern for God's people. As with Abraham's story, we look at Moses' story as a perfect model of calling but our assumptions about calling serve as blinders, limiting our capacity to see that the emphasis is not on the individual called but on God's purposes for the people as a whole.

Paul's encounter with Jesus on the road to Damascus is viewed similarly to Moses' encounter with God at the burning bush: it is awe-inspiring and direct communication. Again, depending on a person's

---

[22]Terence Fretheim identifies six elements of a "typical call narrative" present in Exodus 3: (1) a divine appearance, (2) an introductory word, (3) a divine commission, (4) objection, (5) reassurance, and (6) a sign (Terence E. Fretheim, *Exodus* [Louisville, KY: Westminster John Knox, 2010], 51). What is not clear in this presentation is why Fretheim identifies this pattern as "typical."

[23]See, for example, Richard N. Pitt's description of what he names a "blitzkrieg call" in Richard N. Pitt, "I Heard a Voice from Heaven Say," chap. 2 in *Divine Callings: Understanding the Call to Ministry in Black Pentecostalism* (New York: New York University Press, 2012), 41-71.

[24]Fretheim, *Exodus*, 57.

theological tradition, this expectation to hear directly from God can be held up as a norm. And again, as with Abraham and Moses, we ignore the progressive development of Paul's ministry. We gloss over the years of quiet and isolation between Acts 9 when the believers in Jerusalem sent him off to Tarsus and Acts 11 when Barnabas went to Tarsus in search of Paul.[25] We think of Paul as the fully developed, apostolic presence we read about at the end of Acts or in his latter letters, failing to think about the years of formation that this entailed. Again, Paul's personal history and social location—his origin, the place of his birth, his early education, and so forth—was the cultural context in which God prepared Paul for the work to which God would call him.

In some of our theological communities, the collective element of calling has been rendered abstract. We may acknowledge, for example, that a person's primary calling is to membership in the body of Christ, but in practice, that truth gets waved aside in the rush to get to the identification of our specific, individual task. In other communities, the identification with the body of Christ focuses on separation from the world. The calling to be a child of God becomes a matter of identifying who is "inside" and who is "outside." In either case, we don't regard our cultural context as being a meaningful part of God's work in our lives and we lose the biblical sense of being called together as God's people for the purpose of reaching the world.

THE BIBLE MATTERS FOR CALLING

As people who desire to be faithful followers of Jesus, we look at the stories of called people in the Bible and seek to identify a reliable road map that relegates God to a sort of cosmic GPS: "go three miles north and turn right." Because our cultural assumptions shape how we approach Scripture, we focus on identifying our particular task or role and emphasize the biblical examples of individuals who experienced God directing them to a specific task. We functionally ignore the communal

---

[25]For a careful discussion of what we know and surmise about Paul, see Udo Schnelle, *Apostle Paul: His Life and Theology* (Grand Rapids, MI: Baker Academic, 2005).

nature of calling, for Israel and for the church. For some of us, our contexts de-emphasize our shared humanity and devalue the common good. The competitive nature of our capitalistic society has shaped our way of engaging the community.

Perhaps rather than looking to the Bible for a road map, we should see the Christian Scriptures as the testimony of brothers and sisters who, like us, have encountered God in the midst of their ordinary life circumstances. Perhaps, like them, we seek to make sense of who God is, who we are, and what that means for how we live our lives. The central narrative of the Bible is God engaging the humanity God created. We are God's beloved children. As joint heirs with Christ (Romans 8:17), we are invited to be engaged in the family business.

As much as a person may desire a single, authoritative model of calling, that's not what God provides in the Bible. Instead, we have the stories of the people of God recorded in Scripture—faithful women and men through history testifying to God's work in them and their communities in particular times and places. Rather than a single map, these biblical stories offer challenge and encouragement for the journeys of our own communities as well as suggest some compass headings or markers that help us navigate our life experiences toward the "north" of God's purposes.

As we seek to live faithful lives, learning to discern where God is at work and how we are being invited to participate in that work is a lifelong process of development. Learning to discern where and how God is at work in the present is aided by looking at where God was at work in the past, in the biblical accounts and in our lives. How is it that we come to form a sense of identity as a called person across time? How does our context shape this process? To these questions we now turn.

QUESTIONS FOR REFLECTION AND DISCUSSION

1. If you grew up in a faith context, what did you learn about the nature of the Bible? How did your view of Scripture change over time?

2. What of the "common elements of calling" described in this chapter—God as caller, the individual as the called, a task or role as the calling, and the centrality of knowing—are familiar to you? What do you think is missing from this model?

3. Is the concept that the Bible records God's interactions with people in specific cultural contexts a new one to you? What reactions does this idea provoke for you?

EXPLORING A BIBLICAL NARRATIVE: NEHEMIAH

1. Read Nehemiah 1:1-4 and Nehemiah 2:1-5.

2. In your church and/or family context, would this story be considered an example of a calling? Why or why not?

3. What elements of the "common model of calling" described in this chapter are present in Nehemiah's story? What elements are implied? What elements are missing?

SUGGESTIONS FOR FURTHER READING

Garber, Steven. *Visions of Vocation: Common Grace for the Common Good.* Downers Grove, IL: InterVarsity Press, 2014.

Imes, Carmen Joy. *Bearing God's Name: Why Sinai Still Matters.* Downers Grove, IL: InterVarsity Press, 2019.

James, Richard. *Misreading Scripture with Individualist Eyes: Patronage, Honor, and Shame in the Biblical World.* Downers Grove, IL: IVP Academic, 2020.

Sherman, Amy L. *Kingdom Calling: Vocational Stewardship for the Common Good.* Downers Grove, IL: InterVarsity Press, 2011.

Woodley, Randy. *Living in Color: Embracing God's Passion for Diversity.* Downers Grove, IL: InterVarsity Press, 2001.

3

THE JOURNEY OF CALLING

*Now the LORD said to Abram, "Go from your country and your
kindred and your father's house to the land that I will show you."*

GENESIS 12:1

ON A FAMILY TRIP SOME YEARS AGO, we made a connection in an
airport I had never been in before. Seeing the opportunity to expand the
skills of my teenage children, I gave them the task of figuring out how to
get to our next flight. At first, the two of them stood looking at me blankly.
"How do we do that?" one teen asked. "Figure it out," I said. They looked
at one another. Then the other teen said, "Let's look for an airport map."
Off they went.

If you have traveled through airports, the process of navigation may
have become second nature to you. You know to check your boarding
pass for the flight number. You know to check the gate number against
the gate number published on the departures board. You know to look
for an airport map to see where the gate is located. If you are familiar
enough with an airport, you may even know where the gate is located
without having to consult the map. And you also know where the best
place is to get a cup of coffee and your favorite travel snacks on the way.

My teenagers didn't know any of that. Watching their process was
interesting. My husband and I stayed in the background to keep an eye

on them. They made mistakes and we let them so that they could learn. I was more interested in my teens developing the knowledge and skills necessary to navigate an airport than I was concerned about getting to the boarding gate in the least amount of time.

Much of the conversation about vocation focuses on knowing the specifics of our own callings with certainty. Many of us assume that, once we know, we will have the trajectory of our lives laid out before us. We would prefer that God give clear and unmistakable directions to our destination. We also assume that arriving at a destination of knowing our calling is the necessary first step toward a purposeful life. Instead, God seems to be more interested in the process of our development.

The development of a person's calling is akin to a journey. We have a sense of direction. Sometimes it is as specific as a particular destination, such as my family and I had on our trip with the city we were going to visit. Much of the time, though, the process of vocational formation is more like the passage through the airport: we need to navigate the next step in the journey. This chapter explores the metaphor of journey and how that metaphor helps us to interpret and manage our desire for certainty.

PHASES OF CALLING DEVELOPMENT

Many of us who are evangelical Christians in the United States tend to think of our biblical heroes in a gestalt: the whole of their life and the entirety of their accomplishments. We don't generally think about the processes they went through or the journey of their life across time. We don't actually think of them as people who had anxieties and concerns similar to our own. More often we see them as sort of super-humans whom God used in unique ways that are inspiring but also intimidating.

Consider Moses and the burning bush, for example. We see this narrative as an example of someone having a clear and unmistakable calling, and we read the entirety of Moses' life through the lens of this single event. This is the moment of clarity; this is the moment that set the trajectory of the rest of Moses' life. We generally do not think about all the other parts of Moses' life and the experiences that formed him. Because Moses' life, from birth to death, is one we have a fair amount of information about, his story is a good one for reflecting on calling as a lifelong process. In taking a closer look at his journey, we can see that the process of understanding God's purposes for his life and living into them falls roughly into three phases of formation: foundations, revelation, and fulfillment.[1]

Calling foundations. Examining Moses' early sense of purpose suggests something about how God establishes foundations in our life for our callings. We know that Moses was born into a Levite family (Exodus 2:1) and grew up in Pharaoh's household (Exodus 2:10; Acts 7:21-22). The biblical narrative does not give us details about the forty years Moses spent as a member of Pharaoh's household; we only get a glimpse in Stephen's message in Acts in which he notes Moses "was instructed in all the wisdom of the Egyptians" (Acts 7:22). But consider how significant those years of training were for preparing Moses to confront Pharaoh and lead the Israelites for forty years. Forty years of being trained in Pharaoh's household were key for Moses' development as a leader.[2]

We don't know what prompted Moses to go out among his people (Exodus 2:11; Acts 7:23). Nor do we know the details of *how* Moses came to have a sense of ethnic and cultural identity as a Hebrew. We just know that this identity was significant to him. Exodus 2:11 says Moses was forty years old when he "went out to his people and saw their forced labor." In this context he saw an Egyptian beating a Hebrew. The murder that followed was violent, tragic, and ill-conceived and also implies something of a sense of purpose. Stephen suggests the motive for Moses' actions: "He supposed that his kinsfolk would understand that God through him was rescuing them" (Acts 7:25). Here we have an event, forty years before

---

[1]This threefold construct is based on the work of J. Robert Clinton identifying patterns in leadership emergence. See J. Robert Clinton, *The Making of a Leader: Recognizing the Lessons and Stages of Leadership Development* (Colorado Springs: NavPress, 2012), 248.

[2]T. Desmond Alexander, *Exodus* (Downers Grove, IL: IVP Academic, 2017), 66.

the burning bush incident, that demonstrates Moses had a sense of purpose: he wanted to deliver his people. He was wrong in the method and the timing but he was right in terms of that purpose. Forty years later, it would become his mission from God to see the Hebrews set free from bondage to Pharaoh.

Moses spent the next forty years in the desert, taking care of sheep (Exodus 2:19-21; 3:1). Consider how these years and the knowledge Moses gained prepared him for the work that was ahead. He learned about desert survival and what it takes to keep people and flocks alive in an arid environment. He learned about how to find water. Forty years of sheep tending equipped Moses for forty years of Israelite tending.

One additional thing we know about this forty-year desert sojourn is that Moses went from being a brash, arrogant murderer to being a humble, uncertain shepherd (see Numbers 12:3). Important character development took place in him during those years in the wilderness. We affirm Moses' humility as one of our heroes; we rarely think of the importance of the life circumstances that shaped this humility.

Often in our own lives we're impatient for the burning-bush marching orders to give us a clear sense of the task to which God is calling us. We allow our cultural maps of "success" to press us toward a confrontation with Egyptian guards, assuming people will see our good intentions and believe we are acting on God's behalf. We seek to avoid the God-ordained, back-side-of-the-desert inner-life formation and ministry skill development. We are as quick to overlook God's shaping work in the foundations of our lives as we are to dismiss the first eighty years of Moses' life as significant for his leadership.

Calling revelation. Moses' experience at the burning bush stands as an exemplar of an awe-inspiring encounter with God. In this event we see all of the elements of what I identified in the previous chapter as a common model of calling. God is the caller, establishing a supernatural event that captures Moses' attention. The specific task to which God directs Moses is to confront Pharaoh to set God's people free. Moses is the called person, given the responsibility and authority from God for the task. The narrative in Exodus 3 and 4 is full of God's assurances for Moses that he is indeed the one chosen for the task as well as proofs that confirm this to Moses and, in anticipation, to Pharaoh and to the Israelites.

In some theological environments, this burning-bush narrative is the perfect model of a true calling. A calling is not really a calling if there isn't a clear sense of having heard directly from God; there must be some element of the supernatural work of God. Furthermore, the called person must demonstrate Moses-like reluctance to take up the call. Otherwise, others suspect that the sense of calling originated in the person's ego or desires.

❯ NAVIGATION POINT
On the Use of Names and Titles

Remember when you were a child. What did you call your grandparents? Your aunts and uncles? How about elderly people in the community? Or teachers at school? At what point in your development did you begin to address adults by their first name, if ever? Now that you are an adult, what do younger people call you? Do the children in your family have a special name for you, for example? How about children in your community or at your workplace?

The norm in some groups is never to call a person significantly older than yourself by their first name, at least not without some form of honorific—Miss Marge, Brother Thomas, Dr. Li, Reverend Garcia. The norm in other groups is to default to first name regardless of age and position unless there is some formal reason to use titles. In higher education, some educators with doctorates invite their students to call them by their first name; others assume students will address them by the title that comes with the degree they have earned. Some people come from communities where honorifics are the norm while others come from communities where the use of a title is seen as an attempt to enforce a hierarchy. There is a difference from community to community as to what the use of titles means.

The individuals who contributed their calling stories for this book come from a variety of communities and contexts. People reading this book also come from a variety of backgrounds. In the space of these pages, we form a community of learning and practice. As the author, I establish the community rules, so to speak. Stories that appear with a full name are from individuals who have given permission for their story to be included in this text. I choose to refer to these individuals by their titles to honor them. As Dr. Joyce del Rosario, whose story we will hear in chapter four, says, "It took my village to get me where I'm at so every time (my students) call me Dr. del Rosario, it honors the whole village."[3]

For some contributors and readers, this will feel overly formal. For other contributors and readers, this is a mark of respect and honor. I invite you, as you read "Dr." and "Ms." and "Pastor" with a person's name, to allow this practice to be a reminder to ask yourself, "How do I show honor to people in my own group? How do I show honor to people in other groups?"

Bishop Tony Dunn's calling story, set in the context of a short-term mission trip, is an example of a modern-day burning bush–type narrative. Notice, as you read, the way Bishop Dunn tells his story and what dynamics of the experience he highlights to emphasize his sense that this was an encounter with God.

CALLING STORY
Tony Dunn—Pastor, Bishop

Walking through the lush foliage of a mountainous area of the Dominican Republic to meet the team for morning devotions, I experienced the tangible presence of God. What made it so significant to me is that I had not been fasting or seeking God about anything specific at that time. Some people say, "I have been fasting, seeking the Lord, tarrying for the Lord," but that was not the case for me at that time; nevertheless, God literally met me there that morning.

---

[3] Dr. del Rosario was interviewed on a podcast: Dr. Joyce del Rosario, "Disruptive Potluck: What Are You Bringing to the Table?" interview by John Williams and Erin Takeuch, *Disruptive Peacemakers*, February 15, 2021, player.fm/series/disruptive-peacemakers/disruptive-potluck-what-are-you-bringing-to-the-table.

I felt the presence of God: the level of peace that overcame me, the comfort that I had, as well as there seemed to be a suspension of all things natural. Instantly I knew that it was God. I also knew something was being asked of me.

When the team got together, we were praying and I walked away to face the valley, a huge valley with a mountain on the other side. Facing the mountain, I began to pray. I was saying, "Speak to me. What is it that you are asking of me?" It began to rain: one of those Caribbean rains. We're under a tin roof and it was loud. The guy across from me— Pastor Hugo—began to cry out, "I need clarity! I need clarity!" I was asking the Lord the same thing; I just wasn't calling out like Hugo.

There was a pastor from Puerto Rico, Pastor R. He said, "I have a word for the people." He came to me and said, "God has called you to preach. He wants you to preach the gospel. Eat the word, devour the word. For you have been so insecure." And then he moved on to the next person.

Well! That gave me clarity: God wants me to preach. But it raised other questions also. I was overwhelmed, so I walked away from the team, and began to cry. Then I began to really sob. I could not deny it. God wants me to preach.

Notice how this calling story fits with the common model suggested in the previous chapter. God was the initiator of this experience. In Bishop Dunn's tradition, "tarrying for the Lord" is an important practice when seeking God's intervention or guidance. The fact that Bishop Dunn's experience came when he wasn't specifically seeking God for something emphasized God's initiative to speak to him in that moment of time. Bishop Dunn perceived God directing him personally to a specific role: preacher. The experience of the presence of God and the "double confirmation" of something sensed personally and spoken out by an individual with no prior knowledge of him are, for Bishop Dunn, important aspects of the story that indicate this was indeed an encounter with God on which he can base his sense of knowing his calling.[4]

---

[4]This is a contemporary example of the "double confirmation" dynamic noted earlier as present in the life of David and of Paul. See Clinton, *The Making of a Leader*, 115-17.

In other theological environments, the expectation of hearing directly from God is framed as a task of discernment in the providential circumstances of life. Examining one's own heart and passions, considering personality and giftedness, looking at the circumstances in life, and seeking the counsel and guidance of key people are seen as elements of God's gracious, superintending activity in human lives.

Mae grew up in a Mennonite family in rural Ohio. Her parents, particularly her mother, esteemed missionaries as "the really good Christians." Serious about wanting to serve and honor God, Mae became a missionary. Was that role a calling? From the perspective of her community, becoming a missionary was a good thing. Mae did not articulate an internal sense of being called by God, but what she did articulate was a sense of wanting to do something valuable with her life. Since her community saw mission work as valuable, that is what she did.

Do community expectations and values constitute a call from God? Depending on your social and theological context, the answer could be yes or no. For many people, particularly those from Pentecostal and charismatic backgrounds, because Mae could not identify a particular moment of clarity and certainty about having been directly appointed by God to the role of missionary, the answer would be no. For other people who either come from more collectivist religious traditions—as Mae did—or are part of ethnic groups with a more collectivist approach, the values and direction of the extended community are legitimate means of God's direction, sometimes more so than the individual's desires and impressions.

The revelation of calling is the element that most people focus on when thinking about their vocation. The question "How do I know my calling?" is an expression of a deep yearning for clarity and certainty. Moses is an exemplar of calling for many of us less because of the exact nature of his encounter with God and more because his encounter resulted in an absolutely clear, God-given task. We long to know as Moses knew. His doubt and fear resonate with us. Even as God was angry at Moses for his reluctance (Exodus 4:14), God still provided a way for him to move forward in what God had called him to do. We long for God to meet us in our anxieties and give us a similar sense of certainty.

Calling fulfillment. Many of us would name Moses as a person who finished well, having faithfully completed the work God set for him to do. When we think about Moses' story, the fulfillment elements we tend to focus on are the release of the Israelites from Egypt and then, forty years later, the preparation to enter the Promised Land. But did Moses fulfill his calling? How we answer that question depends on what we understand Moses' calling to be.

In the process of speaking to Moses from the burning bush, God said, "I have observed the misery of my people who are in Egypt . . . and I have come down to deliver them from the Egyptians, and to bring them up out of that land to a good and broad land, a land flowing with milk and honey" (Exodus 3:7-8). This was the specific task God assigned to Moses: "I will send you to Pharaoh to bring my people, the Israelites, out of Egypt" (Exodus 3:10). This task was further emphasized when God then said, "This shall be the sign for you that it is I who sent you: when you have brought the people out of Egypt, you shall worship God on this mountain" (Exodus 3:12). At one level, Moses had completed his assigned task when the people were gathered together at Sinai in worship in Exodus 19.

During the ongoing struggle with Pharaoh and the complaints of the people as their oppression increased, God gave this message to Moses for the Israelites:

> I am the LORD, and I will free you from the burdens of the Egyptians and deliver you from slavery to them. I will redeem you with an outstretched arm and with mighty acts of judgment. I will take you as my people, and I will be your God. You shall know that I am the LORD your God, who has freed you from the burdens of the Egyptians. I will bring you into the land that I swore to give to Abraham, Isaac, and Jacob; I will give it to you for a possession. I am the LORD. (Exodus 6:6-8)

Note that not once is there a direct charge to Moses that his task was to bring the people into the Promised Land. Always, this was what *God* would do. Moses' specific task was to confront Pharaoh and to bring the

Israelites up out of Egypt. Everything that follows in the book of Exodus is the working out of this specific assignment. Clearly, God's ultimate purpose was to bring the people into the land that God had promised. This was the broader context of Moses' calling; this was the larger purpose toward which his specific assignment was aimed. Yet, it is significant to note that God never said to Moses, "You are to bring the people into the Promised Land."

When we consider the revelation of calling and the fulfillment of that calling for someone, we tend to focus on the product of that one person's labor and disregard the broader context of their work. When we seek to know our own calling, we are anxious to know our individual assigned task. We understand, theologically and theoretically, that any Christian calling has to be grounded in God's broader purposes, but that knowledge has a limited impact on our search for clarity. It also has a limited impact on how we assess the fulfillment of a calling. We focus on what an individual does in their single lifetime more than we focus on God's broader purposes in the world. In chapter nine we will return again to the idea of calling fulfillment, looking at the legacies that people leave as their contribution to God's work in the world. Before we can think about the end, however, we need to continue to think about how God has formed us in the past and is forming us in the present moment.

Let us consider this three-part pattern as we read Ms. Laura Gordon's story in her own words. Observe how providential circumstances play a larger part in Ms. Gordon's story than they do in Bishop Dunn's story.

CALLING STORY
Laura Gordon, MDiv—CEO, Business Manager, CPA

I didn't even know what a CPA was until I was in college. Once I took accounting classes, I just knew that's what I was supposed to do. It was some time after I started my business that I came to see there was no distinction between me as a believer in Jesus and me as a CPA. Being at church or being in the office, God would bring people across my path and open doors of opportunity to pray or to minister the Word. It became clear to me that what I do every day is a sort of mission field of people from all different walks of life and all different backgrounds.

How I came to see my work as a calling involved my pastor, Juanda Green. Sometime when I was in my late thirties, Pastor Green started asking me questions about my work. "What do you do with your employees and colleagues and clients?" she asked. I answered, "Well, this happens and they'll call and we'll pray." She said, "Oh, so you're pastoring people! You are a minister in the marketplace." She defined my role as "marketplace minister." I'm licensed by the church as a marketplace minister.

As a CPA, we're part of the inner circle of trusted advisers. I'm not just a CPA, I'm a business manager for entertainers and professional athletes. We know everything they're doing because we see every credit card statement. There's this immediate intimacy with them because they know that I'm aware of everything going on in their life. Also, there's a fiduciary responsibility. I see things and I pray. They know who I am, they know what I believe as a Christian. I don't preach to them because they're not coming to a church service and they don't want to hear a sermon. But if they ask, I share.

There was an opportunity a few years ago with World Vision; they were raising money to build a network of water wells in Zambia. Because of my relationship with these clients—they have foundations and they give money to different causes—I was able to help point them to this opportunity. We raised a lot of money for the project in Zambia. When we got the reports back about the transformation of that entire region of that country, it felt like God hasn't released me to go there personally but he did require me to raise these funds.

Jesus spent most of his time in the marketplace. So did Paul. But yet we always talk about the pastors in the church. I've come to understand that the marketplace is part of the apostolic anointing. Jesus sent us *out*. We're not supposed to sit under each other in church all day. We're supposed to go out. We come together, we worship, we

build each other up, we equip one another, and all that. But we're supposed to be *out*. It's more than just warming the pews and fighting
over ministry positions. There are too many people out here who
need a word from the Lord. I'm not behind a pulpit but the Lord does
use me to help direct resources and, hopefully, direct hearts to him. So,
I see the marketplace as a calling for me.

Notice the indications of calling foundations in Ms. Gordon's story.
Unstated but present was the family value of higher education that supported her in pursuing a professional degree. She had the inherent inclinations and ability to do well in an educational setting pursuing not one
but two degrees. Also unstated but inferred is Ms. Gordon's faith background. She comes from a believing family and was formed by lifelong
participation in church.

Observe how her calling revelation emerged over time. Her experience in her first accounting class played a part. "I just knew that's
what I was supposed to do," she says. Seeing her role as a CPA and
business manager as a "calling" took time to develop. Ms. Gordon finished her degree, became a CPA, and started her business, working in
this role for a number of years before she thought of her role as "ministry." Her story shows a gradual process of emerging revelation across
time. Identifying herself as a marketplace minister was provoked by a
conversation with her pastor, but notice that the revelation was an
identification of what Ms. Gordon was already doing. She had found
her way to her calling; what she lacked was the perspective and language to recognize her identity as a "marketplace minister." Her pastor
and church community so valued and affirmed her calling in this role
that she was licensed as a minister.[5]

Ms. Gordon's calling fulfillment is yet in process. She narrates one
contribution she has made: facilitating the raising of funds for a World

---

[5]In some traditions, including the one of which Ms. Gordon was a part, ordination happens in
two steps: licensing and ordination. Individual churches and pastors have the authority to license
members for ministry roles the community recognizes.

Vision project. In the years following the interview in which she shared this story, her influence has expanded as she continues to engage in the marketplace and act as a person of godly influence in the entertainment industry in Southern California.

ON IDENTITY FORMATION

Consider this lifelong pattern of calling development in light of what developmental psychology has learned about the process of identity formation across a lifetime. When a person is seeking to know their calling, they are fundamentally engaged in the process of developing an identity as a called person. This means that when people ask the question, "How can I know my calling?" they are often asking decision-making questions. Should I take this job or that job? Should I move to another city or stay here? Should I pursue an educational degree and, if so, which degree and at what institution? The questions are ones of direction and choice. Yet these questions are also about who we are and the kind of people we want to be in the world.

Identity has two primary components: who we see ourselves to be and who we are seen to be by people around us.[6] This is true for our social identities. My identity as a White woman, for example, is partially a matter of my internal sense of racial-ethnic-cultural identity and gender identity and partially a matter of how I am classified by society. This dynamic is also present in terms of our identity as a called person. We have an internal sense of calling and our community has a view of us as called people.

A great deal of psychological research has focused on human development from birth through emerging adulthood. Developmental theories describe the process of normative development of differing aspects

---

[6]New Testament scholar Love Sechrest was the person who first brought this dynamic to my attention. In a class on race and Christian identity in the New Testament, she highlighted the ways that our identities—both as a Christian and as people in the world—are partially internally located in how we identify ourselves and partially externally located in how people see us. See the discussion of this point in chapter two, "The Complexity of Identity," in Beverly Daniel Tatum, *Why Are All the Black Kids Sitting Together in the Cafeteria? And Other Conversations About Race*, rev. and updated ed. (New York: Basic Books, 2017).

of the human being.[7] Erik Erikson's eight-stage model of development from birth to old age is one classic framework for understanding development across a lifetime.[8] We will consider particular aspects of calling development related to racial-ethnic-cultural identity, socioeconomic status and class, and gender identity in the second section of this book. For the present, looking at Erikson's stages helps shed light on some developmental aspects of a lifetime of vocational formation.[9] Let us consider these factors interacting with one another: the individual and collective nature of identity formation across a lifetime of development, and the ways in which these are the context for calling foundation, calling revelation, and calling fulfillment.

Calling foundations in childhood. Psychologists and sociologists think about socialization as the process of learning and internalizing the norms and beliefs of society. This starts even in earliest infancy. How parents and other caregivers interact with babies teaches those small humans about themselves and how they fit in the world. Foundational relationships are powerful for fostering an infant's sense of self and influential in how that person will engage in relationships later in life.[10] For some people, a relatively secure childhood helps to instill in them a secure sense of self. Their early attachments to significant people foster a sense of worthiness. When they encounter challenging relationships later in life, the foundations laid in childhood help them cope with and

---

[7]Many psychologists focus on early childhood development, but a few theorists have considered development across the life span. See Jack O. Balswick, Pamela Ebstyne King, and Kevin S. Reimer, *The Reciprocating Self: Human Development in Theological Perspective*, 2nd ed. (Downers Grove, IL: IVP Academic, 2016), 76.

[8]Erik H. Erikson, *Identity and the Life Cycle* (New York: Norton, 1980). See also Erik H. Erikson, *The Life Cycle Completed* (New York: Norton, 1985). For other authors who draw from this framework and offer additional reflections on experience across the span of adulthood, see Daniel J. Levinson et al., *The Seasons of a Man's Life* (New York: Ballentine Books, 1978); Gail Sheehy, *New Passages: Mapping Your Life Across Time* (New York: Ballentine Books, 1995). See also Gail Sheehy, *Understanding Men's Passages: Discovering the New Map of Men's Lives* (New York: Ballentine Books, 1999).

[9]For a reflection on the relationship between a sociological inquiry of life course with its attention on social context and life-span psychology related to the individual, see Chris Gilleard and Paul Higgs, "Connecting Life Span Development with the Sociology of the Life Course: A New Direction," *Sociology: The Journal of the British Sociological Association* 50, no. 2 (2016): 301-15.

[10]Balswick, King, and Reimer, *Reciprocating Self*, 140.

recover from those challenges. For other people, the traumas of neglect and abuse foster a sense of unworthiness and an anxious engagement with the world. When these individuals encounter difficulties in life, their internal sense of self tells them that such difficulties are what they deserve and should expect.[11]

Many of the calling narratives in Christian circles address childhood in one of two ways. The first narrative is of an idealized childhood, where a person grows up in a functional, healthy Christian home, becomes a follower of Jesus, and experiences an early sense of calling to a particular role in life. The second type of childhood narrative is one of adversity overcome. In this narrative, the child grows up in a non-Christian home that is oppressive or abusive. At some point, often through an encounter with a significant adult, this individual comes to faith. Either as a teenager or as a young adult, they then turn their adversity into the basis for ministering to people with similar life experiences. Their sense of calling draws on their past experience, which becomes the basis of their ministry.

The idealized family narrative and the overcoming adversity narrative are a kind of story template, a cultural map of what a worthwhile Christian life looks like. Yet these two narratives don't fit every person. There are individuals from Christian families who experience traumatic psychological and physical wounds, for example. There are also people who have relatively healthy, functional childhoods in non-Christian homes. All of us have places of wounding from our upbringing as well as areas of functioning and resilience.

God is endlessly creative and capable of working in and through any circumstance. The early years of our lives, from infancy through childhood and adolescence, and then into early adulthood, are profoundly significant in our formation. Some of the formation we experience is in line with God's intentions for us; some of our experiences are directly opposed to God's intention for our flourishing. Nevertheless,

---

[11]For more on the impact of trauma on a person's formation, see Bessel A. Van der Kolk, *The Body Keeps the Score: Brain, Mind, and Body in the Healing of Trauma* (New York, Penguin Books, 2015).

God is always at work. Most of that work is for the sake of healing, development, and transformation as God works in our lives so that we are becoming the human beings God created us to be.

The stereotypical image of the adolescent is of a person preoccupied with themselves and the formation of their individual identity. A popular conceptualization of the work of adolescence is the development of an autonomous identity distinct from one's family, particularly parents. Indeed, differentiation—the formation of a sense of identity as distinct from others—is a major developmental task as adolescents think about their beliefs, values, and goals as well as their boundaries with families and friends.[12] Understanding adolescence as necessarily involving rebellion from family values, however, is a Western and individualistic way of thinking about human formation. Reflecting on this point, professor of social work Lacey Sloan and her colleagues, write, "In collectivities societies, healthy identity development is not about reaching a state of 'autonomous self' but about creating a healthy identity in relationship with others."[13] This kind of work does happen in the United States as well, despite the popular mental map that would characterize adolescents as purely self-absorbed. Professors Jack Balswick, Pamela Ebstyne King, and Kevin Reimer note, "From the perspective of thriving, optimal development is not about individual succuss, achievement or subjective well-being. Thriving can include those things but also involves a commitment to giving back to society in some manner."[14] Adolescence is a significant period in the process of developing this kind of reciprocating engagement with others.

Psychologist Beverly Daniel Tatum observes that "integrating one's past, present, and future into a cohesive, unified sense of self is a complex task that begins in adolescence and continues for a lifetime."[15] What

---

[12]Balswick, King, and Reimer, *Reciprocating Self*, 182-83, 201.
[13]Lacey M. Sloan, Mildred C. Joyner, Catherine J. Stakeman, and Cathryne L. Schmitz, *Critical Multiculturalism and Intersectionality in a Complex World* (New York: Oxford University Press, 2018), 27.
[14]Balswick, King, and Reimer, *Reciprocating Self*, 206.
[15]Tatum, *Why Are All the Black Kids*, 101.

element of our identity is most salient at any given moment changes with the seasons of life and the context in which we find ourselves. For example, as we will explore further in chapter six, an adolescent's development of gendered identity may be very significant and strongly influence what they consider as potential future roles based on what roles and occupations they see women and men engage in their contexts.

Tatum notes that dominance or advantage is one dimension that increases the salience of a particular aspect of identity for us. When an aspect of our identity is the dominant one in a particular social setting, we are less likely to have a conscious awareness of that aspect; as the dominant identity, it is seen as the norm for the group. Continuing with the example of gender, a teenage boy in a conservative theological environment may identify a sense of calling to pastoral ministry without ever thinking about his gender identity. A teenage girl in that same context is likely to be highly aware of her biological sex and gender if she feels a sense of calling to pastoral ministry. I have given the example here of gender identity, but the same dynamic is present in other aspects of identity as well. Particularly in the painful self-consciousness of adolescence, we are keenly aware of social norms and the extent to which we do and don't fit those norms.

Calling in adulthood. God's formative work continues with our emergence into adulthood. The early years of adulthood are a significant time of identity formation, since that is when many people make a number of critical choices for their life path: education, career direction, a life partner, parenthood, and so forth.

The stereotypical image of a person asking vocational questions is a young adult deciding their direction in life. One common mental map of vocation is often demonstrated at this stage of development: the question about direction in life is based on an understanding of vocation as the identification of a trajectory for life. While it is not only the young adult who asks this question or has this understanding of calling, this is a frequent concern at this stage of development. "What is my calling?" has embedded in it the assumption that I need to know what occupation

I should choose and that this will be the path I will follow for the rest of my life.

To some extent, this cultural map of a trajectory established with the choosing of an occupation reflects a structure of society that, at least in the North Atlantic societies, was once true but has largely now passed away. In the past, individuals would take up employment with companies early in adulthood and then work for that company for the rest of their lives. People would settle down in an area never to move from that location. In the twenty-first century, particularly in so-called developed nations, this historic pattern has given way to a flexible and changing journey in which people take up multiple different occupations in a lifetime and possibly move to a variety of different locations. Movement and change are now more the norm than an exception. In an era of history when change is rapid and rapidly spreading, the older mental map of vocation as a single trajectory in life no longer matches many people's experiences.

The understanding of calling as the establishment of a single trajectory for life still exists in some of our congregations and families, however. Young adults, particularly those in conservative evangelical congregations, feel a sense of expectation that they are to find a direction and a life partner in their early twenties. Older adults, even those as young as their late twenties, may have a sense of "missed time" because their life experience has not followed this cultural map. At times, a person in their thirties or forties may have received the overt message that it is "too late" to prepare for a ministry vocation, although this is less common now than it once was.

The late twenties to early thirties can be a time of reevaluation. Individuals who are dissatisfied with elements of their life—career, family, and other aspects—may see this time as a "last chance" to get started on a path of their choice.[16] A person's thirties may be a time of setting into a pattern of relationships and life roles. This is a significant time of

---

[16]Balswick, King, and Reimer, *Reciprocating Self*, 239.

vocational formation as people develop a sense of direction in their family and career. The activity of this season is learning to do things well.

Calling in midlife. When people reach middle life, they encounter what Erikson refers to as the challenge of generativity.[17] Generativity "encompasses procreativity, productivity, and creativity, and thus the generation of new being as well as of new products and new ideas, including a kind of self-generation concerned with further identity development."[18] Balswick, King, and Reimer observe, "Societal norms define success in terms of employment advancement to higher status and earning capabilities. Midlife can be a time of crisis for the individuals who realize that they will not reach the lofty goal that they have set for themselves."[19] This is often a context of reevaluation and reassessment of life roles and occupations. A person's forties may include a midlife crisis when a sense of mortality emerges.

For many people, the socioeconomic experiences related to occupation and other life roles have a spiritual parallel in a process of life maturing.[20] Some individuals may come to faith in these midlife years as their previous assurance of their capacity to control their lives is undermined by events and circumstances. For other individuals who have been living as followers of Jesus up to this point, this season of life is often accompanied by an invitation of the Spirit to a deeper walk that goes beyond accomplishment and production. Individuals may experience "hitting the wall" where they receive God's invitation to go deeper in their formation, surrendering their wills to be healed spiritually and psychologically.[21] Doing well and succeeding in producing are no longer sufficient.

A crisis such as a major illness or a severe economic setback or a trauma such as the loss of a significant relationship through divorce or

---

[17]Erikson, *Identity and the Life Cycle*, 103.

[18]Erikson, *Life Cycle Completed*, 67.

[19]Balswick, King, and Reimer, *Reciprocating Self*, 252.

[20]Clinton, *Making of a Leader*, 133-51.

[21]Janet O. Hagberg and Robert A. Guelich, *The Critical Journey: Stages in the Life of Faith*, 2nd ed. (Salem, WI: Sheffield Publishing, 2004), 114-30.

estrangement or death may be a triggering event for such formation.[22] In some contexts, this midlife crisis is interpreted as a failure of calling. Truly called people are "supposed" to persevere for a lifetime. Faithful people are "supposed" to overcome adversity. Holding to a cultural model of calling that prioritizes success and production will necessitate this interpretation of failure. Consider instead what could happen if we let go of those mental maps and recognize that this midlife reevaluation is part of God's process of development. By seeing calling formation as a lifelong journey, we are able to lean into the discomfort and perceive what God is doing at this point in our lives.

If we pass through the disruption of midlife reevaluation, responding positively to God's invitation to deeper formation, we may come to what J. Robert Clinton refers to as convergence.[23] This is a season of development in which a person's roles, giftings, and experience all come together to result in a satisfying life of doing that flows out of being. Many of the heroes of faith we point to as historical or contemporary exemplars of a called person were living in this phase. Often, people who are seeking to know their calling are looking at individuals in this convergence stage of life and assuming that it is a picture of what calling should be like for the whole of life. This assumption is a source of painful frustration when the gap between one's own experience and another person's experience in convergence is so large. Again, this represents a distortion to our cultural maps that can be addressed by recognizing vocational formation as a lifelong process.

Calling in the elder years. Whereas a century ago in the United States, retirement age was set at sixty-five and few people lived much past that age, life expectancy overall in the United States is currently around seventy-eight years of age.[24] People who reach the age of sixty in good health

---

[22]For a reflection on such events and the work of God in the isolation they create, see Shelley G. Trebesch, *Isolation: A Place of Transformation in the Life of a Leader* (Altadena, CA: Barnabas Publishers, 1997).

[23]Clinton, *Making of a Leader*, 39-40.

[24]"FastStats—Life Expectancy," National Center for Health Statistics, Centers for Disease Control and Prevention, updated April 9, 2021, www.cdc.gov/nchs/fastats/life-expectancy.htm.

can now expect to live into their nineties.[25] Thus, what is referred to as the "third third" of life has become a significant place of meaning making. Vocational formation in late adulthood may include "afterglow," a season of retirement in which a person can appreciate the fruits of their labor.[26] Other adults in late adulthood, knowing they possibly have decades ahead of them, choose a second or third career path. Some of these older adults return to school. Others may focus on volunteer efforts or play a significant role in raising grandchildren. In this season of life, a person potentially "becomes less self-centered and the sense of oneself expands to include a wider range of interrelated others."[27] Balswick, King, and Reimer observe that "persons with high ego integration or strong reciprocating selfhood live with a confidence that their life has meaning, value and direction."[28] These senior years can be full of purpose.

ON MAKING SENSE RETROSPECTIVELY

Most calling stories have this characteristic: we tell the story as it makes sense to us now. We don't tell the story with all its messy complications or with all the twists and turns that were experienced in real time. We might mention some of the struggles that were particularly significant to us, but generally, we narrate our experience in a way that makes a clear connection between our experiences and the present moment.

This characteristic of making sense when we look back is the basis of one of the challenges of discerning calling: we compare our inner state of being with what we perceive of the outward expression of other people. Someone meeting Ms. Gordon now would, understandably, assume that she had always been clear about her sense of purpose. They might miss the hints of the complexities and painful moments when that purpose didn't seem as clear or when it was under reconsideration. We do this

---

[25]Balswick, King, and Reimer, *Reciprocating Self*, 261.

[26]Clinton, *Making of a Leader*, 40.

[27]Erik Erikson and Joan M. Erikson, *The Life Cycle Completed: Extended Version* (New York: W. W. Norton, 1997), 124.

[28]Balswick, King, and Reimer, *Reciprocating Self*, 245. For a discussion of continued spiritual development in old age, see William R. Yount, "Transcendence and Aging: The Secular Insights of Erikson and Maslow," *Journal of Religion, Spirituality & Aging* 21, no. 1-2 (2008): 73-87.

with our spiritual heroes as well by looking at their lives and assuming there was a straight line of "knowing" all through their experience. We are apt to compare our questions to their certainty and find ourselves inadequate. Realizing that we make sense of life in retrospect can help us have peace with the messiness and difficulties of the present season and trust that God is still at work in our lives.

When we're asking the question "What is my calling?" we tend to be thinking about this present moment and the near future. The idea that the formation of our vocations takes a lifetime isn't welcome news to some people. Those of us in the United States live in a context that expects immediate results. But God's invitation to us is to a lifetime of formation. God is working to form in us a sense of purpose—a sense that God's hand is on our lives for God's purposes. Like Moses, our early lives are the context of shaping us for those purposes and tasks that we do not yet know. Our calling develops over time with multiple seasons of reflection. We need discernment not as a one-time event to "know" our calling but as a regular pattern of perceiving God's work and God's invitation to participation in that work.

QUESTIONS FOR REFLECTION AND DISCUSSION

1. This chapter suggests that calling is a lifelong journey. How has this metaphor been part of your thinking about vocational formation in the past? Where does this metaphor challenge what you believe about calling?

2. Consider your early life experiences, before your twenties. Reflecting back, where do you see indications of God shaping your life? If you had a sense of God having purpose for your life, under what circumstances did that sense of purpose develop?

3. Consider elements of your social location—gender, race, social class, age, ability, religion, sexual orientation, education, and geographic location. Which of these identities is most significant for your sense of self at this point in your development?

EXPLORING A BIBLICAL NARRATIVE: ABRAHAM

1. Read Genesis 12:1-2. At this moment in time, what two things did Abraham know about God's calling for his life?

2. Read Genesis 12:7. What did Abraham now know that wasn't clear before?

3. Read Genesis 15:1-6. What new information did Abraham receive about his calling?

4. Compare Genesis 12:4 with Genesis 16:16 and Genesis 17:1. How much time has passed between these events? How does awareness of this passage of time affect your perception of Abraham's calling?

5. Read Genesis 17:1-8. How much of God's promise to Abraham was fulfilled in Abraham's lifetime?

6. What implications does Abraham's lifelong calling journey have for your own experience of calling across time?

SUGGESTIONS FOR FURTHER READING

Balswick, Jack O., Pamela Ebstyne King, and Kevin S. Reimer. *The Reciprocating Self: Human Development in Theological Perspective*. 2nd ed. Downers Grove, IL: IVP Academic, 2016.

Cahalan, Kathleen A., and Bonnie J. Miller-McLemore, eds. *Calling All Years Good: Christian Vocation Throughout Life's Seasons*. Grand Rapids, MI: Eerdmans, 2017.

Clinton, J. Robert. *The Making of a Leader: Recognizing the Lessons and Stages of Leadership Development*. Rev. ed. Colorado Springs: NavPress, 2018.

PART 2

SOCIAL LOCATIONS CONSIDERED

IN THE FIRST PART OF THIS BOOK, I laid a foundation for thinking about the concept of social location as a context for vocational formation. This next section explores three specific areas of socially constructed identity: racial-ethnic-cultural identity, socioeconomic status or class, and gender identity. Each of these identities shapes who we understand ourselves to be. They also influence what we understand calling to be and how we interpret God's work in our lives for vocational formation.

For many of us who come from cultures that have been influenced by the Enlightenment in Europe, considering context seems to contradict the cultural assumption of the primacy of "rational" thought and the value for "objectivity." What we don't realize is how much of what we consider objective is a reflection of looking at the world from a particular perspective. We make our view of reality the norm for everyone.

> **NAVIGATION POINT**
> **Socially Constructed Knowledge**

The concept of "socially constructed knowledge" is a theory of knowledge developed in sociology and communications theory that looks at how humans rationalize their experience and codify that rationalization in language.[1] Social constructions are critical to the function of human societies and cultures. Human groups collectively determine the rules for behaving in ways that are considered appropriate.

There are multiple examples of social constructions in use throughout societies. Money is a socially constructed concept, for example; people collectively agree that a piece of paper represents something of value. The intrinsic value of the piece of paper is low. It is the collective agreement of the group that determines the worth of the currency note as well as the ways for appropriately interacting with it. Law, marriage, and family are all socially constructed institutions as well with the norms and expectations being collectively arrived upon.

The purpose of this exploration is to facilitate greater clarity of discernment. As we see ourselves with increasing accuracy, as we recognize God's fingerprints on our lives, we have the opportunity to recognize how God is working to shape and equip us for participation in God's work in the world. I encourage you to receive God's invitation to growing awareness of our multiple identities. As we develop a healthy sense of who we are, bringing the broken things to God in repentance and lament, we are increasingly free to recognize God's calling. We are increasingly capable of discerning where the Spirit is at work and inviting us to join in that work. We are increasingly able to minister out of freedom and wholeness, unhindered by fear and fragility. To be fully known by God and to know ourselves, broken places and all, is to be able to be fully present and fully engaged in God's work in the world.

---

[1] For a scholarly explication of constructionism, see Dave Elder-Vass, *The Reality of Social Construction* (Cambridge, UK: Cambridge University Press, 2012).

4

THE GIFT OF PARTICULARITY
Racial-Ethnic-Cultural Identity and Christian Vocation

After this I looked, and there was a great multitude that no one
could count, from every nation, from all tribes and peoples and
languages, standing before the throne and before the Lamb.

REVELATION 7:9

Could it be that the Creator made all the diverse ethnic groups so that
they would look to Him not only through their own eyes but the eyes of
those different from themselves, so they might see Him more clearly?

RANDY WOODLEY, *LIVING IN COLOR*

IT WAS A SPRING AFTERNOON. The classroom was full, almost to capacity. The students came from diverse national backgrounds— different parts of the United States, Canada, Uganda, Nigeria, Malawi, China, Korea, Norway, and Germany. We reflected together on the scene presented in Revelation 7. I suggested to this room full of developing Christian leaders that Revelation 7:9, with its picture of multicultural and multiethnic worship, represents the God-given vision of the outcome of the church's mission: we look toward the day when a countless multitude from every tribe and tongue will stand before God. I assumed this biblical framework would help set the tone for a discussion of the impact of ethnicity and race on our work as Christian leaders. Partway into the conversation, Lisa made a comment: "But I don't know anyone in my church who thinks like this," she said. "Revelation 7 is in the Bible but it has nothing to do with our daily life as Christians."

For many years, I was much like Lisa. Despite having been a missionary kid in my early years and then, in the United States, growing up in an ethnically and racially diverse neighborhood, despite more than twenty years as a member of a church that could technically be considered multiracial,[1] I hadn't given much thought to the significance of my racial-ethnic-cultural (REC) identity. I possibly had more passion about the vision presented in Revelation 7 than Lisa expressed, yet I had no sense of how being White was significant for my part in fulfilling that vision. It took time reflecting on my REC identity and many different experiences before I began to see how being White affected my perception of calling in the past and shapes how I live out my calling today.

How we think about calling and vocation is shaped by our experiences in particular social and cultural contexts. A person's racial-ethnic-cultural identity is part of the particularity of their experience. God meets people in this particularity and uses it to equip them for participation in God's work in the world. We'll reflect on this idea and process together in this chapter. I begin by briefly overviewing the concepts of race and ethnicity and then lay out a short reflection on race and ethnicity in Christian Scriptures and in the United States today. After that I reflect on the process of forming a racial-ethnic-cultural identity and how that affects our experience of vocational formation. This discussion is framed primarily for the person who has never thought about their REC identity.

---

[1] According to the multiracial church literature, a multiracial church is one in which at least 20 percent of the congregation is some racial-ethnic-cultural group different from the majority. See, for example, Curtiss Paul DeYoung et al., *United by Faith: The Multiracial Congregation as an Answer to the Problem of Race* (New York: Oxford University Press, 2003), 3.

For those who have thought substantively about their racial-ethnic-cultural identity, I hope to offer language that might be helpful for speaking about the experience. The intention is to provide some common ground for expressing both a sense of identity and how that identity influences vocational development.

RACE AND ETHNICITY: A BRIEF OVERVIEW

Race is a term we use commonly in the United States. When we fill out forms—for school applications, at the doctor's office, to submit our taxes, to name a few—we are asked to indicate a racial identity. Many people in the United State take this practice for granted. It didn't cross my mind to wonder about it until I heard colleagues from other countries comment that they found this practice baffling. They wouldn't consider race (as defined in the US) to be a relevant way of defining and categorizing people.

This approach to categorizing people originated in Europe during the seventeenth century and found its way to the Americas via immigrating Europeans.[2] European and US-American perspectives on racial categories continue to have some similarity, but the ways that US-American society is racialized—a racialized society being "a society wherein race matters profoundly for differences in life experiences, life opportunities, and social relationships"[3]—is distinctive to this national, cultural context. This is one reason why people from other countries have difficulty understanding what one of my Australian colleagues once referred to as "the US-American obsession with race."

Sociologists Michael Omi and Howard Winant observe that the concept of race in the United States is often seen as a social category that is either an objective reality or an ideological construct. They write, "When viewed as an object matter, race is usually understood as rooted

---

[2]The first modern, "scientific" classification system of race was published in 1684 by French physician François Bernier. Bernier divided humanity into four "species"—the "first race" (Europeans), African Negros, South and South-East Asians, and the Lapps. For a full discussion of Bernier and his philosophical antecedents, see Siep Stuurman, "François Bernier and the Invention of Racial Classification," *History Workshop Journal* 50, no. 50 (2000): 1-21.

[3]Michael O. Emerson and Christian Smith, *Divided by Faith: Evangelical Religion and the Problem of Race in America* (New York: Oxford University Press, 2000), 7.

in biological differences, ranging from such familiar phonemic markers as skin color, hair texture, or eye shape, to more obscure human variations occurring at the genetic or genomic levels."[4] This is race as determined by what we observe in a person's body; we see someone's appearance and make assumptions about what group they belong to. When viewed as an ideological construct, note Omi and Winant, race is seen as a concept that "masks a more fundamental material distinction" such as ethnicity, class, or nation.[5] In other words, the informal, popular use of the term *race* stands in as a signifier for more complex identities that are more about cultural affiliation than about physical phenotypes.

Ethnicity is a social classification of people based on common heritage, ancestry, language, religion, social practices, and other cultural categories. Culture plays an important part in this identity formation. People in the United States sometimes identify ourselves by ethnic descriptors— Italian American or Polish American or Mexican American, for example. These terms refer to history and culture, to family ties and language.

The term *racial-ethnic-cultural identity* captures a sense of identity that may include phenotype categories but is far more complex. My use of the term has been influenced by Beverly Daniel Tatum, who notes, "What in the past . . . were referred to as models of racial identity development are now better understood as racial-cultural identity or racial-ethnic-cultural (REC) identity models."[6] Tatum cites the research of William Cross and Binta Cross, who explain that these three identifiers—race, ethnicity, and culture—overlap in lived experience to the extent that there is little reason to discuss them separately.[7]

Using the concept of racial-ethnic-cultural identity helps to capture the distinctiveness of a person's experience. For example, my colleague George's mother is Mexican American and his father is Black. People

---

[4]Michael Omi and Howard Winant, *Racial Formation in the United States* (New York: Routledge, 2014), 109.
[5]Omi and Winant, *Racial Formation in the United States*, 109.
[6]Beverly Daniel Tatum, *Why Are All the Black Kids Sitting Together in the Cafeteria? And Other Conversations About Race*, rev. and updated ed. (New York: Basic Books, 2017), 134.
[7]Tatum, *Why Are All the Black Kids*, 134.

look at George's melanin-rich skin and identify him as African American. Meanwhile, George speaks fluent Spanish and self-identifies as a Black Latino. George's racial-ethnic-cultural identity is far richer and more complex than simplistic racial categories.

ETHNICITY AS GOD'S DESIGN

The English terms *ethnic* and *ethnicity* are derived from the Greek word *ethnos*. This is the word that appears in Revelation 7:9: "After this I looked, and there was a great multitude that no one could count, from every *ethnos*." It also appears in Matthew 28, where Jesus says, "Go therefore and make disciples of all nations" (Matthew 28:19); the word translated as "nations" in English is the Greek word *ethnos*. Matthew 28 and Revelation 7 give us a window into God's purpose and intention for the world and for the people of the world. Jesus' command to make disciples in Matthew 28 includes all the ethnicities of the world. Revelation 7 is a glimpse into the throne room of God, where all the ethnicities of the world are gathered in worship. Put another way, these verses reveal the distinctiveness of all the peoples of the world gathered into the family of God and preserved in the presence of God in eternity. Matthew 28 is the church's mission; Revelation 7 is a vision of that mission fulfilled.

Jason approached me during a break after a class discussion in which I attempted to help the participants reflect on how their racial-ethnic-cultural identity had affected their spiritual formation. He had been very thoughtful and attentive during the entire discussion. Now he brought me his concern. "I hear what you're saying about all people standing before God," he said, "but racial identity is just the way the world defines you. As Christians, we are a new creation." Jason's reference to 2 Corinthians 5:17 was important to his sense of self as a child of God. He had previously shared his personal testimony of a troubled childhood and turbulent young adult years. His story was one of deliverance from addiction to drugs and alcohol. For Jason, being a "new creation" was a way of making meaning of his experience. The "old things" of abuse and addiction had passed away; he was a new creation in Christ.

Jason applied this same framework to his racial-ethnic-cultural identity. Race, in Jason's mind, is a worldly definition that passes away. When we become Christians, we are no longer White or Black or Latinx or Asian or Indigenous; we are God's people. "We should focus on our identity in Christ," Jason asserted, echoing the teaching of his church, "not the identities the world gives us." This teaching—that Christians should set aside their racial-ethnic-cultural identities in favor of a "heavenly" identity—presumes there is such a thing as a generic human existence to which we all aspire. In so doing, it ignores the testimony of Scripture regarding the existence of the *ethnos* in eternity. It also avoids noticing that God works within human cultures throughout the Bible.

Remember, for example, that God chose a particular person, Abraham, in a particular social-cultural location, Ur of the Chaldeans. God's intention for the peoples of the earth was clear in this calling: "I will bless those who bless you, . . . and in you all the families of the earth shall be blessed" (Genesis 12:3). God made Abraham the father of a distinct people with a particular language and geographical location as well as particular social-cultural values. The Israelites were not generic humans; they were an *ethnos*.[8]

Consider too the incarnation. Our very understanding of Jesus as the God-man rests on the history of God's work in the particular people of Israel. God became a specific human being: Jesus. Jesus was not a generic human; Jesus was a first-century, male Jew in Roman-occupied Palestine. God became a particular and distinct cultural and ethnic being. God's self-revelation in Jesus cannot be understood apart from his cultural and ethnic particularity.

The early church struggled greatly with issues of ethnicity and culture, especially the question of whether or not Gentiles had to become Jews in order to be Christians. The discussion in Acts 15—referred to as the Jerusalem Council—was all about whether the *ethnos* had to adhere to

---

[8]I recognize I am using the Greek term here rather than the Hebrew equivalent, *goyim*. How the Hebrews came to view themselves as a people, distinct from the *goyim* of the world, is an important theological discussion but beyond the scope of the present work.

Jewish laws and practices as well as significant markers of Jewish identity to legitimately be considered part of God's people. Cultural and social identity was part of the challenge the early church had with evangelism. Jesus said the disciples would be his witnesses to the ends of the earth (Acts 1:8), but allowing the peoples at the ends of the earth to remain the *ethnos* they were while becoming the people of God was a huge theological and practical stretch for the early church. This was the central challenge narrated in the book of Acts: could the peoples of the earth be the people of God?

Two thousand years later, we are so comfortable with the Gentile takeover of the Way that we have difficulty fully grasping how profound a challenge this was to the early church. Meanwhile, many of us who are US-American assume that our perspectives on Christianity—perspectives rooted in Western European thinking—are a norm for Christians around the world, in essence playing out the same challenge in our own lives. As my German colleague, Birgit Herppich, commented to me in an email conversation, "The Western European way became the ethnic, cultural norm for Christianity which we imposed on all the other ethnicities around the world through the modern mission movement since the late 18th century (that is Protestants, Catholics started earlier). Only in the late twentieth century did we begin to understand the cultural diversity of the church again."[9]

If, at the beginning of God's salvific work through the call of Abraham, God's heart for the *ethnos* is clearly seen; and if the ministry of Jesus and the baptism of the Holy Spirit embrace people from every nation without requiring them to change their ethnicity; and if the testimony of the end of time is that the *ethnos* will stand before God in all of their cultural, linguistic diversity, then an effort now to deny ethnic identity denies something significant about the nature of God's work in the world. God created humanity with diversity in mind. God delights in diversity. Human beings are bearers of the *imago Dei*, the image of God. The *imago*

---

[9]Birgit Herppich, personal communication.

is reflected in our humanity—individually and collectively. There is something particular and special about every *ethnos*, some way each group reflects the nature and character of God. Without every *ethnos*, we miss some element of revelation of God's *imago*.

God calls you as an individual to be a child of God and, as a child, also an heir of God and a joint heir with Christ (Romans 8:17). God calls you in the midst of all of your particularity of identity and experience. In other words, you are a child of God, not separated from your social identities but in the midst of those identities. We do not leave our humanity behind by becoming a follower of Jesus; we pick it up and carry it with us. I didn't cease to be a woman when I became a follower of Jesus. I didn't cease being White or US-American or able-bodied or cisgender or middle class when I became a follower of Jesus. I came to Jesus *with* all of my distinctiveness. I am called by Jesus *in* all of my distinctiveness. God does not erase our particularities; the Spirit works in and through our identities.

ON DEVELOPING A
RACIAL-ETHNIC-CULTURAL IDENTITY

Racial-ethnic-cultural identity has both internal and external components.[10] The internal component is an identity a person has appropriated for themselves; it is their self-identification. A person's conferred identity is an externally constructed group affiliation. It is an identity that is assigned to them by people in the social context. Society—and, in particular, groups with power in society—have taken particular ethnic or racial group identifiers and used them to label and categorize people.

Beverly Daniel Tatum explains, "The concept of identity is a complex one, shaped by individual characteristics, family dynamics, historical factors, and social and political contexts."[11] She observes that who we understand ourselves to be is, in large part, shaped by what the world

---

[10]As noted in chapter 3, it was New Testament scholar Love Sechrest who first brought this dynamic to my attention.

[11]Tatum, *Why Are All the Black Kids*, 99.

around us says we are. Our parents and teachers, our neighbors and colleagues, all reflect back to us what they see. Referencing social scientist Charles Cooley, Tatum writes, "Other people are the mirror in which we see ourselves."[12]

This image of ourselves is not a flat, one-dimensional reflection, however. Our sense of self is mediated by multiple dimensions: gender, ethnicity, race, class, able-bodied or differently abled, religious affiliation, and so forth. According to Tatum, it was Erik Erikson who "introduced the notion that the social, cultural, and historical context is the ground in which individual identity is embedded."[13]

Sometimes a person's internal, appropriated identity and their external, conferred identity match. I am socially identified as a White person and I identify myself as White, for example. Sometimes a person's appropriated identity and their conferred identity will have some degree of disjunction. For example, one of my colleagues is regularly identified as White (conferred racial identity) but self-identifies as Afghani (appropriated ethnic identity). George, mentioned earlier, is often identified as African American but self-identifies as Black Latino.

Numerous scholars have studied the processes by which people come to form a particular internal racial-ethnic-cultural identity, and suggest various models of identity formation. Much of the research focuses on White identity development and Black or African American identity development. Less work has been done on multiracial identity or other racial-ethnic-cultural identities, but this research is increasing.[14]

Additionally, most of the research on racial-ethnic-cultural identities has been conducted in the United States and demonstrates Western perspectives and biases, particularly in focusing on the individual.[15] This potentially limits the benefits of this content for contexts outside of

---

[12]Tatum, *Why Are All the Black Kids*, 99.

[13]Tatum, *Why Are All the Black Kids*, 100.

[14]See Walker S. Carols Poston, "The Biracial Identity Development Model: A Needed Addition," *Journal of Counseling and Development* 69 (1990), 152-55.

[15]See Seth J. Schwartz, Byron L. Zamboanga, Alan Meca, and Rachel A. Ritchie, "Identity Around the World: An Overview," *New Directions for Child and Adolescent Development* 2012, no. 138 (2012): 1-18; and Alan Roland, "Identity, Self, and Individualism in a Multicultural Perspective,"

North America or Europe, but, as the primary location of this particular book is the United States, noting this limitation is sufficient for the moment. It is one example of how our shared cultural maps are useful for our particular needs but may be inadequate for engagement outside of our context.

What follows draws from Janet Helms's model of White identity development.[16] This exposition is not comprehensive. There are many more dynamics that could be explored. Neither is this content intended to suggest that every person who has a particular racial-ethnic-cultural identity has the same experience. Rather, the framework is offered as a means of reflection on experience. Where do you see yourself in your development of a racial-ethnic-cultural identity? How do you see your vocational formation being influenced by that experience? To assist in this reflection, we will look at the calling story of Pastor Phil Allen and consider how his experience reflects different aspects of racial-ethnic-cultural identity development. As you read his story, notice the different geographical locations and social settings that were part of his narrative of calling.

CALLING STORY
Phil Allen Jr.—Pastor, Author, Poet, Storyteller, Justice Advocate

I grew up in South Carolina in a family of athletes. Whenever I applied myself, school was easy, but sports was my life. I was an honor student, achieving mostly As and Bs throughout my grade-school years. I played college basketball and I accomplished everything that I'd dreamed of as a kid except playing professionally. I went

---

in *Race, Ethnicity, and Self: Identity in Multicultural Perspective*, ed. Elizabeth Pathy Salett and Diane R. Koslow (Washington, DC: National MultiCultural Institute, 1994), 11-23.

[16]Janet E. Helms, ed., *Black and White Racial Identity: Theory, Research, and Practice* (New York: Greenwood Press, 1990); Janet E. Helms, "An Update of Helms's White and People of Color Racial Identity Models," in *Handbook of Multicultural Counseling*, ed. Joseph G. Ponterotto (Thousand Oaks, CA: Sage Publications, 1995). See also chap. 6, "The Development of White Identity," in Tatum, *Why Are All the Black Kids*, 185-208.

through a season of depression when basketball was over. My identity had been wrapped up in basketball and, once that was taken away, now who am I? What do I do?

I grew up as a church kid but I really didn't know the Lord. In all the confusion after the end of my basketball career, I got on my knees and accepted the Lord. I still didn't have a sense of direction and purpose, though. I was lost in terms of my faith because I didn't have a mentor. There was not one person in my life seriously walking with the Lord. I didn't understand the Bible. I didn't know anything about the faith.

I later moved to Los Angeles to be an actor but then I found I had no desire to act. I was living in LA, having a great time, partying from Malibu to Hollywood, and all the house parties in between. About two years in, I realized there's got to be more to life than this. I thought, *I'm tired of this. This is empty.*

One of my personal training clients invited me to her church. I went with her to Faithful Central Bible Church and the Lord began to speak to me. I'd never heard a preacher teach before. I've always heard the hoopin', the exhortation, the prophetic, but I'd never really been taught the Bible. I'd walk out now thinking, *Oh, that's what that means!*

I still struggled imagining myself as a Christian man. I hadn't seen it modeled for me. The men I saw in the church as a child were all older men. They were there on Sunday but they were sleeping around with somebody during the week, and I didn't want that to be me. Or they were effeminate and that wasn't me. Or they were geeky, nerdy types; that wasn't me either.

My friend Bobby changed that. I saw him in October 2004 when I went back to my college for homecoming. In college, I had been one of the big men on campus, but I wanted to hang out with Bobby. He used to be a cool dude. Well, Bobby was still cool, but Bobby had changed on the inside. Bobby wasn't getting drunk. Bobby wasn't sleeping around. Bobby left school early to go into the ministry. He was, and still is, a pastor. I felt like the Lord was saying to me, "You *can* walk with me. See, he is."

I came back to Los Angeles on fire.

In May 2005, the executive pastor gave an altar call for those who felt called to ministry. The same friend who invited me to church six months earlier kept elbowing me saying, "You know God's calling you! You know God's calling you." I looked at her and I said, "He's not calling me. Leave me alone. He might be calling you, but not me." In my mind, I began to say, *I can't. I got too many things in my life I have to get right. I'm not ready.* Seconds later, the pastor verbatim says those things going through my mind. Now I don't know if that's just the things that most people typically say, or if that was prophetic and it was for me, but when he said that my heart began to race. I began bawling. I knew that God was calling me to ministry.

Pre-encounter identity. Some people grow up in communities made up exclusively of people who share the same racial-ethnic-cultural identity. What they see in their community, in school, on television, on the internet, in music, and so forth, reflects the identity of their social group. The history they are taught in school is the history of their ancestors. The stories told on television and in movies reflect the values and norms and experiences of their social context. At this pre-encounter phase of REC identity development, people have limited awareness that there are people who are different from them. A person may know intellectually that people exist who are different, for example, but those people don't affect their day-to-day life.

When people in this situation are asked to reflect on racial-ethnic-cultural identity at this phase of development, they often cannot do so because there is no sense of *having* a racial-ethnic-cultural identity. As a result, even though race, ethnicity, and culture affect vocational formation, they cannot recognize the impact for what it is. Their racialized experience is viewed as normal, as if everyone else in the world has the same experience.

Many books on Christian calling reflect elements of this phase of identity development. Some authors come from communities where they have had to do little work to consider their racial-ethnic-cultural identity. Other authors know they are writing for communities for whom REC identity isn't salient, and the topic is therefore left out of the writing. Neither author nor audience considers racial-ethnic-cultural identity to be relevant to the discussion of calling.

Ji-hoon is an international student from Korea who had difficulty comprehending the concept of having a racial-ethnic-cultural identity. Expressing his sense of puzzlement, he said, "We don't think about race in Korea. We're all homogenous Korean." In part, this reflects his distinctive geographical and social location. Race isn't a salient category in Korea. In part, this also reflects an experience that is more about cultural values. For Ji-hoon, being Korean is central to his sense of himself. The homogeneity he mentioned was based on a collectivist cultural value that emphasizes a deep sense of connection to the larger community. Part of Ji-hoon's development was to consider how his "Koreaness" is a distinctive part of his identity and formation.

Some evangelical Christians in the United States at this phase of development seek to embody a "colorblind" approach to race. In a workshop, I overheard a White woman say to a Black man, "I don't see you as a Black person, I see you as a human being." Her intention was to affirm and bless. She was working on the assumption that the tensions around race are created by noting difference. She thought that if we would only see and value one another as individuals and not as members of a group, we would rid ourselves of race-based conflict. What she didn't realize was that "I don't see you as a Black person" was experienced as "I am erasing your Black experience and making it nondiscussable." Author Frances Kendall tells a story of encountering this attitude in a group of administrators in a medical organization. A participant in her training spoke up in an angry and frustrated tone, saying, "Why can't I just be color blind and see myself in the mirror as a member of the *human* race? Isn't that our goal?" Kendall narrated her reply:

> "Well," I said, "I don't think that is our goal. I, for one, don't want to be seen as 'just a human being.' I want to be seen as who I am—a woman, a white person, a fifty-seven-year-old. I don't want to be colorless or

androgynous. What I *do* want is to live in a time when our worth is not based on our skin color or our gender, when all of who I am is important and valuable."[17]

Encounter/disintegration. Individuals enter the encounter/disintegration phase of racial-ethnic-cultural identity formation when they engage people who are different from them in a way that compels an awareness of the "other" existing in their psychological and social space. This was likely the process that Ji-hoon was undergoing through being in the United States and in classes with people from a variety of countries. This kind of encounter can occur within a single country as well, though. Moving from an area that is predominantly populated by one racial-ethnic-cultural group to another area that is predominantly populated by a different group or an area that has a diversity of groups can be a context for developing awareness, for example.

Other times, the encounter happens when people of a different racial-ethnic-cultural background move into the neighborhood we've been living in. In the 1990s and early 2000s, for example, the rise in immigration to the United States meant that cities which had previously been made up almost exclusively of people of European descent now have large populations from other countries of the world. Reyna was in middle school when a Somali family moved in next to her home in a Minneapolis suburb. Becoming friends with Jamilah and her family was a context of Reyna becoming aware of the experience of refugees fleeing civil war in Somalia, an experience very different from her own.

For many BIPOC individuals who grow up in ethnic enclaves, starting school can be the context of this phase as they move from a social circle that is made up of people like them to an educational context in which theirs is not the only ethnicity represented. Other BIPOC individuals know they are different from the majority culture at an early age. Pastor Allen is Gullah Geechee, the descendant of a West African rice-growing

---

[17]Frances Kendall, *Understanding White Privilege: Creating Pathways to Authentic Relationships Across Race* (New York: Routledge, 2013), 45.

people enslaved and imported to work on rice plantations in South Carolina. As we reflected together on race and calling in a conversation a couple years ago, he observed of his childhood, "You knew you were different than the White folks." He told a story of an encounter with a salesclerk in a market, where he noticed she would smile at and talk to the White customers but not the Black customers. When twelve-year-old Pastor Allen handed her the money to pay for his purchase, she refused to put the change back in his hand lest she accidentally touch him. Reflecting on that experience, Pastor Allen commented, "That was my first time when I felt like this skin I'm in is bad."

Whenever individuals first encounter people different from themselves, they can be ushered into a phase of disorientation. Listening to the stories of people different from themselves may cause them to realize that not everyone has the same life experiences as they do. They may begin to accept that there are racial and ethnic differences, but they might feel ambivalent about them or have differing opinions as to their origins and effects.

Many of us who are from the dominant culture grew up never having to process our racial identity and therefore have never developed the stamina to process the discomfort we feel. Often, we feel threatened and attacked, and so react with anger or withdrawal.[18] Denial is also a fairly common response at this stage of development. We have not developed resilience to the stresses of conversations about race, and so we act in ways that shut down the conversation. The trope of White men's anger and White women's tears has emerged from how those of us who are White respond in this phase of development.

The disorientation of this phase can confuse and complicate our vocational formation. We may not see the relevance our REC identity has to it, and we resist the discomfort that comes with the disorientation. The problem we see is not the lack of a healthy and integrated

---

[18]Sociologist Robin DiAngelo refers to this lack of capacity to discuss racism as "white fragility." See Robin DiAngelo, *White Fragility: Why It's So Hard for White People to Talk About Racism* (Boston: Beacon Press, 2020).

racial-ethnic-cultural identity; the problem is the person provoking the painful questions about the impact of REC on our formation.

Kevin was one person who expressed this kind of reaction. He could name his family's ethnic-cultural background: both his mother's and his father's families were Scots-Irish. He just didn't consider this information to be particularly relevant. Kevin had grown up with a sense of pride in being a US-American and in the life his ancestors had built in this country. When asked to reflect on how whiteness influenced his experience of calling, Kevin pushed back, resisting the idea that being White had any effect on any part of his life. He insisted on seeing his family as having benefited from their hard work, not from their racial identity. As the conversation continued, Kevin became increasingly upset until, finally, he lashed out with accusations and recriminations. At that point, Kevin seemed stuck, but that does not mean Kevin would stay stuck at this phase. Further life experiences and continued reflection had the potential to be a context for greater self-awareness.

Reintegration of identity. At the reintegration phase of racial-ethnic-cultural identity development, we come to both see racial and ethnic differences and realize that this includes differences in access or privilege. In the process of making sense of this information, we interpret what we see and ascribe meaning to different aspects. In this phase of development, those of us who are White tend to want to protect or justify our unearned privilege. Tim, an administrator in a nonprofit, saw himself as being attentive and understanding to people of various backgrounds. He cited literature that explained how the low educational attainment of Black and Brown people was a product of poverty and single-parent homes.[19] When he was pointed to the data about the wide difference in median family net worth between people of European descent and people of African descent, Tim revealed

---

[19]See Daniel Patrick Moynihan, *The Negro Family. The Case for National Action,* issues 31-33. (Washington, DC: Office of Policy Planning and Research, US Department of Labor, 1965). For alternative interpretations, see Andrea Flynn et al., *The Hidden Rules of Race: Barriers to an Inclusive Economy* (New York: Cambridge University Press, 2017); and Richard Rothstein, *The Color of Law: A Forgotten History of How Our Government Segregated America* (New York: Liveright Publishing, 2017).

his assumptions that privilege and wealth are due to hard work and good behavior while poverty is due to laziness and poor life choices.

A person of color at this stage may also emphasize individual hard work and attainment as the source of success and resist looking at the impact of group affiliation. Elizabeth was a highly educated woman employed as a lawyer. She identified as Chinese American but resisted the idea that her racial-ethnic-cultural experience had salience for her vocational formation; the implication felt to her like an effort to reduce her to a marginalized identity. She preferred to focus on her education and attainments. Henry, a middle-class, middle-aged Black man, agreed with her. He expressed frustration at the young Black men who "need to pull up their pants" and "stop playing the victim." Both Elizabeth and Henry had believed that if they adhered to the values of the majority culture, they would be given access to the benefits of the majority culture, including open doors in education and occupation. They may have experienced both benefits and discrimination based on their racial-ethnic-cultural identity but internalized those experiences as if they were responsible for what they encountered, not just for how they responded.

This phase of reintegration is a normal part of the process of REC identity development, and naming it as normal is important in facilitating a potential space for reflection and development. People who are at this point of their formation need spaces in which they can process their assumptions along with their fears and anxieties. This does represent something of a dilemma, though. On the one hand, meaningful relationships with people who have different experiences is an important catalyst for growth. On the other hand, these kinds of relationships are costly for the people and communities who hold the space for the reintegrating individual to do this work.

Pseudo-independence. Helms's model of White identity formation suggests pseudo-independence is "the first step in redefining a positive White identity."[20] A White person in this phase of identity development

---

[20]Helms, *Black and White Racial Identity*, 61.

sees the benefits of being White but no longer believes White people inherently deserve privilege. Some may express this new awareness through anger toward and criticism of White people. Others may turn toward and seek affiliation with social groups of other ethnicities, taking on their social practices such as language, dress, and behaviors.

In terms of vocational formation, White Christians at this stage may leap into social justice activism. Having become aware of racial inequities, we want to take immediate action to bring about change. And, like all newly converted, we want everyone to see what we see. Some of us begin to actively engage in social media discussions about justice or show up for protests and rallies. We want change and we want it right now.

As eager White people at the pseudo-independence step, we desire to be allies of our brothers and sisters of color. We haven't yet developed a mature sense of White identity, however, and we haven't fully processed how whiteness affects our beliefs and behaviors. I recall one conversation involving Ben, a young White man who earnestly wanted to be considered a White ally. When another person in the conversation, a person of color, said something about their experience, Ben interrupted them to correct their "facts." And when he was gently confronted with this evidence of enacting whiteness—assuming he had the right to "correct" a person of color on their experience—Ben became angry, arguing that he was an ally and his behavior should be accepted as the behavior of such. He wanted his self-image to be accepted and was deeply offended when it wasn't. This meant he did not notice that his anger shut down the conversation. He hadn't yet developed a healthy White REC identity, but he was in the process.

Immersion/emersion. Another phase of racial-ethnic-cultural identity development is what Helms (looking at White people) and Cross (looking at Black people) refer to as immersion and emersion.[21] This is a two-part phase. The first part is going deeply into one's own identity—immersion.

---

[21]Helms, "An Update of Helms's White and People of Color Racial Identity Models," 185-86; and William E. Cross, *Shades of Black: Diversity in African-American Identity* (Philadelphia: Temple University Press, 1991). See also part 2, "Understanding Blackness in a White Context," in Tatum, *Why Are All the Black Kids*, 111-81.

The second part is moving outward to interact with other people—emersion. Immersion is a process of self-awareness while emersion is a process of acceptance and healthy expression of culture.[22]

BIPOC people in this stage immerse themselves in the experience, history, and culture of their particular group. Initially, this immersion may be overly romanticized. This is, however, a necessary antidote to years (and even centuries) of negative stereotypes.

Part of Pastor Allen's journey was to explore his grandfather's story. He had grown up knowing his grandfather had been killed in 1953 when his father was a boy. This was an experience little discussed in his family. When Pastor Allen asked his grandmother about the story, she had a visceral reaction. "I could see her body constrict; her face got tight," he recounted. "It was almost as if it happened a year ago. . . . She said, 'Leave me alone.'" Ten years later, just a few months before his grandmother passed away, Pastor Allen asked her again. "Grandma, how do you know Granddaddy was shot and killed? How do you know it wasn't an accident?" Pastor Allen thought perhaps she had simply assumed he'd been killed but had no evidence. "Because there was a bullet hole in the back of his head," his grandmother responded. "My father [Pastor Allen's great-grandfather] saw it. He told the funeral director, 'Don't do anything until I come down there; let me see for myself.'" Over the course of the next several years, Pastor Allen developed a documentary, *Open Wounds,* to tell the story of his grandfather's death and its lasting effect on his family.[23]

Some BIPOC individuals at this stage of development form an overtly anti-White identity. When this stage comes in adolescence, Black teens may develop what Signithia Fordham and John Ogbu refer to as an oppositional identity.[24] The anger and resentment these adolescents feel in response to their growing awareness of structural racism in the United

---

[22]Lacey M. Sloan et al., *Critical Multiculturalism and Intersectionality in a Complex World* (New York: Oxford University Press, 2018), 32.

[23]Phil Allen Jr., *Open Wounds,* accessed August 13, 2020, video, www.philallenjr.com/open woundsdoc. See also Phil Allen Jr., *Open Wounds: A Story of Racial Tragedy, Trauma, and Redemption* (Minneapolis: Fortress Press, 2021).

[24]Signithia Fordham and John U. Ogbu, "Black Students' School Success," *The Structure of Schooling: Readings in the Sociology of Education* (2010): 274.

States and the lack of understanding and support they receive from White peers or authority figures leads them to reject dominant White culture and turn to their BIPOC peers for support and identity.

White people in the immersion/emersion stage delve into their honest history—a history no longer "whitewashed" and idealized. They embrace what theologian Justo González calls "non-innocent history,"[25] not glossing over the painful parts but recognizing that the good and the bad both formed who we are today. This kind of healthy White identity recognizes the history of whiteness embedded in the founding of the United States and grapples with White privilege and White normativity.

Internalization/autonomy. In this final phase of racial-ethnic-cultural identity development, the individual comes to a clear, self-actualized sense of racial identity while retaining the capacity to engage their REC identity as an ongoing process.[26] People at this stage are able to engage people of other racial-ethnic-cultural identities without feeling compromised or defensive; they have the ability to not only see differences but also develop communication skills that allow them to interact with those from other groups. White people at this stage are openly committed to being antiracist in all facets of their life and work.[27] A person may focus on social justice activism vocationally or in some other capacity, engaging in ministry in a way that attends to concerns of justice, diversity, equity, and inclusion. The capacity for empathy recognizes a shared humanity while honoring distinctive differences. This stage is the full foretaste of Revelation 7:9.

REFLECTIVE NEXT STEPS

I get a variety of responses when I ask people to consider how their racial-ethnic-cultural identity has influenced their experience of calling.

---

[25]Justo L. González, *Mañana: Christian Theology from a Hispanic Perspective* (Nashville: Abingdon Press, 1990). Thank you to my colleague Johnny Ramírez-Johnson for bringing this concept to my attention.

[26]Helms, *Black and White Racial Identity*, 66.

[27]For a thorough discussion of the concept of "antiracist" see Ibram X. Kendi, *How to Be an Antiracist* (New York: One World, 2019).

At one end of the continuum are people who find the question puzzling or nonsensical, as it seems to be unrelated to their experience and their understanding of the nature of God's calling. They haven't thought about their REC identity, so it has no salience for them. At the other end of the continuum are people who have a well-developed and nuanced sense of their racial-ethnic-cultural identity. They generally understand their people group and know a fair amount of the history of that group in their particular geographical location. They are also aware of how the racial identity ascribed to them by society influences their experience. Considering how their racial-ethnic-cultural experience affects their experience of calling is therefore a relatively short step to make. They are able to identify specific and concrete points of intersection.

Consider Dr. Joyce del Rosario's calling story as an example of someone who has worked through these phases of identity formation and has come to a clear, holistic sense of calling that integrates experience and racial-ethnic-cultural identity. Notice Dr. del Rosario's capacity to name her experiences and to see the ways they have shaped her distinctive calling in the world. Her narrative includes pain as well as a generative processing of that pain as she has been able to take her experiences and see God's redemptive work empowered in and through those life events.

CALLING STORY
Joyce del Rosario, PhD—Assistant Professor in the Practice of Ministry and Director of Community Engaged Learning

I grew up in a Filipino United Methodist Church (UMC) in the Seattle area. The church was made up of people who were interconnected through webs of denominational relationship in the Philippines. It was a tight-knit and fiercely communal church. As with many immigrant churches, church was family and family was church. This is the foundation in which my understanding of church, community, and theology is built.

I never considered that White people could also be Methodist until I attended a UMC youth conference in my teens. This was a disorienting experience for me. I felt like the "other" in my own tradition for the first time. Like most of my early experiences with White American spaces, it was both uncomfortable and alluring. I found the different expressions of worship liberating. It attracted me more than the traditional hymns of my home church. Even though we often talked transmigrationally about church in the Philippines and the United States, my understanding of the American church suddenly widened as it coincided with my marginalized experiences in my school life. While I am thankful for the way in which my view of church broadened, I have also spent a lot of time deconstructing this allure with the White American church and my own social and ethnic location. Suffice it to say, my call has always been informed by the context of feeling "othered."

Later, I had a profound encounter with God while attending an ecumenical Asian American youth retreat as a chaperone in college. I felt like I heard God yelling in my ear—so loud and so silent at the same time. "I don't want to be part of your life; I want to be your whole life." I knew then I would go into youth ministry and then I would later teach (presumably youth ministry). At the age of twenty-one, I knew life's call.

I decided that if I was going to be a professional youth minister, I needed more equipping. I enrolled in a somewhat progressive master of divinity program where I didn't have to defend my call as a woman in ministry. While I was ready to be trained in preaching and biblical hermeneutics, I wasn't prepared to have my marginality feel so highlighted once again. In seminary, I felt "othered" once again by the dominantly White institution. The turning point was when a professor encouraged me, "Joyce, you speak a lot of languages." For the first time, I understood I am a Filipino woman on purpose. Up until that point I had considered my identity as something to "overcome" or navigate. She pointed out—what I would later come to understand—the different intersections in which I lived. The professor showed me how my intersectionalities were assets and not liabilities.

It was at that time that I started with who I was rather than what I wanted to become. My personal experience of marginalization became a measure for choosing ministry. As I read through the Gospels, I realized that Jesus always walked on the margins. I decided that's where I wanted to locate my ministry as well. I look around with the question, "Who is on the margins here?" The answer to that question guides my choices. I have never felt so "othered" as in the White American church, but I also know that my living out my call must start with who I am and that is more than enough.

My experience of Dr. del Rosario as a colleague has shaped my own work, including influencing why I have chosen to refer to my guests in this text—those who have contributed their calling stories—by their formal titles. As I noted in chapter three, Dr. del Rosario recognizes she is the product of four hundred years of ancestors who have collectively made possible her academic attainments. When I call her Dr. del Rosario, I am honoring her entire family. As I listen to and learn from her, I think also of my own life and experiences. How has God been at work in *my* context and how does that work affect the distinctive shape of my calling?

With that question in mind, I suggest some action steps that are beneficial for continued development around REC identity and for our development in engaging God's work in the world. I echo what Pastor Allen has written in his book, *Open Wounds*, as a process to move forward: listen, learn, lament, and labor.[28]

First, listen to the stories of your family. Dr. del Rosario's story demonstrates she has embraced her family's heritage, in all its complexity, as a distinct part of her formation. Listen to the stories of people who come from similar REC backgrounds to you. Listen to the stories of people who come from different REC backgrounds. Many of the stories in this book are the fruit of my own practice of listening and are offered to you for engaging in this work. I have found that, as I listen to other people's stories, I come to understand my own story better.

Additionally, learn about your history—the real history. For those of us who are White in the United States, this means being willing to hear the hard stories that our cultural mythology has sought to set aside for

---

[28]Allen, *Open Wounds*, 163-75.

hundreds of years. For those who do not identify with the dominant group, that means knowing your own stories. This may require the kind of effort reflected in Pastor Allen's experience of finding out about his grandfather's death. Stories may be buried under years of pain and denial. All of us need to know and honor the stories of our families—stories of persistence, hardship, courage, service, fortitude. We also need to see them with clear eyes rather than through rose-colored glasses that deny the complexity of our history and experience.

Pastor Allen says, "Listening and learning should lead to lament."[29] As we listen to our family stories and community stories, there will be much to celebrate and there will be much to grieve. We need to cry out to God personally and collectively. Pastor Allen recounts the experience of telling the story of his grandfather for the first time and seeing tears in the eyes of his hearers. "There is healing potential in shared lament," he writes. "My body began to relax as I shared my thoughts, but when I saw the tears of my classmates, there was an overwhelming sense of peace that overcame me. Suddenly, grief gave way to make space for joy and a sense of the beginning of healing."[30] Tell your story. Give room for the healing grace of lament.

Labor is the step that people often want to rush to as a priority. Yet to labor well requires first listening, learning, and lamenting well. Labor is the fruit of that inner formation. Give yourself permission to pause and reflect. The inner soul work of reflection and self-awareness is space in which the Spirit works. As we become more aware of the Spirit's active engagement in our lives, we can more faithfully respond to the invitation to our particular places of engagement with God's work in the world.

QUESTIONS FOR REFLECTION AND DISCUSSION[31]

1. What do you know concerning the ethnicity and national origins of your parents, grandparents, and earlier generations? If this is

---

[29] Allen, *Open Wounds*, 170.
[30] Allen, *Open Wounds*, 171.
[31] This list is adapted from Mark Lau Branson and Juan F. Martínez, *Churches, Cultures and Leadership: A Practical Theology of Congregations and Ethnicities* (Downers Grove, IL: InterVarsity Press, 2011), 24-25.

different from the heritage of the household in which you were raised, describe those differences.

2. When were you first aware of ethnic (or racial) categories? When were you first aware of persons who are different from you?

3. How did your parents and grandparents voice ethnic matters or convey to you what they perceived or what they thought was important? How did other members of the household contribute to your understandings about your own ethnic heritage?

4. Think about the phases of your life—childhood, adolescence, early adulthood, perhaps middle and later adulthood. How did your ethnic identity affect you? What difference did it make in relationships, where you lived, what activities you participated in, how you experienced school, and how you experienced your society (city, nation)? How has your awareness changed?

5. In what sense was who you are in your race/ethnicity considered normative or in what sense was that aspect of your identity marginalized or suppressed? What do you remember about being treated unfairly because of cultural identity? Or of treating others unfairly?

6. How have you experienced significant boundary crossings (in travel, through relationships, or in some organization)? What did you learn about others and yourself?

7. What is the relationship between your ethnic identity and your faith? What difference did or does it make in church? In your beliefs or theology?

8. In what ways do the stories, values, and practices of your ethnic heritage parallel the gospel or facilitate and nurture being a Christian? What elements of your ethnic heritage make being a Christian difficult?

9. What do you value most in your ethnic and/or racial heritage? What do you value least?

10. How has your ethnic and/or racial identity affected your understanding of the nature of vocation?

11. How have the assumptions and values within your racial-ethnic-cultural context shaped what you believe is possible for you in relation to vocation?

EXPLORING A BIBLICAL NARRATIVE: DANIEL

1. Read Daniel 1:3-21.

2. Where does Daniel express a sense of ethnic-cultural identity as an Israelite? How important was it for him personally?

3. Consider the Jewish food laws. (See Leviticus 11.) What was at stake for Daniel in eating the food from the king's table?

4. How significant was this event for the development of Daniel's "call"? What might have happened if he and his friends simply complied with the charge to eat the king's food like the other (unnamed) Israelites did?

SUGGESTIONS FOR FURTHER READING

Allen, Phil, Jr. *Open Wounds: A Story of Racial Tragedy, Trauma, and Redemption.* Minneapolis: Fortress Press, 2021.

Brown, Austin Channing. *I'm Still Here: Black Dignity in a World Made for Whiteness.* New York: Convergent Books, 2018.

Crespo, Orlando. *Being Latino in Christ: Finding Wholeness in Your Ethnic Identity.* Downers Grove, IL: InterVarsity Press, 2003.

Hill, Daniel. *White Awake: An Honest Look at What It Means to Be White.* Downers Grove, IL: InterVarsity Press, 2017.

Reyes, Patrick B. *The Purpose Gap: Empowering Communities of Color to Find Meaning and Thrive.* Louisville, KY: Westminster John Knox Press, 2021.

Shin, Sarah. *Beyond Colorblind: Redeeming Our Ethnic Journey.* Downers Grove, IL: InterVarsity Press, 2017.

Tatum, Beverly Daniel. *Why Are All the Black Kids Sitting Together in the Cafeteria? And Other Conversations About Race.* 2nd ed. New York: Basic Books, 2017.

5

SOCIOECONOMIC STATUS, CLASS, AND CALLING

*My brothers and sisters, do you with your acts of favoritism really believe
in our glorious Lord Jesus Christ? For if a person with gold rings and
in fine clothes comes into your assembly, and if a poor person in dirty
clothes also comes in, and if you take notice of the one wearing the
fine clothes and say, "Have a seat here, please," while to the one who
is poor you say, "Stand there," or, "Sit at my feet," have you not made
distinctions among yourselves, and become judges with evil thoughts?*

JAMES 2:1-4

*Meaning is discerned at the intersection of the stories we
tell ourselves and the worlds we build and inhabit.*

PATRICK REYES, *THE PURPOSE GAP*

I MET DAVID DOUGLAS WHEN he walked into my seminary classroom.
I saw a middle-height man with brown hair and a gregarious, friendly
manner. David engaged his fellow students and participated in lively

An early version of this chapter was presented as a paper to the 2019 annual meeting of the
American Society for Missiology at St. Mary's College, South Bend, Indiana. My thanks to the
colleagues present for their feedback.

group discussions. As I led the class in considering how their racial-ethnic-social identity had shaped their experience of vocational formation, David began to question this approach. David identified other parts of his experience that were more significant for his formation than his racial-ethnic-cultural identity. Let's read David's story, told in his own words.

CALLING STORY
David Douglas—Actor, Producer, Contractor, Theologian, Cultural Apologeticist

I was born in New York city. My mother was a single, Italian, non-practicing Roman Catholic; I never met my dad. My earliest memories of growing up were in the Lower East Side. I remember walking out the door and seeing a dead guy in the doorway with a heroin needle in his arm. I said, "Mommy, what's wrong with him?" And she just turned my head and said, "Let's just walk this way." So that was the beginning.

My mom had clinical depression and possibly had schizophrenia. I remember frequently coming home and seeing her in the corner in a fetal position, out of touch with what I thought was reality. Since I knew no other experience, and didn't know whether other kids had similar experiences or not, I just dealt with it.

When I was about third grade, my mom was having more and more episodes of depression. She was also really concerned for my safety at school. So, she arranged for me to move in with my uncle. I ended up staying with him on and off for periods of two months at a time. That's the first time I had a male guardian in my life. He's probably the closest thing to a dad I've ever had.

There were a lot of complexities about the situation, though. To make a long story short, I was placed in foster care. My mom had to make a decision: would she take me back or would I be put up for adoption? When I was eleven, she gave up her parental rights and I was placed for adoption. It was a tough, tough, tough experience that will always affect my life.

My birth mom, for all of her faults, taught me about generosity. She tried to provide for my material needs. She stimulated my curiosity and expressed interest in my passions. She loved me as best she knew how. But then to feel marginalized by her and then marginalized, even worse, by my adopted mom, who basically took me in but didn't do anything to show me any care, has given me a real lifelong sense of empathy for people that feel like they've been marginalized.

As an adult, I have an extensive background in finance and insurance; I worked as a property and casualty underwriter, institutional fixed income trading settlement manager, etc. I've been an actor, producer, and director. I founded and owned a construction business. My dream as a Christian evangelist/cultural apologeticist is to create faith-based, non-propagandistic stories of truth, beauty, and goodness that inspire people. Trying to make that dream happen is fraught with fighting the secular monopolistic institution of Hollywood and trying to catalyze the church as a whole to see the value in offering a different platform of content than what they see from the pulpit.

I haven't been able to establish myself in a career that suits the aspirations, talents, and desires of my heart. But through it all, I have lived my whole life trying to fight for truth. Maybe that is why I've had so many of these challenges in life: they've enabled me to be sensitive to people because I felt a lot of hurt. The things that look like losses and weaknesses to me are the contexts God uses to form me.

What I came to understand from listening to David's story is that, while everyone else looks at David and sees an articulate, personable, White man, David looks at himself and sees the child living with the consequences of poverty and mental illness. His apparent resistance to recognizing the benefits of being White in the United States was, I gradually realized, an expression of a sense that other significant aspects of his social location were being disregarded. I saw that he, and others with similar experiences, wanted their distinctive circumstances to be seen, acknowledged, and validated. From this experience, I learned I had to find a way to help students consider the implications of class—both those implications that foster a person's formation for vocation and those that hinder it—as well as consider the intersections between REC identity and socioeconomic status.

As I talk about racial-ethnic-cultural identity in relationship to calling, I'm often asked this question: "Are you talking about ethnic/racial identity or are you *really* talking about socioeconomic status?" This chapter is an attempt to engage that question. I will focus on the experience of class in the United States as a way to give the discussion a grounded starting point. This is the context that has shaped me and in which I do much of my work. The existence of class is not isolated to the United States, of course; every nation and social group has experiences with socioeconomic status. But the particularities of class and its relationship to race in the United States is distinctive to our history and current experience.

One cultural value that profoundly influences the discussion of socioeconomic status in the United States is the concept of meritocracy, so I begin with an analytical description of this particular cultural map before moving on to respond to a number of concerns that seem to be behind the question "Are you *really* talking about socioeconomic status?"

CULTURAL MAP: MERITOCRACY

A meritocracy is a social system in which what each person has is based on their personal assets and efforts. A common origin narrative in the United States is based on this principle and goes something like this: My forebearers immigrated to this land, worked hard, and made a life for themselves and their descendants. I have what I have (status, possessions, standard of living, social position, and so forth) because my family worked hard. I continue to work hard and earn what I have.

This story is shared by immigrants from many nationalities, and it is told over and over again in many different ways.[1] French and Spanish

---

[1]This narrative takes a different shape for people who were involuntarily brought to the Americas. Starting in the early 1600s, a large percentage of that group were enslaved Africans; a small percentage were British convicts. This narrative is also different for the people groups whose land this was when European colonizers arrived.

explorers came to the continent seeking gold and other trade goods. English colonizers followed. Poor Irish immigrants fled the potato famine and Chinese workers sought the prosperity of the "Gold Mountain." It is the story of a backwoods child who studied law and became our sixteenth president. It is the story of Thomas Edison, who was devalued as a child in school but ended up as a renown inventor. It is the story of people with names like Vanderbilt and Rockefeller and Huntington who built railroads, banks, and businesses. It is the story of people who started by building a computer in their garage and end up with multibillion-dollar companies.

These individuals are heroes because they embody cultural values we hold dear. They start with little and, through their hard work and ingenuity—so our narrative goes—they make something of their lives. They demonstrate self-sufficiency, not asking for help or complaining about their conditions but doing something constructive. To quote a common idiom, they "pull themselves up by their bootstraps."

Within evangelical Christian contexts, we tell similar stories of our spiritual heroes. We love to tell about those who started with little and built big ministries. We honor the people who start with a Bible study in their living room and now have a multicampus megachurch with thousands in attendance every Sunday. We respect the self-sacrifice of missionaries who gave up everything and left home to pioneer new fields before building up new agencies with hundreds of missionaries.

Notice that the hero stories we tell all tend to end in success as measured by numbers and size. Hudson Taylor is esteemed for his emphasis on living like the people he worked among in China, but his story would not be told if not for the 150-year history of China Inland Mission (now Overseas Missionary Fellowship). Mother Teresa is esteemed as a humble woman, but her success in building a famous ministry was what gave her access to people of power, not her humility. Pastors of megachurches are invited to church-growth conferences and end up publishing many books describing what they did—books that assume that if we do the same, we will have identical results.

Whether we're talking about people who build businesses or institutions, churches or mission agencies, the size of the organization is frequently the definition of success. The higher the church attendance, the more successful the pastor. The greater number of staff and locations, the more successful the mission organization. Further, we assume it was the skills and character of the founders that account for the success of the institutions; such people earned that success by their innate capacities and hard work.

The flip side of this message is also assumed to be true: a person's *lack* of success is grounded in their lack of personal ability and effort. Entrepreneurs with small businesses are assumed to have been less visionary than founders of large businesses. Pastors of small churches are assumed to be less skilled and capable than pastors of large churches. A failed business or a failed church plant are assumed to be the result of limitations in the founders' capacities and efforts.

Historically, many in the United States have viewed poverty as a direct result of poor choices and lack of hard work, although this perspective seems to be shifting somewhat in recent years.[2] In resources ranging from academic texts to popular media, people who are poor are often blamed for their poverty. The cultural map of meritocracy orients our assessments in one direction: people have what they have because of their own efforts. People are rich because they work hard; people are poor because they do not.

The cultural map of meritocracy complicates our vocational development. For one, meritocracy focuses on each person's individual capacities. We are encouraged not to think of ourselves as participants in social systems and structures. More specifically, we are actively discouraged from thinking about our racial-ethnic-cultural identity or social class—or any other group identity—as a factor in social success. In ministry, in work, in any area of endeavor, we are

---

[2]"Why Are People Rich or Poor? Most Americans Point to Circumstances, Not Work Ethic," Pew Research Center, last modified October 2, 2020, www.pewresearch.org/politics/2020/03/02/most-americans-point-to-circumstances-not-work-ethic-as-reasons-people-are-rich-or-poor/.

expected to work hard and produce results, ignoring the effect of context on the outcome. Meritocracy acts to distort our perception of our experience.

With the cultural map of meritocracy in mind, let us now consider the question "Are you really talking about racial-ethnic-cultural identity or are you *really* talking about socioeconomic status?" There are generally three possible reasons people ask this question: (1) the desire to see their own experience of poverty acknowledged, (2) the desire to deny the role that structural racism plays in poverty in favor of emphasizing individual choice, or (3) the desire to understand the complex intersections between racial-ethnic-cultural identity and socioeconomic status.

THE IMPACT OF POVERTY ON
VOCATIONAL FORMATION

Multiple studies have identified the effects of poverty on a person's quality of life and on their self-identity.[3] These scars of poverty—wounding a person's self-perception and sense of agency—can exist in anyone of any racial-ethnic-cultural identity. In other words, poverty is not the exclusive experience of some ethnicities nor is there any racial identity group in the United States that does not have some experience with poverty. For example, recent popular books such as *Hillbilly Elegy* and *White Trash* have narrated the stories of people of northern European descent and their experience of generational poverty.[4] For people groups experiencing chronic poverty, class status has played a significant role in their identity. The experience of being shamed for

---

[3]See, for example, Charlotte Brown et al., "Depression Stigma, Race, and Treatment Seeking Behavior and Attitudes," *Journal of Community Psychology* 38, no. 3 (2010): 350-68; Patrick W. Corrigan, Jonathon E. Larson, and Nicolas Rusch, "Self-Stigma and the 'Why Try' Effect: Impact on Life Goals and Evidence-Based Practices," *World Psychiatry* 8, no. 2 (2009): 75-81; and Eileen Sutton et al., "Stigma, Shame and the Experience of Poverty in Japan and the United Kingdom," *Social Policy and Society* 13, no. 1 (2014): 143-54. My thanks to Bobby Lynch for bringing these resources to my attention.

[4]J. D. Vance, *Hillbilly Elegy: A Memoir of a Family and Culture in Crisis* (New York: HarperCollins, 2016); and Nancy Isenberg, *White Trash: The 400-Year Untold History of Class in America* (New York: Penguin, 2017).

their poverty and the internalized sense of incapacity become central to how they see themselves.

Citing Lee Rainwater, sociologist Robert Bellah and his colleagues observe that "poverty—income insufficient to maintain an acceptable level of living—operates to deprive the poor not only of material capital but of social capital as well." Social capital refers to "features of social organization, such as networks, norms, and trust, that facilitate coordination and cooperation for mutual benefit."[5] Limitations in social capital, including restricted access to education and jobs, have a profound effect on the vocational opportunities afforded the working class and working poor. But, due to the cultural map of meritocracy, they are expected to "pull themselves up by their bootstraps" and "not expect a handout."

Practical theologian Patrick Reyes comments on this cultural idiom, reflecting, "for the community I come from, this 'Pull yourself up by the bootstraps' mantra is simply not possible. The world stole our laces and our boots."[6] Reyes reflects on the vocational implications of his childhood experiences in a working-class community. "For Christian with stories similar to my own," he writes, "the first call to life from God that needs to be named here is a survival to adulthood. My first vocational call was exactly that: simply a call to *live*, to *survive*."[7]

In thinking about vocational discernment, meritocracy can create a hostile environment for people who don't fit the class norms present in a particular context. If the pursuit of a specific vocation is difficult for an individual because of social class reasons—for example, the challenge of paying for a graduate education on a working-class or middle-class income—we still expect people to take responsibility for their own development and not "whine" about their circumstances. Patrick Reyes

[5]Robert N. Bellah et al., *Habits of the Heart: Individualism and Commitment in American Life* (Berkeley: University of California Press, 2008), xxiv; Robert Putnam quoted in Bellah et al., *Habits of the Heart*, xxii.
[6]Patrick B. Reyes, *The Purpose Gap: Empowering Communities of Color to Find Meaning and Thrive* (Louisville, KY: Westminster John Knox Press, 2021), 84.
[7]Patrick Reyes, *Nobody Cries When We Die: God, Community, and Surviving to Adulthood* (Saint Louis, MO: Chalice Press, 2016), 15.

narrates an event that took place during his graduate studies. With no family wealth that could help provide for him, Reyes worked hanging Sheetrock to help cover his expenses in school. One day, he got a call from the contractor he worked for asking if he would put in extra hours to quickly finish a job. He writes:

> This was a chance for a lot of money. So I took the job and we worked all through the night. No sleep before class. It was also a midterm. I had prepared a bit, but I hadn't dedicated many hours to the subject. I came into class, covered in that white power. In many ways, being covered in white powder was fitting considering I just wanted to be respected and listened to like my white classmates. I sat down and started taking my test. I felt like I was doing okay, until about halfway through the class, the professor asked to see me outside. I stood up and went outside with the professor.
>
> "If you are going to be a grad student, you need to act like one or you probably shouldn't be here."
>
> "What?"
>
> "Look at you. You smell. You are covered in who knows what. You don't dress appropriately." I admit my work boots, pants, and flex cap that was covered in sweat was not my best look. "You aren't doing well on your exams. And you are distracting my more serious students."
>
> "Well . . ."
>
> "No. You know, grad school isn't for everyone."[8]

Reyes had not only to pay for graduate education with hard, manual labor but also bear the burden of being viewed as not being seen as a capable student because of this fact. "Serious students" don't hang Sheetrock. Reflecting on this event and other life experiences, Reyes observes his story is an example of someone encountering a "rigged game" in which some people are predetermined to do well and some are not.[9] That Reyes succeeded in completing his degree and gaining a PhD is a testimony to his persistence but also to the emotional and spiritual support of his community. Too often, though, the exceptional individuals

---

[8]Reyes, *Nobody Cries When We Die*, 53.
[9]See chapter three, "The Game Is Rigged" in Reyes, *Nobody Cries When We Die*.

from an impoverished background who excel are offered as the "proof" that individual effort is all it takes to succeed. Reyes counters this assessment, both by narrating the burdens and pains of his experience but also by noting that a focus on the "stars" exacerbates what he refers to as "the purpose gap." He writes, "the purpose gap exists because institutions find and extract the shining star in a community and leaves it without a star, also known as 'the brain drain.'"[10]

RACIALIZED POVERTY AND WEALTH

For some people who suggest that the conversation about racial-ethnic-cultural identity is really about socioeconomic status, the heart of the challenge is a desire to deny the existence and impact of race on everyday life in the United States. In other words, they seek to deny the existence of racialized experience. This position ignores the racialization of poverty in the United States.[11] Others who make the same suggestion are equally ignorant about the intersections between poverty and ethnicity. The difference is that they genuinely want to understand the relationship. The task for both groups is to listen and learn with open hearts.

As noted in chapter four, sociologists Michael Emerson and Christian Smith define a racialized society as "a society wherein race matters profoundly for differences in life experiences, life opportunities, and social relationships."[12] Systems that distribute and withhold economic benefits such as access to jobs, training, goods, and residences are based on racially oriented social rubrics. For example, in a frequently cited study, two economists sent out five thousand fictitious résumés, which were identical in every way except for the name of the person. The résumés with typically White names such as Emily and Greg received 50 percent

---

[10]Reyes, *The Purpose Gap*, 86.

[11]For the purposes of this chapter, I focus on data from the United States. For a survey of the impact of Pentecostalism on poverty in other parts of the world, see Donald E. Miller and Tetsunao Yamamori, *Global Pentecostalism: The New Face of Christian Social Engagement* (Berkeley: University of California Press, 2007).

[12]Michael O. Emerson and Christian Smith, *Divided by Faith: Evangelical Religion and the Problem of Race in America* (New York: Oxford University Press, 2000), 7.

more callbacks for interviews than the identical résumés with typically Black names such as Lakisha and Jamal.[13]

Socioeconomic status and racial-ethnic-cultural identity are not correlated one-to-one. In other words, there are White people in the United States who live below the poverty line and there are BIPOC people who are among the 1 percent most wealthy. To suggest poverty is racialized is not to suggest that only persons of a particular racial-ethnic-cultural identity are poor or only persons of a particular racial-ethnic-cultural identity are rich. Rather, it is to suggest that the experience of economic well-being is significantly influenced by the racial-ethnic-cultural identity a person is assigned by society.

Emerson and Smith found that "a pivotal and dearly held assumption for a large majority of White evangelicals is that all Americans have equal opportunity."[14] If everyone has equal opportunity and everyone's socioeconomic status correlates to the amount of effort they've put in, then anyone experiencing poverty would necessarily be "at fault" at some level, either through not working hard enough or through mismanagement. Poverty is then viewed as the fault of the persons of color who are poor rather than a product of systems that reward or punish based on a person's racial-ethnic-cultural identification. Tatum refers to this as a power evasion: "when someone minimizes the impact of racism, claiming that everyone has the same opportunity to succeed and those who don't only have themselves to blame."[15]

The consequences of the racialization of poverty can be seen when looking at the socioeconomic status of people in the United States. As a group, White people have a greater amount of economic resources on average than do Black people. In 2017, the median household income of White, non-Hispanic people was $68,145 while the median household income of Black people was $40,258.[16] Additionally, the median net

[13]Marianne Bertrand and Sendhil Mullainathan, "Are Emily and Greg More Employable Than Lakisha and Jamal? A Field Experiment on Labor Market Discrimination," *American Economic Review* 94, no. 4 (2004): 991-1013.

[14]Emerson and Smith, *Divided by Faith*, 98.

[15]Tatum, *Why Are All the Black Kids*, 227.

[16]Kayla Fontenot, Jessica Semega, and Melissa Kollar, "Income and Poverty in the United States: 2017," *Current Population Reports* (September 2018): 60-263.

worth—a measure of what resources a family has minus what it owes—is significantly higher for White people than for Black people.[17]

If wealth was the essential aspect of a sense of well-being, then anyone who has a higher socioeconomic status would necessarily feel more positive about their life. A 2016 Pew Research study found that White people are more likely to say they are very satisfied with the quality of life in their community (48 percent) than are Black people (34 percent).[18] If this difference were solely a result of socioeconomic status, then both White people and Black people with higher incomes would have similar views. Instead, 57 percent of White people with a family income of $75,000 or more are more likely to be very satisfied while only 38 percent of Black people with a family income of $75,000 or more gave the same answer.[19]

Since a person's racial-ethnic-cultural group plays a factor in their access to financial resources, then poverty is, at least in part, a product of systemic racism. Nevertheless, perceiving and accepting the effect of racial-ethnic-cultural identity on socioeconomic status is hard for many people to process despite clear evidence of the racialization of wealth in the United States. The difficulty lies, at least in part, in the fact that the data contradict the deeply held value of meritocracy.

An important point to note here is that this content is descriptive, not predictive. Noting the significance of poverty for the process of vocational formation is not to say that those difficulties are defining of a person's potential or possible flourishing. The challenges need to be named; they do not need to be submitted to as if they are the final word. Consider, for example, Christa Lopez's story. Notice in particular how she processes her experience and forms her sense of self.

---

[17]US Census Bureau, "Wealth, Asset Ownership, & Debt of Households Detailed Tables: 2015," accessed July 27, 2021, www.census.gov/data/tables/2015/demo/wealth/wealth-asset-ownership .html. Note that a major difference between groups is equity from property (home ownership and other real estate assets such as rental property). See also Robert B. Williams, "Wealth Privilege and the Racial Wealth Gap: A Case Study in Economic Stratification," *The Review of Black Political Economy* 44, no. 3-4 (January 2017): 303-25.

[18]Pew Research Center, "On Views of Race and Inequality, Blacks and Whites Are Worlds Apart," June 27, 2016, www.pewresearch.org/social-trends/2016/06/27/on-views-of-race-and-inequality -blacks-and-whites-are-worlds-apart.

[19]Pew Research Center, "On Views of Race and Inequality."

CALLING STORY
Christa Lopez—Photographer

I am the daughter of a Latina immigrant, single parent. I was raised by a strong woman to be an independent thinker and to pursue life and everything in it without question or insecurities. That foundation set me up in life to not allow anyone to define me or put me in a box.

As early as maybe three or four years old I was talking to Jesus. I recall kneeling beside my bed and reciting a prayer next to my mom. I remember the recited prayers quickly changed to conversations about everything and anything that happened during the day. I stayed up late and usually fell asleep talking to Jesus. That closeness, developed in my early years, set me up in life to have deep conversations with Jesus, intercede for others, and be able to hear the Spirit speak to me.

I was probably in middle school when, one day at lunch, my mother asked me, "What do you want to do when you grow up—what do you want to be?" In that moment, I heard the Spirit say, "You are to be a helper." Hearing the Spirit's voice was as natural as breathing to me and so I did not question what I heard but embraced it. From that point on, I pursued activities, whether ministry, school, volunteering, etc., to help others.

In one of my Humanitas classes (college-bound high school honor classes), as I was prepping for an essay exam, my teacher had a documentary on TV. I heard a list of statistical data of how Latinas who grew up in single-parent homes turned out. That list was grim and suggested a life of poor choices that led to a life of dependency and poverty. I vowed then that I would prove them wrong—and I have! My life does not reflect those statistics. As I worked as a social worker and later a photographer/videographer, I continued to defy the expectations others had. Ultimately, I am someone that has not let what others think hold me back. I keep coming back to what I learned early in life: hearing the voice that loves me like no other and hearing my mother's voice encouraging me. Those two voices are the ones that matter the most.

CONSIDERING CLASS AND CALLING

Given the complications that meritocracy creates for processing vocation from a variety of socioeconomic statuses, thoughtful attention to class and its impact on vocational discernment requires a fair degree of self-awareness and capacity for noting when unnamed social status is contributing to the conversation. Much of the literature on vocation published in the last twenty years in the United States demonstrates a fundamental underlying assumption: that individuals are free to choose their vocational path. Among other things, this assumption establishes the relative socioeconomic privilege of the authors and their intended audience. To be able to consider one's inclinations, passions, and desires as a primary factor of vocational guidance assumes there are few economic pressures at work. This approach to vocational discernment also ignores all the ways that people are interconnected and the fact that vocational choices affect more than just the individual making them.

For example, Parker Palmer's excellent and popular book *Let Your Life Speak* expresses his Quaker perspective on vocational discernment as "waiting for the way to open."[20] This is a helpful point of reflection, particularly for Christians from other theological traditions. Yet embodied in that work is the social space Parker has as a White man with sufficient resources to make it possible for him to spend extended seasons of time waiting for the open door. Palmer has position and finances and social esteem enough to be able to take that time. Many other people feel a sense of urgency, pressured by an immediate need to provide an income, that they don't see reflected in Palmer's articulation of his experience. Asking people to engage in lengthy discernment processes without acknowledging the economic pressures they face leaves people feeling trapped. They are seen as "less spiritual" if they express their concern about their economic needs.[21]

---

[20]Parker J. Palmer, *Let Your Life Speak: Listening for the Voice of Vocation* (Hoboken, NJ: John Wiley & Sons, Inc., 1999).

[21]Notice the assumption of middle or upper-middle-class financial resources in other, also excellent and well-known books on vocation, including Lee Hardy, *The Fabric of this World: Inquiries into Calling, Career Choice, and the Design of Human Work* (Grand Rapids, MI: Eerdmans, 1990);

Consider, by contrast, Russell Jeung, *At Home in Exile*.[22] There is immense social-cultural pressure on men to have a job that provides for their family and that maintains the trappings of a middle-class lifestyle. Part of Russell Jeung's story is the pressure he felt when, contrary to the expectations of his Chinese American family, he chose to move into East Oakland's "Murder Dubs" neighborhood. He writes of the life trajectory expected of him and his peers in an academic magnet high school in San Francisco: "Among the Chinese Americans, so many went on to join the top Silicon Valley tech firms that we joked about our educational and career trajectories: 'Lowell, US Berkeley, Hewlett Packard: proof there is no free will.'" This trajectory was encouraged and supported by members of his church, who "took upward mobility for granted. It was a sign of blessing and a witness to our families."[23] His story illustrates how difficult it can be to discern God's invitation to particular areas of engagement when that engagement contradicts cultural economic norms and values.

Yet, in the midst of these "distorting" challenges in our cultural maps of vocation, God continues to be at work in our lives. Consider the example of renowned scholar and educator Anne Streaty Wimberly, whose family gave up home and jobs, moving from middle-class security to a period of homelessness in order to seek a climate that would help her mother survive tuberculosis. In this period of time, the family spent their first Thanksgiving eating in a soup kitchen. The event became an important part of Wimberly's vocational journey. She tells the story this way:

> But later on in my life—many, many years later—there was a connection between that event and another event. When my husband and I moved from Tulsa, Oklahoma, to Evanston, Illinois, I found myself for the first

---

Amy L. Sherman, *Kingdom Calling: Vocational Stewardship for the Common Good* (Downers Grove, IL: InterVarsity Press, 2011); Gordon T. Smith, *Courage and Calling: Embracing Your God-Given Potential* (Downers Grove, IL: InterVarsity Press, 2011). Note, in particular, how these authors approach concepts like stewardship and work and the socioeconomic status implied by that approach. These books can be, and have been, helpful to many yet without challenging those who fit the implied socioeconomic status to consider the significance of their relative economic wealth.

[22]Russell Jeung, *At Home in Exile: Finding Jesus Among My Ancestors and Refugee Neighbors* (Grand Rapids, MI: Zondervan, 2016).

[23]Jeung, *At Home in Exile*, 27-28.

time since undergraduate work without a position. I thought, well, God had brought me that far, to continue my vocation as a teacher. But at that point in time, absolutely nothing opened up. And I found myself yelling to God, "God, now what's going on?" . . . And I was looking in the Evanston newspaper and found myself in the want ads. And there was a little tiny article that simply said, "Wanted, a director of a shelter for homeless people." That little tiny article loomed as big as the page. . . . And I thought, okay, I get it, that's what I'm supposed to do.[24]

Initially discouraged from taking the position, Wimberly felt confirmation during a worship service in which she felt the Holy Spirit saying to her, "Don't you remember? You do remember, don't you, when you were homeless? So you know what it's like, and I'm calling you to give back."[25] The twists and turns of experience, including the experience of homelessness, were part of the journey of vocational formation for Wimberly.

Let us return, then, to David Douglas's story. Part of his process was to reflect on the various aspects of his social location. Part of my process was to learn to hear him more clearly. What initially seemed to me a reluctance to acknowledge the privilege he carries as a White man I eventually came to see was more a desire to have his story seen in its fullness and complexity. David's reaction to the conversation about race suggested that he felt his experience of poverty was being overlooked or disregarded because he was White. Part of his vocational journey was to make sense of how God was present in all of his experiences, including on the streets of New York, and how God is working redemptively in and through the various events of his life.

REFLECTIVE NEXT STEPS

A recurring theme of this book is that we cannot examine what we cannot recognize. To the extent that we have separated questions of socioeconomic status and a sense of our class identity from concerns about

---

[24] Anne Streaty Wimberly quoted in Mary Elizabeth Mullino Moore, "Stories of Vocation: Education for Vocational Discernment," *Religious Education*, 103, no. 2 (2008): 223.

[25] Moore, "Stories of Vocation," 223.

developing in our callings, we will continue to unconsciously live out the values and assumptions of our socioeconomic status, even when those suppositions get in the way of discerning God's invitation and faithfully responding. Likewise, insofar as we inhabit middle- and upper-class social standing and continue to separate that social location from our vocational formation, we will be blind to our privilege and callous toward the difficulties of those in a poverty experience. An essential starting point is to begin to notice our assumptions and values.

One place to begin is to reflect on the stories told in our families of origin. How did your family come to live where they do? Perhaps there's an immigrant story to reflect on. How is that story told? What values are embedded in that narrative? Notice as well when stories are missing and consider why those stories are missing.

Consider also what occupations are valued in your family and social groups. How did family members come to have the occupations they do? Is there a family business either literally or in the sense of multiple family members pursuing similar lines of work? Is there an ancestor hero story that established that tradition? In some contexts, the roles that are valued are ones that require university or graduate school education, such as lawyer or doctor or engineer. In other contexts, jobs that require substantial skill but little formal education, such as plumber or carpenter or electrician, are valued. Some families value community helper roles such as teacher, police officer, and fireman. Other families have a tradition of military service that is deeply formational for both life-path choices and a sense of what it means to serve community and country.[26] Would these various roles be thought of as "callings" in your church? Why or why not? Notice the values evident in your judgments.

Additionally, reflect on how meritocracy has played a part in your family and social groups. Observe the hero stories. Notice how the

---

[26]An investigation of what roles and occupations are considered callings/vocations in a particular group of Pentecostal adults is found in Susan L. Maros, "Knowing My Call: A Cultural Model of the Experience of Call in a Pentecostal/Charismatic Context" (PhD diss., Fuller Theological Seminary, 2014).

"self-made" person is viewed. Is the emphasis placed on individual effort
or on social structures that determine status? How are wealthy people
viewed in your family? Are upper-middle-class and upper-class people
seen as having earned their wealth? Also consider how your family self-
identifies in class terms. Then look at statistics for what constitutes poor,
working class, middle class and upper class in your geographical region.
Does this data match your family's self-identification? Is your class status
seen as a badge of honor or of shame? Why?

In my own family, my husband's parents were both immigrants to the
United States. His father came to the United States as a refugee, fleeing
the aftermath of the Hungarian Revolution in 1958. He had painful
stories that he was never able to tell us, answering our questions with,
"You don't want to know." We did (and do) want to know; he didn't want
to speak of them. We've benefited as a family from his courage and ability
to persevere. My husband wouldn't be alive without them. His dad
learned English; he worked hard; he had his own shop as a machinist; he
bought a home, married, and raised two sons. He took the pathway of
assimilation into US-American whiteness, and this pathway worked for
him. We can honor his hard work and resilience and tell the story (the
little that we know!) of his journey from Hungary to the United States to
our two children to encourage them to have a sense of identity of coming
from people who endure, persevere, and make a new life. We can, at the
same time, acknowledge the power systems and racial inequities that
made it possible for my father-in-law to participate in the "American
dream." He would not have been able to purchase the home he did, for
example, if he had been a person of color. He benefited, my husband
benefited, and we continue, as a family, to benefit from the lingering effects of overtly racist housing practices. We can know both the good and
the bad, acknowledge both the effort and the unjust systems. Acknowledging both denies the power of neither.

I offer these personal reflections as one who is also on the journey of
discovery and processing. As we become aware, we can consider our
values and whether the cultural and social assumptions about social

status are ones we choose to own and uphold, ones we choose to challenge, or some mixture in between. In an increasingly globalized world, we need thoughtful, self-aware, and nuanced understandings of our contexts. Our identities—as individuals and as group members—are God-given contexts of formation (Ephesians 2:10). We must acknowledge how our racial-ethnic-cultural identities and our socioeconomic status have formed us and deformed us for engagement with God's mission in the world.

QUESTIONS FOR REFLECTION AND DISCUSSION

1. How would you characterize the socioeconomic status of your family when you were a child? When you were a teenager? What were you taught to believe or feel about this status?

2. What messages did you receive from your family about the nature of work and money? What was expected of you?

3. "You can accomplish anything if you work hard enough for it" is a common social message in the United States. Was this a message you heard as you grew up? Did you believe it applied to you? Did you believe it applied to other people?

4. How have your vocational choices been affected by socioeconomic expectations?

EXPLORING A BIBLICAL NARRATIVE: RUTH

1. Read Ruth 1:1-6.

2. A famine is the context of this story: famine provoked Elimelech to move to Moab with his family as an economic refugee, and the end of the famine as well as widowhood provoked Naomi to move back to Bethlehem. What does this say to you about Naomi's social status or class?

3. Read Ruth 1:16-17. Was Ruth "called" to become a part of the community of faith? What in this story would suggest yes? What are reasons you would give to answer no?

4. Ruth is a marginalized person in at least three ways: she is a Moabite, she is poor, and she is a widow. She is also the grandmother of King David and an ancestor of Jesus mentioned in Matthew's genealogy. What do these two facts—her marginalized social status and her place in the lineage of the Messiah—suggest about God's view of social class?

SUGGESTIONS FOR FURTHER READING

Jeung, Russell. *At Home in Exile: Finding Jesus Among My Ancestors and Refugee Neighbors.* Grand Rapids, MI: Zondervan, 2016.

Reyes, Patrick B. *Nobody Cries When We Die: God, Community, and Surviving to Adulthood.* Saint Louis, MO: Chalice Press, 2016.

6

ON BEING A GODLY (WO)MAN

Sex, Gender, and Vocation

> *Then God said, "Let us make humankind in our image, according to our*
> *likeness; and let them have dominion over the fish of the sea, and over*
> *the birds of the air, and over the cattle, and over all the wild animals of*
> *the earth, and over every creeping thing that creeps upon the earth."*
> *So God created humankind in his image,*
> *in the image of God he created them;*
> *male and female he created them.*

GENESIS 1:26-27

FOR MANY YEARS IN A LEADERSHIP CLASS I taught, when I came
to the discussion of the nature of spiritual authority and how leaders
develop it, I often began the lecture with a "Bible quiz." I would tell my
students I was going to give them a set of clues to a leader in the Bible
who led primarily from the basis of spiritual authority.[1] Play along and
see if you figure out who I am referring to.

I began with clues like this:

---

[1]The questions for this quiz were originally developed by J. Robert Clinton, longtime professor of
leadership at the Fuller Theological Seminary School of Intercultural Studies. He was always
generous with sharing his content, freely giving permission for its use. I have gratefully used his
work in my classroom for more than two decades.

> The Bible records two prophecies I made. Both came true as prophesied.

> The people of Israel came to me to settle their disputes because of my wisdom and my ability to hear from God.

> I became famous enough in Israel that the exact location of my ministry near Mount Ephraim was named after me.

> Poetically I am described by an unusual leadership name.

> I was an inspirational leader. I summoned and challenged a military leader to a great victory over the forces of the king of Hazor.

By this point in the quiz, usually I had a room full of people scratching their heads, wondering who in the world I was talking about. Rarely was the person guessed after those first clues. Sometimes the next clue would bring a light of recognition on someone's face:

> The military leader would not go into battle unless I agreed to come also. I agreed and prophesied that the credit for defeat of the enemy would go to another.

> I may be best remembered for the great victory song I wrote and sang. My victory song is one of two duets recorded in Scripture.

At this point, I would give the last of the clues:

> My gender is female. My leadership is based on spiritual authority.

Usually, when I got to the last clue, there would be some kind of verbal and physical reaction from the people in the room. I saw eyes blink in surprise and heard a startled "oh!" due to a shift in perception.

The person described in this quiz is the judge Deborah, whose story appears in Judges 4–5. My goal in beginning this chapter with Deborah is not so much because of her story per se, although she is a biblical leader worthy of examination. My desire instead is to highlight the surprised responses to the quiz's answer as an example of cultural maps affecting the reading of the biblical text. Many of my students unconsciously assumed that a biblical model of a leader with spiritual authority was going to be a man. Even people who hold a theology that affirms women in leadership roles—in the church and in society at large—will anticipate a male biblical character as an exemplar of spiritual authority or leadership or calling.

My purpose in this chapter is not to argue for or against a biblical theology of women in leadership or women in ministry roles.[2] I do, however, want to name my position at the outset because it is implicitly clear, even if I don't state it: I believe the Bible supports women in leadership roles. Having said that, I can tell you that my specific goal in this chapter is to facilitate reflection on how gender role expectations shape a person's experience of vocational formation—for women and for men—in a variety of theological settings. I begin by explaining the difference between gender and biological sex. I then discuss insights from psychology regarding the development of gender identity, and end by reflecting on the implications for vocational formation.

ON GENDER IDENTITY AND SEX IDENTITY

Sex is a biological category related to our chromosomes—XY for men and XX for women—and to the resulting related physiological differences in primary and secondary sex characteristics. Though more recent research has shown that, in reality, biological sex may be more complicated than the simple binary of male and female,[3] many of our cultures still tend to emphasize this biological binary.

---

[2]There are many excellent books written on this subject. See, for example, Linda Belleville, *Women Leaders in the Church: Three Crucial Questions* (Grand Rapids, MI: Baker Academic, 2000); Carolyn Custis James, *Half the Church: Recapturing God's Global Vision for Women* (Grand Rapids, MI: Zondervan, 2011); Alice Mathews, *Gender Roles and the People of God: Rethinking What We Were Taught About Men and Women in the Church* (Grand Rapids, MI: Zondervan, 2016). See also Alan F. Johnston, ed., *How I Changed My Mind About Women in Leadership: Compelling Stories from Prominent Evangelicals* (Grand Rapids, MI: Zondervan, 2010).

[3]For example, there are "intersex" individuals who are born with a variety of genetic and chromosomal anomalies, such as those who are born with an XX-XY chromosome configuration. See Anne Fausto-Sterling, "Dueling Dualism," chap. 1, in *Sexing the Body: Gender Politics and the Construction of Sexuality* (New York: Basic Books, 2000) for a discussion of the scientific and medical challenges inherent in identifying a person's biological sex.

Gender, on the other hand, is a socially constructed concept that is used to "encompass the social expectations associated with femininity and masculinity."[4] Gender norms exist related to gender roles—what activities and behaviors are expected of men and women—and gender identities—the internal sense of self. Social groups determine what defines a man and what defines a woman, and people enact their gender through behaving in ways that are considered "appropriate" for that gender.

Working in the area of organizational dynamics and leadership, Dutch social psychologist Geert Hofstede looked at cultural dimensions across the world and identified one that he labeled "masculine/feminine."[5] "Masculine" cultures maintain a strong distinction between what are seen as male traits and behaviors and what are seen as female traits and behaviors. "Feminine" cultures observe more of a blending or overlap in gendered traits and behaviors. For example, many South American countries score high on the "masculine" side of Hofstede's scale, displaying traits that other authors have referred to as *machismo*.[6] On the other hand, Scandinavian countries tend to score high on the "feminine" side of Hofstede's scale, with greater cultural emphasis on egalitarian gender roles.

That the gender rules change from culture to culture, and change across time in a given society, is indicative of the socially constructed nature of gender. Nevertheless, for some social and cultural groups in the United States and elsewhere in the world, the foundational assumption about sex and gender is that they are correlated: masculine gender traits belong to the male sex, and feminine gender traits belong to the female sex. Cisgender identity—defined by the *Oxford English Dictionary* as

---

[4]Hilary M. Lips, *A New Psychology of Women: Gender, Culture, and Ethnicity*, 2nd ed. (New York: McGraw-Hill, 2003), 6.

[5]Geert Hofstede, Gert Jan Hofstede, and Michael Minkov, *Cultures and Organizations: Software of the Mind: Intercultural Cooperation and Its Importance for Survival*, rev. and exp. 3rd ed. (New York: McGraw-Hill, 2010).

[6]For a discussion of *machismo* and its impact on the leadership development of women and men, see Wilmer G. Villacorta, *Unmasking the Male Soul: Power and Gender Trap for Women in Leadership* (Eugene, OR: Wipf and Stock, 2019).

"designating a person whose sense of personal identity and gender corresponds to his or her sex at birth"[7]—is understood to be the human norm in these groups.

> **NAVIGATION POINT**
> **Regarding LGBTQ+ Concerns**
>
> In the church in the United States in the twenty-first century, the debate around LGBTQ+ inclusion involves a great deal of contention, pain, and anxiety. Adequately addressing sexual orientation or gendered identity other than cisgender male and female is beyond the scope of this present work. As with other areas of social location identity in this book, I encourage readers to be aware of their churches' or organizations' history and theological commitments on this subject. My hope is to offer a discussion here in which people can consider how the gender norms in their context have shaped their assumptions about calling, whatever their position on or experience with LGBTQ+ concerns.

The fact that I define gender as a social construct may be a problem for some. Evangelicals (among others) tend to view male and female as concrete, God-given, God-ordained sets of characteristics and roles. Any consideration of social construction is seen as undermining God's order. Thus, the invitation to recognize the ways in which socially constructed gender expectations have shaped a person's vocational formation may be interpreted as an attack against "biblical manhood and womanhood." The fear of losing a cultural norm makes any reflection on that norm feel like a threatening experience. Yet, without this reflection, a person will unconsciously enact the behaviors expected, or unconsciously resist the expectations, and not be able to reflect productively on the experience. Reflecting on gender identity is a means of considering God's distinctive work in a person's life and in their social group. To consider the effect of

---

[7] The term *cisgender* was coined in the 1990s, grew in usage, and was added to the *Oxford English Dictionary* in 2015. Katherine Martin, "New Words Notes June 2015," *Oxford English Dictionary*, accessed May 24, 2021, https://web.archive.org/web/20150814051905/http:/public.oed.com/the -oed-today/recent-updates-to-the-oed/june-2015-update/new-words-notes-june-2015.

gendered norms on the discernment of calling, let us consider how gendered identity forms across a lifetime.

THE DEVELOPMENT OF GENDERED IDENTITY

As with other elements of social location explored thus far, gendered identity is developed and expressed in specific contexts. Our sense of who we are emerges and changes across time. The following is a brief reflection on what psychological research has suggested concerning the development of gender identity.

Gender in infancy. When children are born, they are immediately assigned a biological sex and gender identity: "It's a boy!" or "It's a girl!" In the age of ultrasounds and other in-utero tests, many people host what are called "gender reveal" parties. That we call these parties a gender reveal demonstrates the loose way we interchange the terms *sex* and *gender* in everyday language. Technically, these events are "biological sex reveal" parties.

Consider how much gendered norms are immediately applied to infants, even before birth, with pink balloons for the girls and blue balloons for the boys. This color association is a cultural artifact belonging to certain national cultures and to the current era.[8] In other eras and in other parts of the world, the pink/blue association is not present. For example, in rural India the birth of a boy is celebrated differently from the birth of a girl, but both sexes are usually dressed alike for the first few years of their lives.[9]

Childhood development researchers generally agree that socialization into gender roles begins at birth with parents unconsciously adapting their behavior toward their children based on their own gender role expectations. In one review of gender-related studies of infants,

---

[8]For a history of how we came to associate pink with girls and blue with boys, see Jo B. Paoletti, *Pink and Blue: Telling the Boys from the Girls in America* (Bloomington: Indiana University Press, 2013).

[9]Nandita Chaudhary, "Peripheral Lives, Central Meaning: Women and Their Place in Indian Society," in *Cultural Dynamics of Women's Lives,* ed. Ana Cecília Bastos, Kristiina Uriko, and Jaan Valsiner (Charlotte, NC: Information Age Pub., 2012), 8.

Marilyn Stern and Katherine Karraker noted, "Preconceived gender-based expectations may cause the parent to elicit expected behavior from the infant and to reinforce expected behavior when it occurs, thereby confirming the parent's initial expectations."[10] Simply put, a child's biological sex is a significant determinant in how the child will be treated—beginning with colors of clothing and types of toys presented and continuing on to the ways adults engage the infant.[11] What long-term effect this has on the formation of a child's sense of gender identity is a topic of continued investigation.

The nature/nurture debate is relevant to this point of discussion. Some theological environments come down on the side of nature, asserting that God has defined gendered roles and that people must learn them and act within the God-given gender hierarchy. Other theological traditions come down more on the side of nurture, emphasizing the social construction of gender norms. Research in this area is divided, with some studies demonstrating clear gender differences and others giving evidence of exactly the opposite; increasingly, researchers are suggesting that the issue is not "nature versus nurture" but more accurately "nature *and* nurture."[12]

Whether nature or nurture or both are at work, certainly expectation-based nurture has an impact on early childhood behavior. In some Christian contexts, male toddlers who are physically active and unable to control themselves are referred to as "all boy" while female toddlers who exhibit the same behavior are scolded. Two-year-old girls who cry are likely to be comforted while two-year-old boys may be told to stop crying. In other Christian contexts, children are encouraged to express their emotions and to engage in cooperative play. What is "natural" to the child's temperament and personality is shaped by

[10]Marilyn Stern and Katherine Hildebrandt Karraker, "Sex Stereotyping of Infants: A Review of Gender Labeling Studies," *Sex Roles* 20, nos. 9-10 (1989): 502.

[11]Lacey M. Sloan et al., *Critical Multiculturalism and Intersectionality in a Complex World* (New York: Oxford University Press, 2018), 70.

[12]See, for example, Rebekah Grace, Alan Hayes, and Sarah Wise, "Child Development in Context," in *Children, Families and Communities*, ed. Rebekah Grace, Kerry Hodge, and Catherine McMahon (Docklands, VIC: Australia Oxford University Press, 2017): 3-25.

cultural expectations of how they should behave based on their gender identity assignment.

Gender in childhood. In the United States and other North Atlantic countries, a child's school-age affinity for peers is a key aspect of formation. These years are "a kind of peer-oriented proving ground that can validate or inhibit social development."[13] In most contexts in the United States, the norm is for children to play in sex-segregated groups—boys with boys and girls with girls—with an expectation that children will express hostility toward members of the opposite group. These peer groups play a significant role in reinforcing gender norms. A boy who is unwilling to engage in aggressive play may be labeled a sissy or other demeaning terms that suggest his lack of aggression makes him inferior to the other boys and more like the inferior girls.[14] A girl who engages in activities labeled masculine may be called a tomboy for acting outside of gender role expectations. This label can be derogatory or positive, either meaning that she is failing to behave like a "normal" girl or that she is engaging in a healthier lifestyle that includes exercising and dressing sensibly.[15] Note the inherent sexism in the positive designation of *tomboy* and the negative use of *sissy*: girls who "act like boys" are aspiring to what is seen as good (in other words, what is male) while boys who "act like girls" are deviating from that good.

During this season of life children experiment by trying on different occupations and life roles in play and in imagination. This is why, when children are asked "What do you want to be when you grow up?" they respond with a range of concrete and imaginative answers. Some people point to the affirmation or criticism they received for answers they gave when they were a child as being significant for what they imagined they could become as adults. One wonders how many brilliant children might

---

[13]Jack O. Balswick, Pamela Ebstyne King, and Kevin S. Reimer, *The Reciprocating Self: Human Development in Theological Perspective*, 2nd ed. (Downers Grove, IL: IVP Academic, 2016), 165.
[14]Sloan, et al, *Critical Multiculturalism and Intersectionality*, 70.
[15]Sloan, et al, *Critical Multiculturalism and Intersectionality*, 72-73.

have developed in an entirely different direction had they not been turned toward occupations that were "more realistic" for them based on societal gender norms.

Consider also how many high-performing people such as professional athletes or accomplished actors point to how the encouragement they received from important people in their lives, particularly parents and teachers, was essential to their future accomplishments. This dynamic is particularly significant in light of the studies that have demonstrated that "teachers, often without realizing it, treat boys and girls differently: They pay more attention to boys than to girls in the classroom, spend more time outside of class talking with boys than girls, and respond differently to boys' and girls' successes and failures."[16] Significant adults in a child's life play an important role in helping that child develop a sense of self and agency.

Childhood is also a time when children begin to consciously notice the enactment of gender-specific roles around them, observing their parents and other close relatives, learning from the men they see what it means to "be a man" and learning from the women they see what it means to "be a woman." They also notice how roles and occupations are discussed by their families, as well as what is affirmed by their communities. Children who grow up in faith communities will see gendered roles in their churches, with some being primarily or exclusively filled by men and others filled by women. As a result, they will learn, even without being overtly taught, what roles are available to them as males and females. The experience comes first; the explicit theology comes later.

Team sports is a classic context for development in childhood and adolescence. On the playing field, young people learn to work hard and to collaborate with a group toward a shared goal—something bigger than themselves. Additionally, children and teens who play sports learn lessons in leadership, such as how to prioritize the good of others and how to motivate teammates to persevere in the face of adversity. Prior to

---

[16]Lips, *A New Psychology of Women*, 157.

the advent of Title IX in the 1970s, team sports in schools were largely limited to boys in the United States. Beginning in the 1970s, the development of women's sports teams and the inclusion of girls' team sports in schools meant that more girls had opportunities to be involved in sports and thus to receive some of the same leader formation as their brothers.

Gender in adolescence. Adolescence has traditionally been defined as the phase of development between childhood and adulthood, starting with the onset of puberty and ending with commitment to adult roles.[17] With the arrival of puberty, hormonal changes prompt a growth spurt, the emergence of primary and secondary sex characteristics, and the onset of fertility. Jack O. Balswick, Pamela Ebstyne King, and Kevin S. Reimer explain, "The biological changes in puberty both increase young persons' interest in sex and their awareness of others' perception of them as sexual objects."[18] Girls who have, in their younger years, thrived in school or demonstrated leadership gifts may, in adolescence, draw back from demonstrating these gifts.[19] Peer pressure and social pressure from media representations of women can provoke girls to be critical of their bodies or, conversely, to use their bodies to gain attention. Both adolescent boys and girls move toward identifying with a social group, distinct from their family. The values of this group become influential in the way the adolescent sees themselves and their place in the world.

One common traditional vocational narrative in some Christian communities is the teenage calling story. William's story is a typical example. He grew up in a small city in the Midwest United States in the middle of the twentieth century. He recalls how his parents came to faith when he was a small child and how the family became actively engaged in their local church. William prayed "the sinner's prayer" at his mother's knee when he was about five years old, an event he sees as significant for

---

[17]Balswick, King, and Reimer, *Reciprocating Self*, 184.
[18]Balswick, King, and Reimer, *Reciprocating Self*, 188.
[19]Lips, *A New Psychology of Women*, 162-70.

establishing his sense of identity as a Christian. Then, when he was sixteen, he attended a summer church camp and helped as a junior counselor. At one of the nightly meetings, the guest speaker issued a call for the young people to give their lives in service to God. For William, this was another significant encounter, as he went forward for prayer, feeling a sense of God's call to be a pastor. When he related this event to his family and to his church, he was affirmed and supported. Once William graduated from high school, his family and church also supported him in his decision to attend a Bible college. He began pastoring immediately upon graduation, starting in a small church in a community not far from his childhood home and then pastoring in several different churches for a total of more than five decades.

A traditional calling narrative of this nature—an early commitment to faith with a teenage commitment to a particular role, especially that of pastor or missionary—is powerful enough and dominant enough that it colors how people view calling, even if they don't share the particularities of William's life experience. In fact, in some Christian circles, people who haven't had this kind of experience express a sense of being a second-class citizen in the people of God. And those who did not grow up in the church but came to faith as an adult assume they have "missed out" and cannot be called by God because they were not a Christian as a child.

Another dynamic of this teenage calling narrative is how gendered it can be, depending on the individual's social and theological environment. William's sense of calling to be a pastor was affirmed. He had seen male pastors in his church and could imagine following in their footsteps. Had William been Wilma instead, the ability to perceive herself as called to be a pastor would have been less likely if she saw only men in pastoral roles since, in general, we can't imagine what we've never seen. The community affirmation and support that William received may not have been extended to Wilma. Similar dynamics can be seen in other roles and occupations. A boy growing up in a theological environment that emphasizes men as leaders and providers, and only hears men affirmed in these capacities, for example, may feel a sense of pressure and constraint to fulfill this norm whether or not it fits his distinctive personality and gifts. Perhaps Bill sat beside William at the summer camp and did not feel called to be a pastor; he wanted to be an elementary school teacher. The speaker's call for "Christian service" assumed some roles and excluded others. William was praised by his church as sensing a particularly mean-ingful calling while Bill may not have been similarly affirmed. In their context, William's sense of calling to pastoral ministry was consistent with vocations for men, while Bill's sense of calling to be an elementary school teacher was not viewed as an equally masculine choice.

Gender in emerging adulthood. In the previous century in the United States, adolescence generally ended sometime between eighteen and twenty-two with the individual entering the labor market, getting married, and starting a family.[20] Sociological shifts have influenced this pattern significantly, with some young people leaving home in their late teens but not marrying, becoming parents, or finding a long-term job until at least their late twenties.[21] Currently, some developmental scientists suggest adolescence extends into the mid-twenties, a view that has less to do with committing to adult roles and more to do with brain maturation.[22]

Jeffery Arnett identifies five characteristic features that are distinctive to emerging adulthood: identity explorations; instability in love, work, and place of residence; self-focus; feeling in-between (neither adolescent nor adult); and a sense of possibility/optimism.[23] The phenomenon of not viewing one's self as an adult is more common in countries such as the United States, Canada, Australia, New Zealand, South Korea, Japan, and most of Europe, "where young people are able to postpone entering into adult roles until their mid-twenties or later. In less economically privileged contexts, where less training is required for vocations and

---

[20]Balswick, King, and Reimer, *Reciprocating Self*, 184.
[21]Jeffrey Jensen Arnett, *Emerging Adulthood: The Winding Road from the Late Teens Through the Twenties*, 2nd ed. (New York: Oxford University Press, 2014), 1.
[22]Balswick, King, and Reimer, *Reciprocating Self*, 185.
[23]Arnett, *Emerging Adulthood*, 8-17.

marriage occurs earlier in the lifespan, adolescents seem to transition right into young adulthood with these adult commitments."[24]

For some emerging adults, the sense of exploring identity and of having a wide variety of possibilities to engage can be empowering and exhilarating. Some may participate in short-term missions or explore a variety of occupations. For others, however, the freedom comes with a sense of overwhelming pressure. Tom's experience is an example of the latter. "I am a part of the generation that got trophies for participation," Tom said. "Ever since I can remember, I was told, 'Follow your passion!' and 'You can do great things for Jesus!' and 'You're going to change the world!'" Tom was in his early twenties and working part time as a receptionist in a dental office while also attending college part time. He had changed his major twice and wasn't sure whether his current business administration degree was where he wanted to be. Though he was attempting to consider what God's purpose was for his life, he was finding the process difficult. "Sometimes the pressure is just too much," he reflected. "Everyone expects me to find the perfect job that I just love. Of course, that job is supposed to pay a lot of money too, since a 'good man' is supposed to provide well for his family, even if I don't have a family yet. Sometimes, I just want to drop out and work as a barista for the rest of my life."

Gracie had, like Tom, received many messages from her church community encouraging her to "do great things for Jesus." Her efforts to find herself were complicated by the expectations she felt from significant adults in her life, particularly her youth pastor. Pastor Dustin had been an important mentor for Gracie, including her as part of the leadership of the youth group and encouraging her to co-lead one of the teams for the youth group's summer evangelism outreach. "But I've noticed," said Gracie, "when it comes to hiring interns, Pastor Dustin always hires one of the guys." Gracie asked Pastor Dustin why he didn't hire any of the young women and was told, "Oh, you're going to get

---

[24]Balswick, King, and Reimer, *Reciprocating Self*, 210.

married. Being a wife and mother will be your calling." While the roles of wife and mother were ones Gracie hoped to have some day, she struggled to feel her dreams and interests outside of family had value in the eyes of her church community.

Questions of social relationships, particularly around intimacy and social status, are important issues of development at this stage. Emerging adults may also seek to identify what kind of work they enjoy, are good at, or find meaning in.[25] Strong gendered expectations influence what these emerging adults consider as options available to them. Messages from significant adults intended to support emerging adults in the process of discerning God's calling in their lives can be encouraging when the expectations of the social group are a good fit for the individual's sense of themselves. Those same well-intentioned messages may also function to hinder the emerging adult's capacity to discern God's calling when the gendered norms don't fit the distinctive characteristics of the individual's sense of self or don't fit their particular gifts and interests.

CALLING STORY
Cassie Williams-Demyers—Sound Engineer

I felt God call me at seventeen. That was a season in my life where the Lord was really speaking. I was convinced I was going one way and then, over the next few years, I discovered life had made some twists and turns.

At nineteen, I met someone who I thought I was going to marry. The relationship was based on friendship and on our shared interest in music. He played the bass; I played the guitar and piano. We had a vision for a music ministry. It was great. I thought, *Okay, God, this is what you want me to do. Let's go!* Then the relationship started to go sour. He looked at me one day and said, "You're not the one God has for me." And, basically, there went my entire hope of music ministry. It went completely down the tubes.

---

[25]Balswick, King, and Reimer, *Reciprocating Self*, 219.

> After that, I focused on finishing my undergraduate degree. I just went to school and worked in the church bookstore, and, somehow, just got trapped.
>
> A couple years after that, I had been praying about what to do next. I thought about going back to the sound engineering. I felt the Lord say, "Okay. Go for it," so I looked around and started going to recording school. Soon after, I transitioned from the church bookstore to the media department. I've been doing sound engineering for the last five years.
>
> Looking back, I never thought I'd go back to running sound, but here I am! I just ran the church's biggest show of the year. No in-house engineer gets to run that show, let alone a woman. Seriously, when they see a woman in the sound booth, it's like, "Whoa! Okay."
>
> All that to say, you get called to ministry at seventeen, yeah, but the call changes a lot over the years. I've come to the realization that sometimes ministry is just doing whatever you do where God has you at that point in time.

Gender in middle adulthood. Generally, when people reach their thirties there is a sense of "settling down" and developing an "adult" life structure of job and family connections.[26] For some people, these family and work roles are strongly gendered: men have paid occupations outside the home while women engage primarily in care for children and the home. For other people, the income of both women and men is necessary for the survival of the family. In yet other instances, family and work roles are managed on a more case-by-case basis. The "traditional" family exemplified by the mid-twentieth-century White suburban experience—father working outside the home, mother as a homemaker, and 2.5 children—seems to significantly represent an older generation. A 2019 Pew Research report about fatherhood in the United States notes a rising share of stay-at-home dads and men who see parenting as a central part of their identity.[27]

---

[26]Balswick, King, and Reimer, *Reciprocating Self*, 242.

[27]Gretchen Livingston and Kim Parker, "8 Facts About American Dads," Pew Research Center, June 12, 2019, www.pewresearch.org/fact-tank/2019/06/12/fathers-day-facts.

Randall was in his early thirties when he and his wife were expecting their first child. "I was a mess at the time," he recalled. Randall was the product of a broken home where substance abuse had played a part in the breakup of his parents' marriage. "My mom used to just bury her emotions with an attitude of, 'No use crying over spilt milk' and my dad numbed his feelings with alcohol," he explained. "I learned not to feel and to present a 'successful' exterior." In his late twenties, on the verge of becoming a father himself, Randall struggled with what it meant to be a husband, a father, and a good man. "I was self-absorbed and drowning in negativity," he remembered. "I began to frequent night clubs again and chose relationships that always kept drama in my life. I had no idea how to handle my emotions or relate to my wife. And I really had no idea how to be a good dad!" What changed for Randall was an opportunity that arose in his workplace. He was invited to take over the supervision of an after-school program for at-risk youth. "In hindsight," Randall said of the experience, "the kids were not the ones at risk; I was at risk. I was at risk of falling from purpose, at risk of forgetting what it means to care about others, and most at risk of forgetting to care about myself. I thank God for those kids and for that job because it made me a better person, a better husband, a better father, and, most of all, a better Christian." Randall's experience is one example of the complex nature of development, and the ways that multiple roles and relationships are impacted and, in turn, affect a person's sense of gendered identity.

Some women may adopt the motherhood role as their primary identity and place of vocational engagement. This role is culturally and personally significant for a large number of women who see care for their husbands and children as their God-given call. For these women, their twenties and thirties are heavily involved in raising children and engaging the community from the base of their home. The "motherhood season"[28] itself is often a place of ministry and leadership development, as it includes the formation of women's capacities in key skills

---

[28]Elizabeth Loutrel Glanville, "Leadership Development for Women in Christian Ministry" (PhD diss., Fuller Theological Seminary, 2000).

applicable to other contexts. Overseeing the life skills and character development of small children requires similar capacities to overseeing the formation of skills in a classroom or in a congregation, for example. Household management—whether finances or scheduling or any of the other myriad of things that mothers do—forms similar skills to handling a grant budget or managing an office schedule. Capacities in motivation and marketing can be formed in a marketing firm or in the local parent-teacher association.

Women who have significant work or ministry experience prior to having children are more likely to remain engaged in a work role during their children's early years. One common pattern is to drop below full-time work for a time with the first child and then remain part time with second or subsequent children while they are small. Other women focus on the motherhood role, emerging into other occupations and seasons of calling when children are school-age or when they are grown and have left home. Often, women who come to the conclusion of their child-raising years find they have significant skills to contribute to the marketplace or to ministries.

A cultural view of a woman as homemaker and mother has significant socioeconomic connections. Working-class and working-poor women cannot afford to stay at home with their children; they are too busy participating in keeping a roof over their heads and food on the table. The mid-century, US-American model of the White, middle-class, suburban housewife is, historically speaking, both a relatively recent social development and a relatively isolated social development. Some women of color have similar experiences, particularly if they are middle or upper class socioeconomically, yet this experience is certainly not the norm for all women in the United States or around the world. Indeed, in many places globally, women have always contributed to the economic resources of their families.

Psychologist and practical theologian Chanequa Walker-Barnes has written powerfully about the social-cultural factors that have gone into the formation of what she calls the StrongBlackWoman. This is the Black woman who is the backbone of her church, the center of her family, and the one to whom everyone turns when in need; she is the radically self-sufficient, consummate caregiver. As a result of constantly tending to the needs of others, she is often also morbidly obese, suffers with diabetes and other circulatory diseases, and struggles with chronic depression and anxiety, yet part of one of the least studied topics in health research.[29]

Walker-Barnes notes the long-lasting impact of the 1965 US Department of Labor Report *The Negro Family: The Case for National Action* (popularly known as the "Moynihan Report" after the chairman of the committee), and the "matriarchy thesis" that emerged from the report suggesting that the so-called matriarchal structure of the Black family "feminized" Black men, making them inadequate workers and absent fathers.[30] Together with the preexisting stereotypes of African American femininity that prevailed in popular culture and public discourse, the matriarchy thesis solidified the depiction of Black women as angry, domineering, and unnaturally strong. While the matriarch has little basis in the lived experiences of African American women, it continues to dominate the United States' popular imagination about the personalities and relationships of Black women.[31]

The pressure to produce, and particularly to earn sufficient money to single-handedly provide his family with a middle-class or upper-middle-class lifestyle, constrains some men from being able to openly and freely hear God's call. They know they are expected to provide for everyone financially. Men are also culturally conditioned to be "strong" and "in charge" and to not express emotions that are associated with weakness (read: women's emotions). Anger is an acceptable male emotion; sadness and fear are not. Indeed, men are told both implicitly and directly that to express fear or doubt is to call their masculinity into question, so there

---

[29]Chanequa Walker-Barnes, *Too Heavy a Yoke: Black Women and the Burden of Strength* (Eugene, OR: Cascade Books, 2014), 44-46, 52-60, 75, 160.

[30]For a critique of the report, see also Susan D. Greenbaum, *Blaming the Poor: The Long Shadow of the Moynihan Report on Cruel Images About Poverty* (New Brunswick, NJ: Rutgers University Press, 2015).

[31]Walker-Barnes, *Too Heavy a Yoke*, 117.

should be no surprise when men suppress their emotions. These pressures have serious long-term impact. For one, they render many men emotionally stunted. We should not be shocked at the rate of pastoral burnout, for example, when we expect pastors to care for people but never to express sadness or fear or grief. We've built a cultural system that imprisons men in a set of expectations that they cannot challenge without having their manhood challenged. For many conservative groups, challenging your manhood is the equivalent of challenging your existence.

Consider Daniel Cheung's story. As he articulates his experience as a child in a Korean American church and then how he thinks about calling now, note his reflections on how his experience of privilege has shaped the path of his journey.

CALLING STORY
Daniel Cheung, JD—Nonpartisan Legislative Attorney

I was born in Los Angeles to Korean American immigrant parents. I grew up in a suburb about fifteen miles north of downtown Los Angeles that was mostly White. The community was about 14 percent Korean so I never felt like I was the only one. I also grew up in a first-generation Korean American church. That's where I learned the most about my Korean heritage. My Korean-ness was very much tied to my faith community. Being Korean and being Christian were interwoven.

The message from the pulpit was that the highest calling that you can have is to be a martyr on the mission field. Meanwhile, our parents gave us a different implicit message when they commented on who went to which university or who had what career.

My dad's worldview was shaped in large part, I now understand, because of his experiences as an immigrant. I believe he thought, *You do what you need to do.* That means getting credentials such as a college degree. For him, living out your faith means being a good man, a good provider, a good "leader" of the household, and then serving in the church as much as you can.

I attended law school at NYU and obtained a degree in public administration at the Harvard Kennedy School. During that time, I met the woman who is now my wife; she was studying on the West Coast. We married and moved to Utah where she is now about to complete a PhD, studying Asian American rhetoric and Asian American studies. I serve as a nonpartisan legislative attorney for the Utah state legislature, drafting in the areas of health and data security.

My wife and I have a lot of conversations about what it means to live as Asian Americans and to live as Asian American Christians in the United States. My intentional identification as an Asian American was actually fairly recent and has to do largely with those conversations.

I feel like I might be living my calling if that's the language I would use to describe my work. I enjoy what I do. But I no longer see calling the way I did in my church and in my early twenties. Not everyone has the privileges that allow me to do what I do and be where I am now. I recognize that I am able to occupy this space, in my work and in service in my church, largely because of things that society has privileged: being male, being married, my education, and my profession as a lawyer.

REFLECTIVE NEXT STEPS

Consider another story now—that of Pastora Inés Velásquez-McBryde. Her experience contains both gender and racial-ethnic-cultural norms that have influenced her sense of calling. Notice the embedded socioeconomic elements in the story as well. I'll draw from her experience to suggest some beneficial points of reflection and development.

CALLING STORY
Inés Velásquez-McBryde—Pastor, Chaplain, Church Planter

I was born in Spain and spent my formative years in Nicaragua. My mother was a Spanish diplomat and my father a Nicaraguan pastor. After the revolution, a lot of people left Nicaragua or were exiled. We stayed. When asked why we didn't leave, my father said, "I had to stay because the families of the church needed help. And what would this country become if everybody left?"

Both of my parents were deeply involved in humanitarian efforts. I have fond memories of jumping in my father's Toyota Land Cruiser 4x4 and going deep into the mountains to bring medical care. Because my English was better than his, my father would have me translate. He'd say, "Sit down by this nice doctor from the USA. You're going to translate for him." I learned from very early to be involved in the community; justice was part of my discipleship.

Because of those experiences, I wanted to be a doctor. I saw women doctors from the United States. I saw Nicaraguan women doctors. I saw strength in those women. I saw intelligence in them. I thought, *That could be me.* During my premed studies in the United States, though, I felt a calling to let go of this ambition to be a doctor. I felt a clear sense of call to pastoral ministry.

What I didn't realize then was that God had been calling me for a very long time. My grandfather was a pastor and my father was a pastor. My father discipled me for the ministry. My grandmother and aunts modeled what it was to be strong women of faith. But because I never saw a woman preach and teach and pastor in my church, I never had the imagination to think God might call me to be a pastor. My calling was muddled and confused because of all these layers of social conditioning about what a woman can or cannot do.

After college I was invited to be a part of a church plant. That church said, "You are a pastor!" I said, "Oh, no, I'm not a pastor. Women can't do that." My father had called something out of me. My father said, "You can do anything God calls you to do!" Now, the church was catalytic in my calling.

I want a whole generation of women that come in contact with me to see what they can be, because you can't be what you can't see. I realize I am a holy disruptor of two narratives—race and gender. We're in a complex place in US history right now. I have lost friends and family over issues of race and over issues of calling as a female pastor, both inside and outside the church. I'm having to take a stand and be grounded theologically. I never imagined that I would lose so many friendships with people who are unwilling to dialogue about how we came to have these different theological and social positions. That's been a very painful part of my calling. As a Latina, I represent a whole bunch of marginalized people right now. I sometimes wish I didn't have to do that, but God is calling me to be courageous.

Reflect on gender norms. Pastora Velásquez-McBryde has developed a conscious sense of awareness of the gendered expectations that were present in her family and church as she grew up. Her story is about discerning God's call and the ways in which that discernment process was complicated by what she could and could not consider for herself.

What are the norms that are present in your context? At the end of this chapter are a series of reflective questions designed to help you bring some of those norms and assumptions to the surface. Sit before God with these elements. Give thanks for what has been life-giving and affirming. Surrender to God what has been frustrating or painful or constraining. Trust that your biological sex and your sense of gender identity, as complicated as that may be by experience, is part of who God has deliberately made you to be. There is something about your calling in life that is rooted in and ministered through who you know yourself to be as a woman or a man.

Seek mentors and models. Sometimes when people talk about mentors, they are seeking that all-encompassing counselor who will engage intensively in their formation across many years. Some people do indeed have these individuals in their lives. Many (or perhaps most) of us have a constellation of mentors of various sorts.[32] One type of mentor that we can all seek deliberately is that of a contemporary model. Who are the women you admire? Who are the men you admire? What qualities and characteristics of their lives and ministries do you value?

Note Pastora Velásquez-McBryde's example of her father, aunts, and grandmother as people who deeply shaped her sense of self and her

---

[32]Regarding definitions of mentors and the power of a "constellation" of mentors, see Paul D. Stanley and J. Robert Clinton, *Connecting: The Mentoring Relationships You Need to Succeed in Life* (Colorado Springs: NavPress, 1992), 157-68.

understanding of the nature of engagement with God's work in the world. Who are the significant people in your life? What words have they spoken about what it means to be "a good person"? What have they modeled about what it means to be a good Christian man or woman?

Storytelling. Writer and speaker Kathy Khang reflects on an experience that highlights the significance of remembering and storytelling. She watched poet and spoken-word artist Amena Brown tell a story about her grandmother preparing food for family members who were traveling. Khang writes,

> Her grandmother would carefully wrap a slice of cake in waxed paper and put fried chicken in a paper towel and foil. These lovingly packed meals were important to African Americans in the time before the passage of the Civil Rights Act, when black travelers didn't know if they would be able to find a restaurant that would serve them.
>
> As I recall Amena's performance, mannerisms, and imitation of her grandmother's speech and cadence, I can see how the warm memories of food dovetailed into a story of racial injustice. Amena can tell this story because of who she is and who her people are. And while I can share her story here, I can't possibly embody the story because it's not in my bones or blood.
>
> But I can share the story of how my grandmother, who was a child in Korea during Japanese rule, was widowed before she turned forty while raising five children and how she never remarried. I can tell you how she refused to tell me her Japanese name, but did tell me about why she chose not to remarry—because she would have been forced to prioritize her role as wife over her role as mother, even though it was difficult to live as a single mother in her patriarchal culture.
>
> Amena's grandmother and my grandmother. Two different women, two different periods in history—but injustice didn't silence them or stop them from acting on their own behalf and on the behalf of their families. We need to give voice to these uniquely embodied stories. We need their complexity and beauty.[33]

---

[33]Kathy Khang, *Raise Your Voice: Why We Stay Silent and How to Speak Up* (Downers Grove, IL: InterVarsity Press, 2018), 22-23.

What stories are present in your family? Who are the ancestors and founders? What are the family stories that foster your sense of self, particularly yourself as a woman or as a man?

I am aware, as I write this, that there are many people for whom their gendered identity is a source of pain for a whole variety of reasons. Some of us have been profoundly wounded in ways that have affected our sense of gendered identity, fostering a sense of inadequacy or fear or anxiety. Pastora Velásquez-McBryde's power as a preacher and change agent comes, at least in part, from her struggles in calling formation. God takes our pains and struggles and redeems them, taking what was broken and making something beautiful.

An undergirding conviction of this book is that we are—collectively and individually—God's masterpiece, created in Christ Jesus to do work in the world that God shaped for us and for which we are shaped (Ephesians 2:10). This includes our biological sex and socially constructed gender. In my own journey, I carried a sense of calling to leadership and thought for many years that somehow God had missed out observing my sex/gender when God invested those gifts and callings. I had to come to the point where I realized that God made me female on purpose. I live out my calling *as a woman*. I believe the same is true for every one of us: we live out our callings as the women and men God made us to be on purpose. The more we can consciously reflect on the gendered norms in our social contexts, the more we can recognize God's fingerprints in our lives, embracing who God has made us to be as women and men.

QUESTIONS FOR REFLECTION AND DISCUSSION

1. Starting with your grandparents and parents, how were life roles and tasks divided? Who did what in the home? Outside the home?

2. Who in your family controlled the financial resources?

3. What were the patterns of education in your family? For women? For men?

4. Who did you see serve in leadership and decision-making capacities in your family? In your church? In your community?

5. Who was engaged in childcare in your family? Did this change over time or after some significant event?

6. What did your family teach you about what it means to be a "good man" or a "good woman"?

7. What did your church teach you about what it means to be a "good man" or a "good woman"? What biblical models of manhood or womanhood were referenced and/or affirmed? What biblical examples were condemned?

8. What roles or occupations were you encouraged to consider as you grew up? What roles or occupations were closed to you?

9. When did you first experience a woman in a significant position of leadership—a pastor, a supervisor, a CEO, for example? What was that experience like for you? How did it shape or shift your perspective on what roles women "should" have?

10. When did you first experience a man in a primary caregiver role— for example, an at-home dad or a therapist or childcare worker? How did this experience shape or shift your perspective on what roles men "should" have?

11. How have the gender norms of your family shaped your understanding of the nature of your own vocation?

12. How have the gender norms of society influenced your sense of what is possible for you vocationally?

EXPLORING A BIBLICAL NARRATIVE: DEBORAH AND BARAK

1. Read Judges 4.

2. What do you recall being taught about Deborah? About Barak? What was positive? What was negative?

3. Was Deborah taught to you as a positive model of leadership? As you reflect on this point, what reasons come to mind for why or why not that was the case?

4. Consider what you know about hospitality in the ancient Near East. How are Jael's actions countercultural? How does the text seem to portray her behaviors?

SUGGESTIONS FOR FURTHER READING

Dixon, Rob. *Together in Ministry: Women and Men in Flourishing Partnerships*. Downers Grove, IL: IVP Academic, 2021.

James, Carolyn Custis. *Malestrom: Manhood Swept into the Currents of a Changing World*. Grand Rapids, MI: Zondervan, 2015.

Khang, Kathy, Christie Heller De Leon, and Asifa Dean. *More Than Serving Tea: Asian American Women on Expectations, Relationships, Leadership and Faith*. Downers Grove, IL: InterVarsity Press, 2009.

Lea, Bronwyn. *Beyond Awkward Side Hugs: Living as Christian Brothers and Sisters in a Sex-Crazed World*. Nashville: Nelson, 2020.

PART 3

EXAMINING INTERSECTIONS

IN PART TWO, WE REFLECTED ON SOME OF THE CONTEXTS that shape us. This discussion focused on racial-ethnic-cultural identity, socioeconomic status and class, and gender identity. We could also consider other social location identifiers such as ability, age, theological tradition, and geographical location. The three social location identifiers discussed are not the sum total but rather three categories that are significant to consider.

While I have discussed the three identifiers in three separate chapters, we should also consider how these various social location categories intersect and interact with one another. I am not just a woman, for example; I am a White woman. My experience as a woman shapes my experience of being White and vice versa. Similarly, being middle class affects both my experience as a woman and as a White person. The concept of intersectionality is helpful for thinking about these points of interaction.

> **NAVIGATION POINT**
Intersectionality

Intersectionality is a term coined by law professor and activist Kimberlé Williams Crenshaw in a 1989 article.[1] In the article, Crenshaw wrote about

[1] Kimberlé Crenshaw, "Demarginalizing the Intersection of Race and Sex: A Black Feminist Critique of Antidiscrimination Doctrine, Feminist Theory and Antiracist Politics," *University of Chicago Legal Forum* 1989, no. 1 (1989): 139.

how the "intersection" of race-based discrimination and gender-based discrimination affects Black women's access to justice in the court system. They stood, as it were, in the intersection between these two identities. Crenshaw described the analogy this way:

> Consider an analogy to traffic in an intersection, coming and going in all four directions. Discrimination, like traffic through an intersection, may flow in one direction, and it may flow in another. If an accident happens in an intersection, it can be caused by cars traveling from any number of directions and, sometimes, from all of them. Similarly, if a Black woman is harmed because she is in the intersection, her injury could result from sex discrimination or race discrimination.[2]

Intersectionality is a heuristic framework—a concept that helps make sense of social dynamics. As such, the concept has been utilized in many different fields and disciplines. Much of this work has utilized intersectionality to explore power relationships. What group or groups, within a given social context, are dominant, and what groups are subordinate? How is power apportioned and mediated?[3]

My use of the concept of intersectionality includes a difficulty that should be named here: I am a person writing from a position—indeed, multiple positions—of privilege, appropriating a concept framed to help elucidate the experience of people without privilege. As a woman, I experience some disadvantage, but to suggest that this single disadvantaged identity allows me to claim empathy for or affiliation with marginalized people is problematic.[4] Thus, I draw (with gratitude) on the work of Crenshaw and others while being mindful of the need to continue to recognize my places of privilege.

---

[2]Crenshaw, "Demarginalizing the Intersection of Race and Sex," 149.

[3]Sumi Cho, Kimberlé Williams Crenshaw, and Leslie McCall, "Toward a Field of Intersectionality Studies: Theory, Applications, and Praxis," *Signs: Journal of Women in Culture and Society* 38, no. 4 (2013): 785-810.

[4]For a discussion of the role White women have played in the maintenance of racial and socio-economic systems in the United States, see Frances Kendall, "How White Women Reinforce the Supremacy of Whiteness," chap. 5 in *Understanding White Privilege: Creating Pathways to Authentic Relationships Across Race* (New York: Routledge, 2013).

Like physical world maps with their mix of accuracy and distortion, our context-shaped mental maps both focus and distort our understanding of experience. God works within the limitations and complications of our contexts. This is the same God who did not wipe out humanity and start all over again but, instead, chose the incarnation as the means of redeeming the world, becoming a human being and walking among us. God continues to work in and through our particular social-cultural contexts.

In this third part of the book we will reflect on the ways our distinctive collection of social identities shapes how we engage three particular areas: power and privilege, spiritual practices, and purpose. Because our various social locations affect us in different ways, intersectionality allows us to consider how they interact with one another and shape our vocational journey. The purpose of this reflection is to discern the ways in which God has shaped and is shaping us in particular contexts and to then discern the implications for our next faithful step.

7

ENGAGING POWER

The word of God continued to spread;
the number of the disciples increased greatly in Jerusalem, and
a great many of the priests became obedient to the faith.

ACTS 6:7

JOHN DUCKED AROUND A CORNER in downtown Los Angeles, narrowly avoiding a group of teenagers waiting at the bus stop. He was already fifteen minutes late to the meeting of the elders of Park Street Community Church. He loved this community and all that God was doing in their midst, but oh, the headaches of this latest season! John hoped this meeting would be productive in moving the community toward some solutions to the tensions that threatened to tear them apart.

As John walked, the joys and challenges of the church turned around and around in his head. Park Street Community Church had begun some ten years before with a small core of committed disciples who met regularly to study Scripture and pray together. Most of that first group was made up of working-class people—a janitor, a couple of house cleaners, a bus driver. One family owned a little corner market. Another member was a clerk at city hall. The neighborhood in which they lived had people that spanned the range of socioeconomic status— professionals in multimillion-dollar lofts to homeless families living on the streets. The church gathered in small groups in homes and local parks, reading Scripture and seeking to take seriously the lessons about shared life and caring for the marginalized. They became known throughout the neighborhood as a loving community that lived out its faith in practical, concrete ways. The church grew as more people were drawn into this communal life. Park Street Community Church became a multiethnic, multinational, multigenerational, multisocioeconomic-status community. This was a joy to John but also a source of challenge.

One family in the church owned property in the area. Knowing the needs of the church community and the larger neighborhood, they sold a building and gave the funds to the elders of the church. With this seed money, Park Street Community Church opened a food pantry. The enterprise was a blessing to both the church members and the broader neighborhood. But problems also came with the blessing. John spent increasing numbers of hours every week managing the food pantry. He struggled to deal with government regulations and volunteer schedules. Though he loved this expression of practical care for people, he hated how incompetent he felt in the work and how it took up the majority of his time, leaving him little time to do other necessary work in the church.

The breaking point came for John when murmurs and rumors broke out into open conflict. The food pantry was intended to help anyone in the church who was in need. However, many people struggled with transportation, relying on busses or walking. For some of the older members, particularly the elderly women living on limited means, access to the pantry was restricted by their mobility challenges. John began regularly taking food to some of the church members who were near his apartment. That's when rumors of favoritism and preferential treatment started to circulate. Finally, one of the men in the church openly challenged John: "I thought the food pantry was supposed to be for everyone. Mrs. Ramirez has been sick in her apartment for three weeks. I know you took food to Mrs. Jones. Why haven't you visited Mrs. Ramirez?" Other voices spoke up, referencing additional members of the community who hadn't benefited from the food pantry resources. "It looks to me," said a younger member of the church, "like you're taking care of the old White people and ignoring the people of color."

John was devastated. He loved everyone in the church and never intended to show preference for some over others. He also had never set out to run a food pantry and he wasn't any good at it. When the elders of the church met to talk about the problem, John expressed his desire to give up and abandon the work altogether. But cooler heads prevailed and a strategy was found. Word went back through the small groups of the church: meet together and pick one person from your neighborhood who has godly character, a good reputation, and a history of servant-hearted engagement. John will give up running the food pantry; this group of people whom you choose will have the authority to entirely take over the management of the project and determine how to fairly and effectively distribute the resources.

At the meeting, representatives from the various home groups were present. They offered the names of the people the home groups had selected: Marquis Washington, Mario Ramírez, Precious Johnson, Seo-yeon Kim, Luciana Rodriguez, Rosa Gonzales, and Ha-joon Park. Gratefully, John and his fellow elders prayed for this group of people, presenting them to the church as the new Park Street Food Pantry team.

So God's message continued to spread. The number of believers greatly increased. And even lawyers, government officials, and academics were added to the community.

This retelling of Acts 6, set in the present day, is intended to highlight particular elements of the biblical story. Generally, when Acts 6 is taught, the focus is on the structural/functional issues; Acts 6 is interpreted as the establishment of the differentiation between the role of elder and the role of deacon. Focusing on the task-authority and responsibility elements of the story, we miss the ethnic tensions, the socioeconomic status challenges, the power differential, and the vocational implications. Like my retelling, the early church was an ethnically and a socioeconomically diverse community. People who had means sold property and gave the money to the apostles to share with those in need. But, as in my modern retelling, the apostles were criticized for showing favoritism to the people in their own ethnic group. The solution was to give away power: to give the authority to the community to appoint representatives who could come up with a system of equitable distribution. The individuals the community chose were members of the marginalized group: Greek-speaking Jews.

Consider the implications of these aspects of Acts 6 for our own callings. Think of John and Peter and James struggling to distribute resources fairly in a community with ethnic, social class, and gender diversity. Consider the words "we, for our part, will devote ourselves to prayer and to serving the word" (Acts 6:4) less as a job description of the role of elder and more as the apostles' recognition that they had failed at the job of equitable care for all the members of their community. The statement was, at least in part, a recognition by the apostles that food distribution wasn't their work. The answer was not to abandon caring for the people in need, nor was it to double down and work harder at the task of caring for the widows or to present the community with the apostles' redesigned plan for distribution. Instead, the apostles authorized the community to do the work of identifying the people who would come up with a solution.

Examining one's social location and multiple identities is beneficial as a personal exercise. It can be helpful in discerning one's assumptions about the nature of vocation and how those assumptions help and hinder in discerning particularities of vocation. If, however, the conversation ends there—with a personal point of reflection—then we have only continued the individualistic, self-actualization approach to vocational discernment so common in the United States, just with a different lens of inward reflection. If, on the other hand, our calling has to do with our participation with God's work in the world, then our consideration of social location cannot stop with self-reflection. Where I stand in the world, the groups I am associated with—both those I directly identify with and those that society connects me to—is the context out of which I engage in God's mission. As I cross boundaries of social and cultural groups, I do so from a distinct set of locations and as the particular person God has created me to be. We therefore need to consider the nature of power and what this has to do with the development of our callings so that we, like the apostles, can recognize our cultural blind spots and take action to mend the social wounds that result.

Many of us are in social and theological environments where naming power and privilege triggers all manner of resistance. Socially, as we've discussed, the values of individualism, self-sufficiency, and meritocracy make the discussion of the social elements of power a violation of cultural taboos. Theologically, we absorb messages about power such as, "Human power is bad and God's power is good" or "To acknowledge human power is prideful." As we react to discussions of power, the exposure of the assumptions and values that go with our cultural maps can be distressing. To stop and give thoughtful consideration to the nature of power and how we have personally and collectively engaged in systems of privilege requires a great deal of emotional and spiritual effort. What we individually have to gain is, like the disciples, a focus on what is ours to do. What we have collectively to gain is, like the early church, the flourishing of our communities as we work toward enacting gospel-rooted equity.

REGARDING THE NATURE OF POWER

When people talk about power, the word can refer to a variety of dynamics depending on the context of the conversation. Power related to organizational development is different from power related to community organizing, for example. Talking about power connected to city hall is different from talking about power connected to church elders. Sometimes conversations about power get bogged down in the differences in what we're referring to and how we think about it. We can end up having "unproductive parallel conversations," missing one another's meanings because we assume the other sees power the way we do.[1] I

---

[1]For more on "unproductive parallel conversations" and other strategies that people use to avoid hard conversations, see Chris Argyris, "Teaching Smart People How to Learn," *Harvard Business Review* 69, May-June (1991): 99-109.

suggest that power exists in at least four dimensions: personal, organizational, social structure, and spiritual.[2] I will briefly discuss each of the four dimensions, drawing from Pastor Jean Burch's calling story, which she shares with us in her own words, to illustrate these dimensions at work.

CALLING STORY
Jean Burch—Pastor, Nonprofit Executive Director and President

I had a twenty-year career in corporate America as director of professional development and recruitment for a couple of large law firms. I heard the Lord tell me to go back to school—first a Christian university and then seminary. I thought, *God, I don't know where you're going with this, but if you want me to go to school, I will.* I never thought that God was leading me to be in leadership in our church.

Growing up, my mom was a Pentecostal—in the Church of God in Christ—and my dad was a Baptist pastor. I think I did just about everything that a woman was allowed to do in the church. I was the choir director. I taught Sunday school. I preached, but it was standing behind the small lectern on the right side or standing on the floor. Women weren't allowed to stand behind the big pulpit. I was okay with that because that was my upbringing. But there was just this push and this pull.

I eventually left my dad's church because it was really difficult for me, sensing a calling on my life, to figure out what that really meant in a place where women were not allowed to be pastors. I found a church, and it was there at that church where God did a major healing in my life. This pastor had begun to embrace women in ministry. He was constantly talking about the healing and the deliverance and the calling

---

[2]In 2019, as president of the Academy of Religious Leadership, I facilitated a conference with the theme "Engaging Power." Leading up to that meeting, I was in conversation with author, speaker, and community organizer Alexia Salvatierra, during which these four categories of power became clear to me. For a reading of my reflections at that time, see Susan L. Maros, "Introduction: Engaging Power," *Journal of Religious Leadership*, 19, no. 2 (2019): 1-17.

in your life. I was listening to it and getting healed and delivered all at the same time.

One Sunday, the pastor said, "I want all of the preachers to meet me after church." The benediction came and I began to walk up the aisle to leave the church when the pastor called my name. He asked me, "Why are you leaving? Aren't you a preacher?" It was there that I had the sense that God was saying to me, "You need to accept the calling on your life today." That was the beginning of me being in a place where I could grow and learn and be accepted as a preacher.

A few years later my dad called me and said, "You know, our church is getting smaller and smaller. We need some help. Can you come and teach a Bible class?" So, I came over to teach the Wednesday night Bible study. Then dad said, "Can you preach behind the little podium a couple of times a month?" So, I started preaching twice a month.

My mom passed away in 1999 and soon after my dad made an announcement to the church trustees that he was ready to retire. About six months after my mom passed away, I drove my dad to a trustee board meeting. He told them that he had gone as far as he could go without his partner, and that he believed that God had already called the next person to pastor the church. "Some men want their sons to follow in their footsteps, but God gave me a girl and she's a preacher. I believe she should be the next pastor of our church." Now I had driven this man to the meeting and he didn't tell me anything about what he was going to do or say that evening. I'm sitting there, wanting to disappear under the table, with all of these traditional Baptist trustee board members and deacons looking at him in silence. Nobody said a word. One of them finally said, "Okay, well, we're going to talk about it later."

Traditionally the church would have voted by secret ballot, what my dad called "the good old Baptist vote." The church was full of people that many of us didn't even know, let alone had seen in a while, because they all came out to vote for the next pastor. On that night, my dad informed the congregation there would be an open vote. He holds the ballots up and he says, "I know you all came to vote and here are these ballots. But I'm tired of Baptist people doing things in secret. So, everybody who wants my daughter to be the next pastor, stand to your feet." There was no table for me to go under this time. I'm sitting there looking around to see who is going to stand up. They were looking at each other and, one by one, every one of them in the room stood to their feet. I decided at that point that God has an ejection button in heaven and he ejected all of them up out of their seats. That's how I became the first female pastor. And, here I am, over twenty years later.

I met Pastor Burch while she was pursuing a master's degree. She was already a seasoned leader, well established in her community. As we talked about leadership and organizational dynamics, Pastor Burch's ministry examples were particularly helpful in the class coming to understand something about the nature of power at work in a ministry context. Consider the definitions of the four dimensions of power as I've identified them, and consider how Pastor Burch engages in these four dimensions in her ministry.

Personal power. One way to think about power is the area of personal power: an individual's capacity to be an active agent. This includes a person's ability to live out of a set of values of their choosing and to make decisions based on those values. Vocationally, personal power can be expressed by the individual who chooses to sacrifice for his family as well as the person who chooses to go against her family's wishes in her choices. Having the capacity and resources to choose education, a job, and a location to live in are all expressions of personal power.

Personal power engaging with a group comes from what the group sees as the individual's characteristics—their personality, their experience, their capacities, their character. A person's competencies and gifts, an individual's personality or skills, can influence a church group, a family gathering, or a team in a business. A person's history of service or collaboration can be a resource for change. This social capital becomes the fount of influence.

In Pastor Burch's calling story, we see a person who was not considered qualified for a pastoral role by her church communities due to her gender. Meanwhile, Pastor Burch's family had nurtured a sense of personal agency, encouraging the development of her leadership capacities. Her father and her pastor who embraced women in ministry were significant people in affirming Pastor Burch and opening opportunities for the development of her leadership. Her gifts as a teacher and preacher made a way for her further work as people responded to her ministry.

Organizational power. Another way to think about power is in terms of organizational power. This is positional power—the authority that comes with a role that has a set of collectively acknowledged responsibilities. A pastor of a church has certain positional power—the nature of which varies from one tradition to the next—which is different from the positional power exercised in that same church by an usher or a nursery worker. Each of these positions carries with it a certain amount of authority regardless of the person who is in the position.

Pastor Burch's calling story has significant moments of organizational power at work, particularly through the agency of her pastor father. He utilized his positional authority to make a way for Pastor Burch's development. He called on her gifts to benefit the congregation. He took an active role in confronting organizational norms to facilitate her emergence as the pastor of the church. Note, though, that focusing entirely on the role of Pastor Burch's father in her vocational development means we would miss the ways in which Pastor Burch herself engaged the organization. She tells of multiple roles she filled over a lifetime of church engagement, from Sunday school teacher to choir director to Vacation Bible School director.

When Pastor Burch became the pastor of Community Bible Church, she inherited the role of director of a nonprofit organization connected to the church. The church's founding pastor had created the nonprofit in 1970 and had overseen the development of a property with 133 units of affordable housing. Thirty years later, this property continued to be a source of pride for the church and an acknowledged benefit to the community. Sometime after taking up the role as pastor and nonprofit director, Pastor Burch took a walk in the neighborhood. She tells the story this way.

One day after I had just started as pastor, I sensed the Spirit of the Lord telling me, "Walk around your Jerusalem and see what's there." I took off walking down the street.

There was a property near our church, thirty acres of land with 313 units—just down the street from our 133 units—owned by a slumlord who had allowed the property to go to the ground. The residents there were living in unsuitable conditions.

I walked around this property. I saw a group of young men talking. I'd heard about gangs but I didn't know a whole lot about them. So, I just walked up into the group and introduced myself as the new pastor on the block and invited them to come to church. They looked at me and all busted out with a great big laugh. I thought to myself, *Okay, this doesn't look good*. When I got back to the church and told someone where I had been, they looked at me and said, "Thank God you're still alive. You interrupted something that was going on with one of those gangs."

That Sunday I got up to preach and I was just on fire. "We have got to do something more in this neighborhood. We can't allow this to go on across the street from our church. How can we be so satisfied that we built 133 units down the street when the residents in the 313 units across the street from us need our help?"

Pastor Burch recognized a need in the community. She felt impassioned and empowered by God to speak to the issue. She utilized her organizational power as pastor to address the church regarding this community problem. What followed was the action of the church as a whole, engaging their collective power as a congregation to do something in their community. Notice how the church enacted organizational power in terms of engaging in negotiations alongside their spiritual power as the people of God.

The trustee board chair and the deacon board chair called me into the office. They began to tell me that they were in negotiations with a developer concerning that property but they couldn't agree on anything. I thought, *If there was one thing that God spoke to me about while I was*

> *walking in my Jerusalem, it was that we had a new opportunity.* So, I said to
> the congregation, "We've got to pray and ask God what we should do."
>
> We prayed, went back to the table, and figured out a way to come up
> with a deal that we could live with. So, in 2000, we became the nonprofit
> partner of the largest affordable housing units in the city. This little
> church that always thinks they can do big things has become the largest
> provider of affordable housing in the city.

When people focus on vocational formation in terms of role or occupation, often they're focusing on organizational power. They assume that a person cannot engage in a calling without having a specific role: you can't bring change in a church unless you are the pastor, you can't bring change in a business unless you are the CEO, you can't bring change in a town unless you're the mayor or on the town council, and so forth. Vocational discernment, when thinking about power from this perspective, becomes job guidance or career development. Granted, legitimate authority is a useful vocational tool, and some problems and challenges are best addressed with positional power as a part of the solution. Nevertheless, people engage personal and spiritual power, as well as engage together as a group to maximize their collective power, to bring about change "from below" and lead from the middle of organizations and societies all the time.

Social systems power. Pastor Burch's use of organizational power points toward a third way to think about power: the power resident in social systems. Within any social system, be it a family or a church or a neighborhood, the dominant group exercises power to determine the norms and values of the whole group. Sociologists study this kind of power by looking at social group norms. Critical race theorists and womanist theorists look at social power, considering systems and structures of dominance and inequality, for example. Liberation theologians focus on hierarchical structures of power and the ways those structures retain power for the privileged and enact injustice for the marginalized. Community organizers help groups to activate their personal and collective power to address inequities and injustices within a given context.

Pastor Burch talks about Community Bible Church as "the little church that can." She says, "Our church has never grown to a very large size. People come to the church, they get healed, they get delivered, and they move on. So, the church has never been really big, but it's done really, really big things." Pastor Burch continues, "We know that at least part of our mission as a church is providing housing for 'the least of these' in our city."

The development of the affordable housing property is an example of a "big thing" done by a small church, an organization addressing a larger social issue. A further example is the development of the Clergy Community Coalition (CCC). Pastor Burch tells the story of its development this way.

> In the 2000s, we began to see an uptick in gang violence in our city. We decided at our church that something needs to be done about this. A couple pastors in the area came to me and said, "Can we talk about what we can do?" At the same time, the chief of police called and said, "I think maybe pastors can help us." The superintendent of schools called. "Gang violence is up. People are moving out of the city because they can't afford to live here, so enrollment is down. We need to sit down together and try to figure out what to do."
>
> At the beginning of 2005, there were four pastors and myself who met periodically to talk about issues concerning the city. God brought us together around the issues of lack of affordable housing and the increase in gang violence. We formed a group called the Clergy Community Coalition to help bring peace, justice, and equity to our community. The first thing we did was started trying to plan all these activities we were going to do.
>
> We had a visiting pastor that came to pray with us one day and he had a prophetic word from God. He said, "Listen, God is not calling you to have programs yet. What he's calling you to do is to come together as pastors to pray together, to put down all of your differences—all of your denominational differences, all of the things that have separated you for so long—and simply pray." God called the moratorium on this little organization that we had founded and, for a couple of years, all we did was come together and pray.

> When we decided to start meeting again, we had asked the super-
> intendent of schools and the police chief if they would come and talk to
> us and give us a sense of what's going on in the community. Soon after,
> in addition to the superintendent of schools and the police chief, the
> sheriff captain, the city manager, and the public health director all came.
> Sixteen years later, we are still meeting every second Wednesday of the
> month with about forty clergy, civic leaders, and community leaders.
> The community leaders in our city come not only to give their reports
> every month but also with prayer requests for the community. While I
> was president of the CCC, we received an award from the police depart-
> ment, who said, "They showed us that things can happen through the
> power of prayer."

This is an example of social systems power at work. Pastor Burch was a
catalyst and an organizer for the work; the whole of the community engaged together to put resources toward common concerns.

Principalities and powers. Pastor Burch and the Clergy Community
Coalition is also an example of the fourth way to think about power, that
of "principalities" and "powers" (Ephesians 6:12 KJV). These are the
spiritual powers in conflict with God's power and purpose for humanity.
Within some theological traditions, these powers are literal entities set
in opposition to God and to human flourishing. For other theological
traditions, these powers (if considered) are the philosophical and symbolic representation of social systems power.

Pastor Burch and her colleagues initially intended to utilize organizational and social systems power when faced with their community concerns. The prophetic word brought by the visiting pastor, however, focused them on engaging principalities and powers through prayer. The
history of churches within the community was one of competition and
criticism. There were denominational barriers and personal relationship
barriers. Behind these personal and organizational obstacles were principalities and powers seeking to keep the church in the city divided. The
pastors needed to set aside their traditional divisions and pray together.

This was not a one-time meeting but a practice that developed over the span of years. Now, more than a decade after the founding of the CCC, members of this group will openly say that there is one church in the city with many local congregations. Their presence and work continue to be important as they shepherd the community.

When we talk about power, we often think of one or more of these four definitions and then interpret other people's words related to power through the grid of our own assumptions. Some White evangelicals, for example, hear the social systems power discussion of inequalities around race through the filter of personal power. That filter focuses on individual action and merit, ignoring the existence of social systems. Any effort to point to the history of laws and practices that favor one group over another is considered excuse-making or "playing the race card," or, to put it another way, failing to take personal responsibility for personal actions. The White evangelical mental map prioritizes personal agency. Progressive White Christians, on the other hand, may emphasize social systems and ignore the existence of spiritual power. Systemic injustice is viewed as being entirely of human origin, ignoring the existence of evil actively at work against human flourishing. Pastor Burch, as the leader of a historically Black church in an area of the city that has been racially and ethnically diverse since the early days of the community, takes a multifaceted approach to power. Her ministry is an example of one person engaging multiple levels of power for the sake of the well-being of the entire community.

THE CHALLENGE OF EXPLORING PERSONAL POWER

Reflecting on personal power presents a number of challenges. I want to focus on two: the challenge of seeing ourselves as having personal power and the challenge of recognizing the social systems power we benefit from. Both of these points of reflection are particularly pertinent for people who, like me, come from backgrounds of significant social resource.

The power we have. I would argue that, at a fundamental level, every person has a measure of power. At first glance, this is a hard statement to make as a generalization. There are people we can think of—from small children to the severely disabled, from persons in extreme poverty to individuals who are incarcerated—who seem to have little to no power. Yet even people who have little positional or social power still retain some measure of personal agency, even if their capacity to influence their circumstances is severely limited.[3]

For most of us the places we feel a lack of power are much more obvious than the places we exercise power. This is, in many ways, an effect of assuming that what we have is normal and experienced by everyone. In other words, whatever power I am able exercise, I assume to be human, meaning that I believe everyone has the same power I do. What I pay attention to, then, are the places where people have power that I don't have.

Let me give a personal example. I am an educator and work in graduate education. In different institutions where I teach, I experience varying levels of resistance due to my gender. My personal anecdotes display dynamics that have been identified in empirical research. For example, studies of student evaluations of professors reveal that women generally receive lower evaluations than their male counterparts.[4] Other studies show that men and women faculty who do not meet gendered expectations are sanctioned differently, with women being more harshly assessed.[5] Similarly, in a study conducted in an online class where teaching instructors facilitated multiple groups, one under their own identity as

---

[3]For a discussion of human agency in relation to psychological theories of development, see Jack O. Balswick, Pamela Ebstyne King, and Kevin S. Reimer, *The Reciprocating Self: Human Development in Theological Perspective*, 2nd ed. (Downers Grove, IL: IVP Academic, 2016), 99-102. For a famous example of someone reflecting on people with little to no organizational or social power who have agency to find purpose for their lives, see Viktor E. Frankl, *Man's Search for Meaning*. (Boston: Beacon Press, 2006).

[4]Susan A. Basow and S. Montgomery, "Student Ratings and Professor Self-Rating of College Teaching: Effects of Gender and Divisional Affiliation," *Journal of Personnel Evaluation in Education* 18, no. 2 (2005) 91-106; Sophie Adams et al., "Gender Bias in Student Evaluations of Teaching: 'Punish[ing] Those Who Fail to Do Their Gender Right,'" *Higher Education* (March 2021): 1-21.

[5]For example, Susan A. Basow and Nancy T. Silberg, "Student Evaluations of College Professors: Are Female and Male Professors Rated Differently?," *Journal of Educational Psychology* 79, no. 3 (1987): 308-14.

a man or woman and one under their colleague's identity, the gendered identity of the man was rated significantly higher than the gendered identity of the woman, regardless of the actual gender of the teaching instructor. In this study, the authors note that female instructors have a "double bind . . . where gendered expectations (that women be nurturing and supportive) conflict with professional expectations of higher-education instructor (that they be authoritative and knowledgeable)."[6] Simply put, the more likable I am as a person, the less competent I'm considered as a professor. The more competent I am, the less likable I'm considered. I know also, depending on the environment I'm in, that I will have students—women and men both—who don't think a woman should be teaching men. I know all of this and am not surprised when I encounter resistance. To be faithful to my sense of God's calling on my life, I've had to learn to manage this dynamic. I am aware of the power differentials related to gender, and I see how they affect the classroom as a group as well as how they affect individual students.

At the same time, what I am less aware of is how I exercise the power of whiteness and how my being White affects students in my classroom. Indeed, for many of my years as a professor, I was entirely ignorant as to how my racial-ethnic-cultural identity shaped the classroom experience. Though I was vaguely aware of the fact that I was White, it wasn't a salient identity for me. Being female was a much more salient identity, particularly because I constantly ran up against social norms in my occupation. Even though being White wasn't an important identity marker for me, I brought my White self into every classroom. My lack of awareness of my White identity facilitated my tacit support of White norms in the contexts in which I taught. The fact that my intentions were good did not in any way moderate the effects of my behaviors on students. For example, it was many years before I understood student critiques suggesting the content of courses was not applicable to their contexts. Since I have

---

[6]Lillian MacNell, Adam Driscoll, and Andrea N. Hunt, "What's in a Name: Exposing Gender Bias in Student Ratings of Teaching," *Innovative Higher Education* 40, no. 4 (2015): 291-303, esp. 295.

always been deeply concerned with the immediate applicability of course work to my students' lives and ministries and have habitually designed course readings and assignments to take context into account, I found these recurring critiques baffling and frustrating. It took me years to realize that students were responding to the dominantly White (male) authors of the required reading and to the White-normed conceptual frameworks I used. I had been formed in contexts that exposed me only to White authors talking about their White social contexts as if the dynamics and experiences in these contexts were universal. My intention was to create learning spaces in which every student could process their distinctive experience; my impact was to reinforce White normativity and to marginalize the experiences of students from different backgrounds.[7]

You may not be a professor or White or female. But you are a human located in a specific social and geographical context. You can see places where you lack power. You may or may not have given thought to where you exercise power. I encourage you to consider the personal "space" you take up in your social settings. Where is your voice heard? Where do you have influence? The next time you are in a group—whether in a Bible study or a business meeting or any other context where a group of people is interacting—notice who speaks and who does not. Notice whose voice is heard and recognized. Consider not just what you intend in your interactions with people but look for clues as to the effect.[8]

The power we benefit from. Recognizing the different aspects of our personal power can also help us see where we gain from social systems power. Social system power is benefit we accrue not from our own efforts but from our group affiliation. We experience a measure of privilege simply by being a member of a particular group that has social power.

---

[7]For a penetrating analysis of this dynamic in Christian education, see Willie J. Jennings, *After Whiteness: An Education in Belonging* (Grand Rapids, MI: Eerdmans, 2020).

[8]A helpful text that looks specifically at power, space, and group interactions is MaryKate Morse, *Making Room for Leadership: Power, Space and Influence* (Downers Grove, IL: IVP Books, 2008).

> **NAVIGATION POINT**
> **Defining Privilege**
>
> *Privilege,* defined by the *Merriam-Webster Dictionary,* is "a right or immunity granted as a peculiar benefit, advantage or favor." Author Andy Crouch defines it as "the accumulated benefits from past successful exercises of power" and notes that "privilege is the name for all the good things we do not need to try to acquire, because they simply flow to us as a result of past exercises of power."[9]

Privilege is, on its own, inherently neutral and sometimes beneficial. For example, when traveling, everyone who is a citizen of the United States has access to countries that individuals from other nations are not able to visit without a lengthy and expensive visa process. Simply by being a citizen of the USA, I acquire the benefits of agreements made by my government. We can also often get by speaking only English when we visit other places. We've done nothing to earn the privilege of our language being the most widely spoken modern language, but we certainly benefit from it.

Bible scholar Love L. Sechrest names some other advantages privilege offers:

> Though recipients of privilege are often unconscious of its influence, privilege confers advantages for both the pursuit of happiness and the cultivation of character; it not only smooths the way for its beneficiaries, but it also confers a poise and self-possession that can function as intangible but nonetheless genuine social resources that confer competitive advantages on the bearers of privilege.[10]

Reflecting on this point is complicated, though. The cultural map of meritocracy influences the way we approach conversations about privilege. Privilege, as a concept, is generally viewed as inherently a

---

[9] Andy Crouch, *Playing God: Redeeming the Gift of Power* (Downers Grove, IL: InterVarsity Press, 2013), 150. See especially chap. 8, "The Lure of Privilege," for a discussion of the nature of privilege and its relationship to power.

[10] Love L. Sechrest, "Identity and Embodiment of Privilege in Corinth," in *1st and 2nd Corinthians,* ed. Yung Suk Kim (Minneapolis: Fortress Press, 2013), 11.

bad thing in the United States. We see privilege as the opposite of merit; merit is earned and privilege is unearned. We disdain social elites who inherit money and social status without having to work for it and praise people who acquire large fortunes through their talents and efforts. The cultural map of meritocracy makes discussions of privilege based on group affiliation offensive and thereby influences our ideas about vocation formation. To suggest that we have attained a certain position or status because we are the recipient of unearned benefits is to suggest we don't deserve or haven't earned our place in the world.

The conversation about racial-ethnic-cultural identity and how some White people in the United States react negatively to this conversation is one example of the challenges of thinking about power and privilege that comes with group affiliation. Peggy McIntosh famously likened the benefits of whiteness to "an invisible weightless knapsack of special provisions, maps, passports, codebooks, visas, clothes, tools and blank checks."[11] Frances Kendall points out several reasons why unpacking this knapsack is so difficult. First, many of us who are White do not feel particularly powerful or privileged. Being told we are the recipients of White privilege feels like a slur against our character and a denial of our painful experiences in life. Beverly Daniel Tatum observes, "Understanding racism [in the United States] as a system of advantage based on race is antithetical to traditional notions of an American meritocracy."[12] Second, according to Kendal, even if we're aware of White privilege, we generally only think about privilege in terms what we gain from it, not what White privilege costs us. Third, "understanding how we are both beneficiaries and losers because of social system power requires that we face the fact that this system didn't just magically appear; it was intentionally constructed and put

---

[11]Peggy McIntosh, "White Privilege: Unpacking the Invisible Knapsack," in *Revisioning Family Therapy: Race, Culture and Gender in Clinical Practice* (New York: The Guilford Press, 1988), 148.
[12]Tatum, *Why Are All the Black Kids*, 89.

into place, ostensibly for us, by people who look like us."[13] These dynamics make it difficult to give thoughtful attention to what God is exposing in terms of our power and privilege as well as difficult to discern God's invitation to a next faithful step.

When we feel threatened as people, we default into fight or flight behaviors. In response to questions about privilege and power accrued because of our social location, some of us become angry and defensive. The action is meant to shut down the exploration, to deny the existence of the power, and even to attack the person who is bringing this power differential to our attention. Others don't even get to the point of having this conversation because we act preemptively to shut down the possibility. Still others of us flee the conversation through emotional or physical withdrawal.

In the midst of this struggle, God continues to invite us to reflection on our social locations and identities. God's purpose is to set us free and empower us to be and become the people God created us to be. The more we can see ourselves clearly and accurately—the good and the bad—the more we can be recipients of grace and agents of grace in other people's lives.

INTERSECTIONS OF POWER

Profound healing comes with realizing our worth and authority as God's children. We have been rescued from the power of darkness and transferred into the kingdom of the beloved Son (Colossians 1:13). We are heirs of God and joint heirs with Christ (Romans 8:17). We have access to approach the throne of grace with boldness (Hebrews 4:16). Seeing people transformed by the realization that they have profound value in the eyes of their Creator and Redeemer is one of the joys of the calling of the people of God.

When our work as the people of God stops with our personal sense of being reconciled to God, and when it focuses solely on individuals

---

[13]Frances Kendall, *Understanding White Privilege: Creating Pathways to Authentic Relationships Across Race* (New York: Routledge, 2013), 23.

becoming reconciled to God, we fail to engage in the fullness of God's work. Facing up to power and privilege is an important part of our work in the world as children of God. Consider examples we have in the Bible of God challenging social power. Jesus welcomed a woman, Mary, to the place of a disciple. He had dinner with social outcasts. Paul challenged Philemon to turn his back on the social norms that would have allowed him to physically abuse his runaway slave, Onesimus, and instead accept him as a brother in Christ.

As children of God, we are invited to "let Christ himself be your example as to what your attitude should be" (Philippians 2:5 Phillips). "For he," the passage continues "who had always been God by nature, did not cling to his prerogatives as God's equal, but stripped himself of all privilege by consenting to be a slave by nature and being born as mortal man" (Philippians 2:6-7 Phillips). Living into this level of discipleship is extremely challenging. Yet this is part of our vocational formation. We have areas of personal, organizational, and social power. To deny the power we have, and the privileges that come with the power, is not humility. Instead, we seek to hold them with open hands before God so that we're as equally willing to let go of privilege and power as we are to steward these resources at God's direction.

Everyone needs to think about marginalization and power, maybe especially people like me, whose privileged status allows us to avoid the subject if we choose. I invite you to join me in this reflection of life experience to see it in a new light. My hope is to encourage you to see that part of our calling as privileged people is to steward and engage in actively using that privilege to deconstruct systems of oppression.

My colleague Dr. Kutter Calloway is a White man who appears to be the epitome of privilege. Like David Douglas, who we met in chapter five, Dr. Calloway was influenced by his experience of poverty. This experience shaped him in significant ways that stay with him to this day. Consider Dr. Calloway's story as he tells it in his own words. Notice how he processes both his places of disadvantage and of privilege, weaving them into his sense of God's calling in his life.

CALLING STORY
Kutter Calloway, PhD—Associate Professor of Theology and Culture

I was ordained as a Southern Baptist minister nearly two decades ago, but I often joke that, as the son of a Southern Baptist church planter (a Church Planter's Kid or CPK as I like to call us), I was ordained in the womb. Because we were a church-planting family, we moved quite a lot. I attended no less than ten different schools during my K-12 education. Each move came with its own unique form of dislocation and disorientation. But in terms of how my parents talked to us about these numerous transitions, the common refrain my siblings and I heard was that we as a family were simply responding to God's call. I remember wondering why God couldn't seem to make up God's mind regarding where my family should live and serve. Then again, God was a God-on-the-move, so who was I to question God's repeated promptings for us to do the same, even if it did seem arbitrary and sometimes capricious?

In addition to (and in certain respects because of) our frequent moves, we were also very poor. Of course, as a kid, I didn't know what it meant to be poor, much less how poor I was—not until someone labeled me as such. Children can be cruel. I knew that from firsthand experience as an overweight adolescent. But in spite of my ability to eventually move beyond my peers' cruel remarks regarding my weight, I've never been able to shake from my memory the first time I heard another kid refer to me as "poor white trash" and then join with others to openly ridicule me for the way I looked and dressed. In this and numerous other encounters like it, I remember feeling not only hurt, humiliated, and vulnerable, but also a deep sense of shame that I still can't quite explain, along with a brooding sense of anger at how helpless I was to do anything about it. Even now, as an adult who has escaped poverty, that same sense of shame and rage will occasionally rise to the surface of my conscious awareness, manifesting itself in unusual and unpredictable ways.

To be clear, I don't mention growing up in poverty or my family's constant moves in order to gain anyone's sympathy. I am a White, cisgendered, heterosexual male, so in all other respects, I inhabit an undeniably privileged position in society. However, I highlight these elements of my story because, as my sense of calling has expanded and deepened over time, I have come to the realization that, as a theological educator, my ability to stand in solidarity with students and colleagues who are infinitely more marginalized and vulnerable than I am has little to do with my strengths or skills or the resources I am able to access. Rather, it has everything to do with allowing my own relatively minor but deeply formative experiences of marginalization and alienation to (re)shape my vocation on a fundamental level.

In other words, as a professional theologian, it is one thing to recognize how your personal experience of social or economic disadvantage enables you to identify more readily with those who experience numerous intersecting forms of marginalization as a way of life. But it is something else altogether to make the active pursuit of justice on their behalf the central focus of one's research, writing, and teaching. So, the question I now face is not so much whether or how I might interpret my past experiences as indications of the unique ways in which God has called me, but whether I will have the courage of my convictions.

POWER AND VOCATIONAL FORMATION

As God calls us to participation with God's work in the world, there is a concomitant call to bravery. Bravery is not the absence of fear; bravery is making hard choices in the face of fear. Am I so committed to discerning God's purpose and responding to God's invitation that I'm willing to grow as a human being? Consider the idea that attending to social location is an expression of discipleship and spiritual formation. Do I have the courage to allow the Spirit of God to show me truly who I am? God's purpose is not to shame and freeze us. God's purpose is an invitation to repentance and healing as well as to celebration of all that God has created us to be in all of our distinctiveness. If I cannot face the implications of my social identities, I cannot fully recognize, embrace, and enter into God's purposes. Moreover, how can I truly engage the ministry of reconciliation to which God has called us (2 Corinthians 5:18) if I am denying the existence of dividing walls and, by my behaviors, actually adding stones to those walls?

Thankfully, the mercy and grace of God is that God continues to work in the midst of our limitations. God has done great things in the world through privileged people, despite our limitations. It's also true that the purposes of God have been hindered by the social and cultural blindness— unintended and willful—of God's people. But we see throughout Scripture that God chooses to work through flawed people. Look at many of the heroes of faith. David was a man after God's heart and an adulterer and murderer. Moses was humble and angry and avoidant and a murderer. Paul was self-righteous and arrogant and violent as well as an apostle. Peter was reactionary and confused as well as a rock. The early church was a multicultural, multiethnic, multiclass community through which the testimony of the gospel shone. And the early church had difficulty living together as members of different ethnic communities, and they struggled to see how to include Gentiles as full members of the community of faith.

Over and over again in Scripture we also find examples of people of faith who are in contexts of systems of power. Joseph, Nehemiah, Esther, and Daniel, to name a few, were people of God geographically located within empires opposed to the things of God, with systems and structures that were antithetical to God's purposes. Part of the message of the lives and work of these individuals is that God is still at work, even in hostile environments. God can and does use systems and structures to further God's purposes in the world. Our task is like that of Joseph and Nehemiah and Daniel and Esther: to be faithful people who are skilled and wise in the management of cultural power while growing in our identity as the people of God.

The challenges we experience in grappling with power and privilege are the challenges faced by our sisters and brothers who walked with Jesus. They are challenges we share with sisters and brothers in the faith across time and around the world. The goal is to live faithfully to God, responding to God's call to participate in God's work in the world, knowing that, ultimately, the goal we work toward is that day when people of every language and social group and ethnicity and socioeconomic status and gender identity will stand before the throne of God.

QUESTIONS FOR REFLECTION AND DISCUSSION

1. Think about your faith tradition. Of the four dimensions of power—personal, organizational, social systems, and principalities and powers—which one is most often emphasized? Which one is ignored?

2. Consider your multiple identities, particularly racial-ethnic-cultural identity, socioeconomic status/class, and gender identity. Which of these has elements of privilege and power? In which do you most experience a sense of lack of power?

EXPLORING A BIBLICAL NARRATIVE: ESTHER

1. Read Esther 2:5-11, 19-20.

2. Esther is a Jew who initially hides her ethnic identity from the king. What do you infer as Mordecai's motive for instructing Esther to hide her identity?

3. Imagine: how important was Esther's identity as a Jew to her sense of herself?

4. Read Esther 4:5-17.

5. What organizational or social power did Esther have as queen? What were the limits of that power?

6. What social systems power was at work limiting Esther and Mordecai? Think about their ethnic identity and Haman's actions and attitudes. Haman, the villain in the story, is referred to as an Agagite, possibly a descendant of Agag, king of the Amalekites referenced in 1 Samuel 15. How does viewing the story of Esther

as a story of ethnic and racial tension affect your perception of Esther as a called person?

7. The principalities and powers are not named in the book of Esther. Indeed, God is not named directly in the book of Esther. Where do you see God's presence implied? Where do you see powers in opposition to God implied?

8. Imagine: as Esther fasted and prayed for three days, what powers were in her mind?

SUGGESTIONS FOR FURTHER READING

Crouch, Andy. *Strong and Weak: Embracing a Life of Love, Risk, and True Flourishing.* Downers Grove, IL: InterVarsity Press, 2016.

Villacorta, Wilmer G. *Tug of War: The Downward Ascent of Power.* Eugene, OR: Wipf and Stock Publishers, 2017.

PRACTICES FOR THE JOURNEY

As a deer longs for flowing streams,

so my soul longs for you, O God.

My soul thirsts for God,

for the living God.

PSALM 42:1-2

Come to me, all you that are weary and are carrying heavy burdens,

and I will give you rest. Take my yoke upon you, and learn from

me; for I am gentle and humble in heart, and you will find rest

for your souls. For my yoke is easy, and my burden is light.

MATTHEW 11:28-30

LES WAS EXHAUSTED. He cared about his congregation and wanted to be a good pastor, but he felt wrung out and used up. Despite years of fruitful ministry, Les had begun to question his calling. The ministry he had entered twenty years before with passion and excitement now felt like a grueling, never-ending battle with the same struggles year after year. In an effort to find help, Les started meeting with a spiritual director. In an early meeting, this man asked him, "Tell me about the rhythms of your life." Les had a hard time comprehending the question. "Rhythms?" he asked. "Do you mean my schedule? Or my spiritual disciplines?"

The fact was, at that point in his life, Les had no rhythms. Les had grit and determination. Les was a reliable pastor, doing whatever he had committed to do to the best of his ability. He had drive and discipline that fostered professional success. Now, all that energy had run out. His emotional, intellectual, and spiritual well were dry.

Les had grown up in a Christian home and came to faith in Jesus early in life. In his early twenties, Les was deeply ambitious to "change the world for Jesus." During college, he participated in a church that emphasized spiritual disciplines as essential for living a godly life. Les studied the lives of great people of faith in Scripture and in history. He saw that they all had spiritual disciplines as the foundation of their spiritual greatness. Desiring to be a faithful and fruitful Christian, Les read the Bible every day and read through the whole Bible every year. He learned to pray, grounded in the conviction that God is present and active in his life. He also learned to give of his resources—money, time, gifts—as well as fasting every week and attending church Sundays and Wednesdays. Les understood these disciplines to be something like spiritual calisthenics; what exercise is for the physical muscles, spiritual disciplines are for spiritual muscles.

There is an extent to which the analogy of muscles is true: what we develop in the habits and patterns of our souls either sustains us or reveals the limits of our resources when difficult times arise. But this truth, for Les, was lost in the achievement orientation of earning his way toward a life of meaning. He read the Bible less to encounter God and more to acquire the familiarity and knowledge that he saw in the lives of the spiritual heroes he sought to emulate. He prayed less to experience the presence of God and more to develop spiritual power. He gave of his money and his time not so much to participate in God's economy and be set free of the world's systems of value but more to earn God's favor. When Les looked back on the first half of his life, he saw a driven, task-oriented existence. He didn't have rhythms of work and rest; he had schedules and task lists and goals. Yes, Les had been "successful" in his calling as a pastor, yet his soul was dry and he was burned out.

When we think about vocational formation in the context of the United States, we generally think about our role or occupation. Spiritual formation and discipleship get slotted into a different category as if vocational formation and spiritual maturity have nothing to do with one another. We step into production-oriented lives. Yes, we hear the message that God loves us and that who we are is far more important to God than what we do. We condemn the busy "Martha" in favor of a spiritual "Mary"—all while bustling around "distracted by many things" (Luke 10:41). Discipleship, we think, is for "beginners." We want to hurry on to do great things for Jesus.

Think about how we preach the idea of calling to emerging adults. You are supposed to find what you're passionate about and go out and change the world, we tell them. There's much less preaching about vocation that says, "Jesus is in the lifelong process of transforming your whole being." There's little connection between soul transformation and God's call. Spiritual formation is seen as an inward, individualistic experience; calling is task-oriented, production-focused work. Some of us see cautionary tales from Scripture of people who fail, like Saul or Judas, and respond with a spirituality that becomes steeped in fear and rule-keeping. Calling is made into a process of winning God's favor.

Psychologist Archibald Hart has noted, "People in our age are showing signs of physiological disintegration because we are living at a pace that is too fast for our bodies."[1] What if spirituality, emotional maturity, and flourishing in our calling were not separate topics but different facets of one experience? Hear the invitation of God to be formed into the likeness of Christ. We are being transformed and, as the people whom God is in the process of transforming, we are invited to participate in God's transforming work in the world. We have a place in the family business. Let

---

[1]Quoted by Adele Ahlberg Calhoun, *Spiritual Disciplines Handbook: Practices That Transform Us* (Downers Grove, IL: InterVarsity Press, 2015), 74.

us therefore consider several practices that seem to be particularly related to the development and sustaining of our callings.

CULTIVATING SUSTAINABLE RHYTHMS

Amy Carmichael, missionary to India and founder of the Dohnavur Fellowship, is attributed with saying, "I would rather burn out than rust out."[2] This phrase has been echoed by numerous other Christians. To be called is seen as the charge to actively *do* something. We have difficulty thinking about rest as a vital aspect of our calling. Rest is viewed more as a necessity for our frustratingly frail bodies than as part of a rhythm of life God has designed for us to live. Alternatively, we may view rest as the necessary evil that makes us more productive if we pay attention to it. We rest for the sake of production, not because rest is a value in and of itself.

Sometimes the sense of urgency in the work we're doing seems to preclude rest. How can we rest when people are literally dying? Then there are the socioeconomic and class elements of rest. One pastor I know questions how he can rest and take vacation when his congregants —largely working class and working poor—have no such capacity.

One of the biblical rhythms of rest is that of a weekly sabbath. We know that the Bible says, "On the seventh day God finished the work that he had done, and he rested on the seventh day from all the work that he had done" (Genesis 2:2). Some of our church communities have emphasized sabbath as a regular, God-honoring practice. Often we assume it should take place on a Sunday and include church attendance. Old Testament scholar Walter Brueggemann frames the practice differently, however, suggesting that sabbath is an act of resistance that says a holy "No!" to a culture that insists on being busy doing.[3] Cultivating rhythms of rest and play, activity and stillness, is

---

[2]Elisabeth Elliot, *A Chance to Die: The Life and Legacy of Amy Carmichael* (Old Tappan, NJ.: F. H. Revell, 1987), 122.

[3]Walter Brueggemann, *Sabbath as Resistance: Saying No to the Culture of Now*, rev. ed. (Louisville, KY: Westminster John Knox, 2017).

a spiritual practice that confronts the places in our souls that have been conditioned to serve the idol of busyness and accomplishment. We need this practice for our own well-being. We need this practice as a place of being formed by the Spirit for our participation in God's work. We need this practice in order to be renewed and sustained for a lifetime of participation in mission.

Some of our resistance to rhythms of rest reflects our theology of the human body. We relegate our physical selves to something "less than," particularly when compared to the life of the mind or the life of the soul. Some traditions equate the physical body with the "flesh" and tend to view the body as inherently sinful. We point to hedonism in culture as something to be avoided and thus reject our physicality. Challenging this and similar views, Ruth Haley Barton notes, "The spiritual discipline of honoring the body helps us find our way between the excesses of a culture that glorifies and objectifies the body and the excesses of Christian tradition that have often denigrated and ignored the body."[4]

To engage in rhythms of rest and activity is to engage in a spiritual practice of honoring our bodies. This is a practice that "challenges us to remember the sacredness of the body in every moment of our lives," Stephanie Paulsell notes. "The Christian practice of honoring the body is born of the confidence that our bodies are made in the image of God's own goodness. . . . As the place where the divine presence dwells, our bodies are worthy of care and blessing."[5] She goes on to say,

> Embodiment is central to the Christian faith. The Christian emphasis on the incarnation of God's presence in Jesus and the Christian understanding of community, which describes the church as the body of Christ, both put embodiment at the center of Christian meaning. Jesus' command that we love our neighbor as we love ourselves makes it clear that our faith has everything to do with how we live as embodied people.[6]

---

[4]Ruth Haley Barton, *Sacred Rhythms: Arranging Our Lives for Spiritual Transformation* (Downers Grove, IL: InterVarsity Press, 2006), 82.
[5]Stephanie Paulsell, "Honoring the Body," in *Practicing Our Faith: A Way of Life for a Searching People*, ed. Dorothy C. Bass (Hoboken, NJ: John Wiley & Sons, Inc., 2009), 14-15.
[6]Paulsell, "Honoring the Body," 16.

In the First Testament, God called Israel to observe rhythms that were linked to the natural rhythms of the day, the lunar cycle, and the seasons. The early church, already grounded in these practices, carried them forward. The liturgical calendar, with its rhythms of celebration and fasting and its seasons of the church, reflects the rhythms of life.

Rhythms can include daily rhythms of rest and activity, exercise, eating, and practical care for the body. Sabbath is one example of a weekly rhythm. Some families practice a weekly family night or a weekly small group where souls are connected and refreshed. Some people engage in monthly practices, such as a half-day retreat once a month. Some churches celebrate the Lord's Table once a month as part of the rhythm of the community. Other rhythms might be quarterly or yearly.

When we practice rhythms of rest, we demonstrate with our bodies that we are trusting in God as the one who motivates and fulfills our callings. By slowing down, we actively contradict our culture's mandate to produce to establish our value. In addition, practicing rhythms of rest "is a way we honor our limits and the fact that God is found in the present moment. Through slowing we intentionally develop margins in our lives that leave us open to the present moment."[7] Rhythms of rest help foster a pattern of life that is open to God's presence and power, a pattern that is sustainable across decades of life.

LISTENING DISCERNMENT

When Christians in the United States ask questions about calling, many of those questions focus on knowing: how do I *know* what God is calling me to be and to do? We want to discern what job to take or what ministry to engage in. We want to discern whether we are supposed to move from one city to another or whether we are to pursue a particular educational degree.

In addition, we are asking how we can know what God desires. Jesus said, "My sheep hear my voice" (John 10:27). As children of God and

---

[7]Calhoun, *Spiritual Disciplines Handbook,* 89.

followers of Jesus, we want to be certain we're able to distinguish between God's desires and our own, between God's voice and our own or our culture's voice.

Discernment can be defined as "the intentional practice by which a community or an individual seeks, recognizes, and intentionally takes part in the activity of God in concrete situations."[8] We desire to recognize what God is doing and what we are supposed to do in response. Many people who yearn to "know" their callings treat the practice of discernment as a means to an end, however. Discernment is seen as the process; knowing is the goal. People yearn for a sense of inner certainty, clearly articulated, with the ability to reference particular events as supporting this inner certainty.

What we understand discernment to be is significantly influenced by our theological environment. Pentecostal/charismatic individuals may focus on direct communication. Samuel's experience hearing God's voice in 1 Samuel 3 is a biblical model of this. Just as Samuel needed Eli to help him learn that the voice he was hearing was God's voice and learn how to respond, so too do we need to learn to identify God's voice so that we may respond as Samuel did: "Speak, for your servant is listening" (1 Samuel 3:10).

For brothers and sisters in Reformed traditions, the emphasis is more on discerning God's work through the wisdom and council of elders or of the community. They may also focus on discerning God in the circumstances of life, since they strongly assume those circumstances are being providentially shaped by a sovereign Creator. The end goal is similar regardless of the means by which it is reached: How do I know?

Why is it we hunger for inner certainty? What is it we believe will be true about our lives if we are able to know with assurance what God has called us to be and do? There is a great deal in our US contexts that emphasizes the agency of the individual. We transfer cultural values to God, quoting idioms like, "Pull yourself up by your bootstraps," and "God

---

[8]Frank Rogers Jr., "Discernment," in *Practicing Our Faith: A Way of Life for a Searching People*, ed. Dorothy C. Bass (Hoboken, NJ: John Wiley & Sons, Inc., 2009), 105.

helps those who help themselves," oblivious to the fact that this saying is nowhere in Scripture. I alone am supposed to identify a life path and make my way, we think. I alone am responsible for myself. I am supposed to be self-sufficient and productive. We see ourselves as being held accountable for what we do with our lives and live in fear of "doing the wrong thing." Influenced by these cultural values, it is no wonder that we focus on knowing.

What people tend to assume, whatever theological tradition they come from, is that God's purposes are somewhere "out there," in danger of being missed. Our anxiety about missing God's purposes suggests that we think God has deliberately made discerning those purposes difficult as some sort of test. If we fail the test, we're out. We claim to believe in a gracious, loving God who is sovereign and powerful. What we demonstrate with our reactions and behaviors, however, is that we believe in a critical, judgmental, and distant God who will penalize us for any wrong choice we make. It is as if we think somehow God is unwilling or unable to deal with our doubts and detours. In this context, we treat discernment like an examination: we must choose rightly or fail.

What if we actually believed—and lived out the belief in action—that God is present and at work in our lives? What if we trusted that God is faithful? When God called you, inherent in that call is God's commitment to develop you fully according to God's purposes in your life. You and I cannot, by our own strength and efforts, fulfill God's purposes in our lives. God does not call us to accomplish tasks; God invites us to participate with what God is doing in us and in our contexts. For this, we need a regular habit of listening and discernment.

Anne Streaty Wimberly suggests that Christians bear a fundamental call to the vocation of listening. This listening is a radical openness to God and a radical openness to one another.[9] The practice of listening is the cultivation of a habit of paying attention. We need to cultivate habits of paying attention to where God is at work. We need to cultivate

---

[9]Anne Streaty Wimberly, "Called to Listen: The Imperative Vocation of Listening in Twenty-First-Century Faith Communities," *International Review of Mission* 87, no. 346 (1998): 331-41.

capacities to recognize what God is doing and where God is inviting us to participate.

Henri Nouwen has said this about discernment:

> The purpose of discernment is to know God's will, that is, to find, accept, and affirm the unique way in which God's love is manifest in our life. To know God's will is to actively claim an intimate relationship with God, in the context of which we discover our deepest vocation and the desire to live that vocation to the fullest.[10]

Calling is more of a process than it is a destination. Developing a sense of vocation is more akin to developing an internal compass than it is to setting a trajectory or gaining a set of destination markers. Calling is more of a journey than it is knowing the right road to take. Discernment is less about knowing than it is about relationship. In other words, discerning my calling is less about knowing with certainty exactly what I should be doing and more about walking daily with God, noticing where God is at work and where and how I am being invited to participate in that work. Our capacity to discern God at work is not a test but an invitation. Where do we sense God working? Pay attention to joy. Pay attention to what wells up inside—whether it is hope or indignation, compassion or rage.

My invitation to you is to press into the uncertainty. God is still God in the dark and in the storm. We tend to want to get out of the storm and into the light. We fear being abandoned. We fear being lost. What we need is to encounter God in the wilderness. This is not an encounter that makes the wilderness suddenly a lush garden. This is not an encounter that suddenly makes the darkness bright. This is an encounter and an invitation to intimate relationship with God.

COMMITTED TO COMMUNITY

Another rhythm we need to sustain our lives of participation in God's work in the world is a regular pattern of engagement with a community

---

[10]Henri Nouwen with Michael J. Christensen and Rebecca J. Laird, *Discernment: Reading the Signs of Daily Life* (London: SPCK, 2013), 25.

of faith. Our US-American individualistic faith has taught us to seek to "be fed," as if the satisfaction of our individual needs is the measure of good church. Sometimes we hear a message about service to the community. Sometimes we hear about the common good. Occasionally, that message takes root in helpful ways. Other times, that message seems to be a self-serving recruitment to give our resources of money, time, and effort to a particular local church.

With our cultural maps inclining us to emphasize Lone Ranger callings, we fail to recognize how vital the community is for discerning and developing calling as well as sustaining our lives as we live out our calling. In focusing on our individual callings, we fail to consider the calling of the community. I have quoted Ephesians 2:10 as a core text: "For we are his workmanship, created in Christ Jesus for good works, which God prepared beforehand, that we should walk in them" (ESV). Note that *we* are God's workmanship. As a good US-American, for years I read this "we" as being a group of individuals who are each individually God's workmanship. Without denying that God is at work in individuals—I believe God is at work in each of our individual lives—this verse is about the collective. We, as a group, are (collectively) God's workmanship. Further, God has prepared for us, collectively, good works for us (collectively) to walk in.

Community is the space in which we develop our sense of self and our understanding of God's character and work in the world. Community is the context in which we process our individual and collective callings, discerning together what God is doing and what God is inviting us to do. Community is the environment in which we do our work and the resource for sustaining our souls in the work. We minister in the community, to the community, with the community, and from the community.

Part of community is hospitality. Christine Pohl notes, "Hospitality is at the heart of Christian life, drawing from God's grace and reflecting God's graciousness. In hospitality, we respond to the welcome that God has offered and replicate that welcome in the world." The practice of hospitality in Scripture is primarily the practice of making space for the stranger.[11] This hospitality of community includes the sharing of stories. In both telling our stories and listening to the stories of others, we learn to recognize the *imago Dei* in ourselves and in others.

In these turbulent times in the United States, as communities are increasingly polarized and increasingly hostile to "the other," there is a desperate need for the people of God to be peacemakers and bridge builders. We don't make peace by shouting down the opposition. We don't make peace by building walls and clear boundaries between "us" and "them." We make peace by following Jesus' model, who,

> though he was God,
>   . . . did not think of equality with God
>   as something to cling to.
> Instead, he gave up his divine privileges;
>   he took the humble position of a slave
>   and was born as a human being. (Philippians 2:6-7 NLT)

Consider what our families and churches and communities would look like if we consciously considered that part of our vocational formation was to follow Jesus' model, surrender our privilege, and lay down our lives for the common good.

To what community do you belong? Who are the people of faith who you know deeply and who know you deeply? There are some patches of this in the United States, but data suggest we are a profoundly lonely and isolated people. Our sense of calling suffers accordingly when we are not known by people with whom we share life. There is little help from the community in discernment and formation when we don't have a community that knows us well enough to speak into this process.

COMPANIONS FOR THE JOURNEY

Many of us hunger for iron-sharpening-iron relationships. We long for wise counselors and for coaches and disciplers. Depending on how we

---

[11]Christine D. Pohl, *Living into Community: Cultivating Practices That Sustain Us* (Grand Rapids, MI: Eerdmans, 2012), 159. Pohl also observes, "One of the main Greek words for hospitality in the New Testament is *philoxenia*, which means 'love of strangers'" (*Living into Community*, 197).

have learned to define *mentoring*, we may be focused on finding that one relationship with a senior leader who will spend time with us and speak into our lives. By seeking this one, all-inclusive discipling relationship, we miss out on the mentors who are all around us.

Paul Stanley of Navigators realized that every leader and Christian minister needs a constellation of mentors.[12] We need those upward mentors who are beyond us in skill or wisdom or knowledge. This is the kind of mentoring that many of us think about when we use the word *mentor*. Stanley's insight was that we also need peer mentors—people at a similar phase of development, whether within our organizational context (internal mentors) or outside it (external mentors). As people who are working through similar questions, we can mentor one another with that iron-sharpening-iron kind of activity. We also need what Stanley refers to as "downward mentors"—people who are in a phase of development in some area that we have acquired a degree of mastery in. People whom we mentor keep us on our toes, asking questions that help us shake off cobwebs of complacency or that help us see our work from a fresh perspective.

Disciplers and spiritual directors are mentors who help us focus on our understanding of the Christian life and the fundamental practices of the faith. These women and men aid us in processing who we understand God to be and who we understand ourselves to be as children of God. Disciplers, in particular, help us understand foundational practices of the Christian faith from prayer to Bible study to accountability in community. Spiritual directors help us reflect on our relationship with Jesus, paying attention to the state of our souls; this is less about the disciplines and exercises of the Christian life and more about paying attention. Disciplers and directors can both be important people for helping us learn to discern God's voice and perceive God at work, something similar to how Samuel needed Eli's help in learning to recognize God's voice (1 Samuel 3).

---

[12]Paul D. Stanley and J. Robert Clinton, *Connecting: The Mentoring Relationships You Need to Succeed in Life* (Colorado Springs: NavPress, 1992), 157-68. The framework of types of mentors in this section draws from Stanley and Clinton's work.

Coaches help us learn skills and develop our capacities. They tend to be people who have developed skills in a particular area, which means they are good at what they do. They are also good at helping other people develop in those areas. We need coaches particularly in seasons of significant development in ministry. We can, of course, learn by trial and error. Self-reflection is a significant resource for learning. Yet having a person who can point out what we have done well and where we can improve significantly increases the speed of our development. A coach may not necessarily be involved directly in our learning of discernment—although a coach may work in the area of, say, training spiritual directors—but they can obliquely help us to perceive what God is doing and learn how to respond effectively.

We also need teachers and counselors. Some teachers may be instructors in a formal education situation. Other teachers are informal educators, people who have a fount of knowledge from which we benefit. This knowledge helps inform us in the how-tos and development of our work. Counselors, too, can be formal counselors such as a Christian counselor or therapist or informal counselors who have the gift of wisdom. These individuals help us gain insight into our interior world as well as develop capacities for engaging our context.

The point of mentioning this diversity of mentors is this: there are a variety of relationships that we need and that will help us grow. To seek that one, central person who will mentor us is to miss out on the range of people whom God has provided to contribute to the forming of our lives. Some people may be a part of our lives for an extended period of time. Others may come and go on a recurring basis. Still others appear in our lives for a particular moment and then are gone. We cannot develop in isolation; we need to be part of a community discerning where God is at work in our context and supporting one another in our collective calling to participate in that work.

THE POWER OF LAMENT

The biblical practice of lament is a powerful spiritual exercise. Many of the psalms are songs of lament. "Where are you God?" the psalmists cry often. This is the songbook of the community of faith. Yes, there are psalms that express confidence in God as a refuge and helper in times of need. Yes, there are psalms that praise God and express gratitude. This is not an either-or binary that requires only one kind of expression as a people of faith. We praise God *and* we cry out, "How long?" We give thanks to God *and* we ask, "Why have you abandoned me?"

Writing about the psalms, Walter Brueggemann notes that many of us do not connect with them because, "in most arenas where people live, we are expected and required to speak the language of safe orientation and equilibrium, either to find it so or to pretend we find it so." By contrast, "the speech of the Psalms is abrasive, revolutionary, and dangerous. It announces that life is not like that, that our common experience is not one of well-being and equilibrium, but a churning, disruptive experience of dislocation and relocation."[13]

Soong-Chan Rah observes this about the practice of lament in US-American churches:

> The American church avoids lament. The power of lament is minimized and the underlying narrative of suffering that requires lament is lost. But absence doesn't make the heart grow fonder. Absence makes the heart forget. The absence of lament in the liturgy of the American church results in the loss of memory. We forget the necessity of lamenting over suffering and pain. We forget the reality of suffering and pain.[14]

The biblical practice of lament contradicts a theology of success or happiness that is central to some of our faith traditions. If the assumption is that the Christian life should be constantly victorious and glorious, then suffering and lack is a spiritual problem based either in a lack of faith or in the sinfulness of the believer. We see a modern version of Job's friends in many of our communities telling us, "If you suffer, it is because of unconfessed sin." The victorious-life-oriented theology that is intended to guide us to faithful discipleship functions as a cultural map that keeps us

---

[13]Walter Brueggemann, *Praying the Psalms* (Winona, MN: Saint Mary's Press, 1986), 7.
[14]Soong-Chan Rah, *Prophetic Lament: A Call for Justice in Troubled Times* (Downers Grove, IL: InterVarsity Press, 2015), 22.

trapped in unproductive and destructive denial of suffering. Unable to lament, we are unable to receive God's presence and comfort in our grief.

Cultivating a practice of lament is necessary for our own spiritual and emotional health. There will be seasons of loss and grief in our lives. A triumphalist theology that requires a cheerful face and expressions of celebration in the midst of pain won't sustain us. Ignoring our pain, burying it under a "glorify God" expression of denial, only covers over the wound and leaves it to fester. Too many of us have interpreted "be angry but do not sin" (Ephesians 4:26) to mean "your anger is sinful." God is capable of hearing our pain, grief, and anger. By our behavior, however, we seem to demonstrate that we believe God has a fragile ego. We act as if speaking what we genuinely feel will result in God lashing out. Our behavior suggests we see God as a vindictive, judgmental, and highly critical presence, waiting to reject us for expressing any criticism.

Borne out of research among Christian activists engaged in nonviolent change in eastern Africa, Emmanuel Katongole identifies the connection between hope and lament this way:

> In the midst of suffering, hope takes the form of arguing and wrestling with God. If we understand it as lament, such arguing and wrestling is not merely a sentiment, not merely a cry of pain. It is a way of mourning, of protesting to, appealing to, and engaging God—and a way of acting in the midst of ruins. Lament is what sustains and carries forth Christian agency in the midst of suffering.[15]

Lament has personal and communal expressions. We need lament as an individual practice to process our dark emotions with God. We need lament as a communal practice to process together the pain of our families and communities. The practice of lament is also essential for the cleansing of our souls. We need to see ourselves accurately and we need to bring our grief about this truth to God. Repentance means stopping, turning around, and going a different direction. We cannot repent if we don't acknowledge the truth.

---

[15]Emmanuel Katongole, *Born from Lament: The Theology and Politics of Hope in Africa* (Grand Rapids, MI: Eerdmans, 2017), 12.

The more we open our eyes to the world around us, the more we see suffering. The more we open our eyes to the world in our communities and in our own hearts, the more we see brokenness of various kinds. Ignoring the spiritual practice of lament leaves us with little recourse to respond to pain and brokenness besides blame and denial.

Because the Psalms are full of violent, vindictive, angry language, beginning with this songbook in Scripture is a way of beginning to grow in the practice of lament. Consider reading a psalm of lament and rewriting it to fit some circumstance in the present moment. Cultivate this practice as a regular part of your spiritual rhythms. If anger, pain, frustration, and fear have been disallowed in our families or our communities of faith, developing in the practice of lament may take an extended time. Meeting with a counselor or with a spiritual director might be helpful for unpacking the cultural and family messages that block our capacity to recognize and express dark emotions.

Some seasons of life may require a lot of lament. The discovery of injustice and our participation in it necessitates deep lament. Seasons of loss, whether in our community or our families, benefit from the practice of lament. Sitting in lament, giving place to grief and pain, is a part of moving through the pain. We will not fully experience God's grace and glory if we refuse to fully experience anger and fear, frustration and sadness. Part of being a faithful minister of the gospel is to be present to pain just as God is present to our pain.

CALLING STORY: DR. JUDE TIERSMA WATSON

Jude Tiersma Watson has for thirty years engaged in two main areas of ministry: she has been part of an intentional community of "urban monastics" seeking to do justice, love mercy, and walk humbly with God (Micah 6:8), and, at the same time, she has been a professor of urban ministry, teaching others who want to learn to do the same. Read through Dr. Tiersma Watson's call story. Notice in particular how she references the presence of listening and discernment as she reflects on the journey of her life.

CALLING STORY
Jude Tiersma Watson, PhD—Associate Professor of Urban Mission

Growing up in a Dutch immigrant family on a dairy farm, looking into the future, I could not have imagined the life that has been gifted to me. I remember being fearful of the future, of how I would navigate life as an adult. Although my parents encouraged education and I did well in school, I had few examples of the possibilities before me. No one in my family had gone to college. People of influence were men, and there seemed to be few options for women leaders. When God came to me as a teenager and revealed that I was beloved, my fears subsided. I determined to follow God wherever God would lead me.

People often think we choose our path, but I have not chosen the adventure that has been my life. Rather, I have learned to say yes to the things God opened before me. Quakers speak of Way Opening, and most of my life has been paying attention to where the way is opening, and surrendering to that. My discipleship encouraged obedience, but I have learned that the core word here is *audire*, to listen. Obedience for me has been listening and responding to what God has put in my heart. My journey has led from teaching migrant children in California, moving to Amsterdam and then Nepal, and then a degree at Fuller's then School of World Mission. The biggest surprise came after graduation with my MA: God's invitation to move into a struggling immigrant neighborhood in central LA, when I had prepared to move to Asia. Central LA was my home for thirty years. I wonder who I would have become if I had not spent those thirty years in a dense urban metropolis.

I have also not chosen my social location, another huge impact in who I have become. Living the immigrant experience but with the privilege of White skin has been a unique spot to be placed. When God invited me to locate myself in a place of struggle and poverty, I learned so much from my wonderful Central American neighbors, many who fled civil wars in their home countries. By moving into my immigrant neighborhood, I began to see how what I thought of as a context-free formation and calling was in fact not context free at all. I began to see the privilege of my place in the world. A large part of my journey was adapting my understanding of spiritual formation from my rural roots to life in a 24/7 city.

This way of seeing grew deeper when I prepared to marry John. He asked if I knew what it would mean to marry someone with Black skin. And really, I didn't. He understood that it would have a cost for me, that it would begin to transform me in ways I hadn't expected. And it has, just has my years in LA formed me, reformed me, transformed me. Indeed, I could not have imagined the life that has been gifted to me. And for that I am deeply grateful.

Elsewhere, Dr. Tiersma Watson expressed the importance of developing "unforced rhythms of grace" (Matthew 11:28-30 *The Message*).[16] Reflecting on her experience as a child growing up in an agricultural area, she noted that grapevines have no internal support. If left to themselves, the vines will grow across the ground, leaving the grapes to wallow in the mud after the rain. The grapevine branches need the support of the trellis as they produce grapes. Similarly, the unforced rhythms of grace provide the support for our spiritual, emotional, and physical formation. These unforced rhythms need to attend to what has connected us with God and facilitated our thriving with God.

Richard Foster observes, "When we despair of gaining inner transformation through human powers of will and determinization, we are open to a wonderful new realization: inner righteousness is a gift from God to be graciously received. The needed change within us is God's work, not ours."[17] Jesus used the metaphor of a vine and branches to express the need for the life of God to flow through us. We do not produce the fruit,

---

[16]Jude Tiersma Watson, "Learning the Unforced Rhythms of Grace: Creating a Rule of Life in a 24/7 World," Fuller Youth Institute, February 26, 2014, https://fulleryouthinstitute.org/articles /learning-the-unforced-rhythms-of-grace.

[17]Richard J. Foster, *Celebration of Discipline: The Path to Spiritual Growth*, rev. and exp. ed. (San Francisco: HarperSanFrancisco, 1988), 8.

neither of formation nor of the work in the world. Instead, supported by unforced rhythms of grace, the life of the Spirit flows through us. Our spiritual formation and our vocational formation are part of the whole of our lives.

Pastor Les's context formed him to think about spiritual disciplines primarily as something you do that develops you as a spiritual person. That meeting with a spiritual director began a season of holy unraveling for Les. Richard Rohr talks about the work of the second half of life, in which we deconstruct the false self we built in the first half.[18] Les's first half of life revolved around a performative faith. His task now was to come to Jesus and learn anew what it means to walk in unforced rhythms of grace.

Similarly, each one of us has received and continues to receive God's invitation to come, find rest, and walk with Jesus. Some of us are like Les, coming from traditions that emphasize spiritual disciplines in a way that cultivates a performative faith. Others of us come from traditions that deemphasize spiritual disciplines. All of us need to cultivate rhythms of grace that nurture and sustain our souls as we engage with God's work in the world.

QUESTIONS FOR REFLECTION AND DISCUSSION

1. What were you taught in your church about the relationship between discipleship and vocational formation? Was this connection made? Was it absent? Why?

2. What are the rhythms of your life currently? What do you engage in daily, weekly, monthly, and yearly?

3. What rhythms do you need to sustain your participation in God's work in the world? Where are you sensing God's invitation right now?

---

[18]Richard Rohr, *Falling Upward: A Spirituality for the Two Halves of Life* (San Francisco: Jossey-Bass, 2013).

EXPLORING A BIBLICAL NARRATIVE: ELIJAH

1. In 1 Kings 18, we have the story of Elijah's confrontation with the prophets of Baal. This is a classic power encounter wherein we see clearly who is God and who is not. Coming off of this "ministry high," Elijah receives a death threat. Read 1 Kings 19:3-4.

2. What do these verses suggest about Elijah's frame of mind? What emotions is he experiencing?

3. Read 1 Kings 19:5-8. What do these verses suggest about Elijah's physical state? What connection do you see between Elijah's body and his emotions?

4. Read 1 Kings 19:9-10. What is Elijah feeling at this moment? What does he want from God?

5. Consider Elijah's exhaustion. When have you felt exhausted and at the end of your capacity to continue?

6. What kinds of questions do you ask of God when you are exhausted?

7. Name some way in which God has "sent an angel" with food and water to nourish your body and soul.

SUGGESTIONS FOR FURTHER READING

Brueggemann, Walter. *Sabbath as Resistance: Saying No to the Culture of Now.* Rev. ed. Louisville, KY: Westminster John Knox, 2017.

Johnson, Jan. *Abundant Simplicity: Discovering the Unhurried Rhythms of Grace.* Downers Grove, IL: InterVarsity Press, 2011.

Rah, Soong-Chan. *Prophetic Lament: A Call for Justice in Troubled Times.* Downers Grove, IL: InterVarsity Press, 2015.

9

DEVELOPING A PURPOSEFUL LIFE

Now the word of the Lord came to me saying,
"Before I formed you in the womb I knew you,
and before you were born, I consecrated you;
I appointed you a prophet to the nations."

JEREMIAH 1:4-5

I REGULARLY TEACH A CLASS that focuses on the discernment and development of calling. I know when students walk into the room on the first day that many, if not all of them, are thinking about calling primarily in terms of what role or occupation they should choose. Indeed, many of them are pursing education specifically to be trained and credentialed for specific roles they envision as their vocation. This is an example of a dominant cultural map, one that can both be helpful and function as blinders. Some people are unable to see how God is shaping their lives for fruitful engagement outside of a specific job. It takes work to facilitate a process of transformational learning that assists these students in becoming aware of this particular cultural map and questioning its primacy. Yet God does indeed assign us tasks, and some of us do live out our callings in the context of specific occupations. In this chapter, I present a framework for thinking about calling development that includes, but is not limited to, identifying a major role.

Rob Dixon's narrative has embedded in it a variety of common traits of calling stories that we have already considered together in this book. As you read it, with the lifelong nature of the development of calling in mind, notice in particular how he begins with a statement of a sense of purpose and then talks about how this purpose shaped his development over time in a number of different roles.

CALLING STORY
Rob Dixon, DIS—Campus Minister, Author, Speaker

I understand that my contribution to God's mission in the world is to challenge the people of God to embrace a theology and practice of gender equality, and do that work with my whole heart.

When I was in my twenties, I probably went through ten different statements of calling. "I'm called to students." "I'm called to lead worship." "I'm called to develop leaders" was a huge one. I focused on that for years and years. One of the things I've realized is that in your twenties and thirties you have to try a bunch of stuff. You try everything, and then at some point, what you're really supposed to be doing becomes clearer and clearer. What gets you out of bed in the morning becomes more and more obvious.

When I look back on my life, I see a pattern of development over time. In part, my current sense of call has its origins in the women who influenced me early on. For instance, I resonate with what Paul says about Timothy (2 Timothy 1:5); my mom and grandmothers were super influential in my life as a young Christian. In addition, I grew up in a church that had women pastors. And as a part of following Jesus in college, I was mentored by an InterVarsity staff worker named Úna. My experiences with these and other women in leadership sparked an interest in how faith and gender go together, and particularly in how men and women can partner together effectively.

During my early years with InterVarsity Christian Fellowship, every year someone would raise an objection about women in ministry. When I became a staff worker, and later a staff leader, that yearly conflict around women in leadership became mine to own. It's one thing to see the conflict; it's another thing to try to steward it. In my first year as a staff leader, I went to meet with a student and he'd brought a local pastor who was opposed to women in ministry. That pastor eviscerated me for an hour. I left in tears, mad and frustrated. Now, I look back on that experience as a turning point; for me, the value for women in leadership became less of a general agreement and more of a sense that "this is a hill to die on." I dug into the Scriptures. I studied and read everything I could. I developed my theology. I also became kind of militant about it. A mentor warned me: you need to have your convictions but hold them with humility because you're becoming like that pastor, just on the opposite side of the argument.

After I'd been in InterVarsity for fifteen years or so, my colleague Tina enrolled in Fuller's Master in Global Leadership program, and she suggested I consider applying along with her. This seemed like a good opportunity for further growth, so I did. In the program, I found myself increasingly writing my papers about women and men in ministry partnership. In one class, talking about identifying our ultimate contribution, it occurred to me, "Maybe my contribution is supposed to be around gender." I felt God invite me to consider taking something that had been more on the periphery of my staff work and bringing it into the center.

Since then, I've been able to find a way to do that work of challenging the people of God to embrace a theology and practice of gender equality in my job with InterVarsity. For instance, Tina and I developed a curriculum that we teach during spring break looking at women in the Bible from Genesis to 2 Timothy 2. I'm also deliberate in mentoring women staff. And in 2018 I completed doctoral work researching how to foster flourishing ministry partnerships between women and men. My sense is that, eventually, all my staff time will be focused on challenging the people of God to embrace a theology and practice of gender equality.

I want to focus on four different aspects of calling in this chapter: a sense of purpose, a major role, ministry competencies, and a legacy.[1] Our cultural mental maps of calling generally focus on the second of these aspects: a major role. Yet all four are present when we think about our heroes of the faith. We'll consider each in turn and reflect on Rob Dixon's experience as an example. As we do so, consider how you have seen each of these concepts at work in your own context in other people and in your own life.

CALLING AS A SENSE OF PURPOSE

Life purpose has to do with what a person senses is God's intention for their life. It is about the overall trajectory of their journey. Purpose is their God-given "north" toward which their internal compass is pointed. Discerning purpose may include reflection on providential elements of calling: passions, personality, giftedness, strengths, and so forth. Discernment also includes reflection on life experiences and seeing patterns of God's activity in events and circumstances. God has wired people in a particular way to care about particular things. God uses context and environment to shape a person's heart and perspectives. Part of vocational discernment is to pay attention to indications of God's prompting.

Rob Dixon's story demonstrates a theme that has been present throughout his ministry life: the development of leaders. Anyone who is around Dr. Dixon—from the staff he supervises to the people in his workshops to the students in his classes—knows that he is a great coach and advocate for the formation of leaders. This thread of purpose is woven through his experience. How he has thought about leader formation has changed over time, with an increasing focus on ministry partnerships between women and men. What specific role he expresses this purpose through has also shifted across time. Yet that thread of purpose continues to tie together his experiences.

---

[1]This fourfold framing of calling is based on Robert Clinton's leadership emergence theory. See J. Robert Clinton, *Strategic Concepts That Clarify a Focused Life: A Self-Study Manual Defining and Applying Focused Life Concepts to Leaders Today*, rev. ed. (Altadena, CA: Barnabas, 2005).

Notice also that Rob Dixon's story demonstrates a common character-istic of calling stories: we make sense of our lives retrospectively. He can look back to his twenties and thirties and make sense of his work as an InterVarsity staff worker with a focus on leader development and under-stand this focus in a different way now that more time has passed. A person could look at Dr. Dixon's ministry now and hear his calling story and think that his development happened in a straight line. This is the way we tell our stories—making sense of what happened looking back. We edit out the long seasons of questioning and the detours on the path.

Another major characteristic of Rob Dixon's calling story is how he reflects on his personal sense of purpose. What lies in the background of this story is all of the resources and limitations of his social identities. Dr. Dixon's racial-ethnic-cultural identity, his socioeconomic status, and his gender identity have offered him resources for considering many paths in his life. He has worked hard and been a faithful steward of what he has been given. His growing emphasis on ministry partnerships be-tween women and men is an example of a person coming from a place of privilege—in this case gendered privilege—and stewarding that priv-ilege for the sake of the flourishing of God's people.

One of my intentions in this book is to reflect on collective aspects of calling since many of us automatically think largely in terms of indi-vidual purpose. You might have also noticed how Dr. Dixon's calling story reflects the influence of the cultural map of individualism and in-dividual journeys. Rob Dixon tells his personal calling story; he doesn't tell the story of his community, though he does reference his community and some of the individuals who have been significant in his formation. This is a very common trait of calling stories, particularly in the United States: we tell our personal story, and, if the community is included, it is a narrative of how the community helped us in our personal formation.

Consider, then, these two parallel questions. First, what is distinctive about the community (or communities) of which you are a part? What elements of God's character does this community particularly embody? What would be missing in God's work in the world if this community did not exist? This distinctive contribution reflects God's purpose for that group.

For example, I am a citizen of the United States and have spent the majority of my life in Southern California. I am shaped by my experiences in this geographical and cultural context. One specific instance of seeing the impact of my geographical location came in the process of writing this book. A former student from Georgia read an early draft of chapter four and commented that the manner of my discussion of race reflected more of my location as a White person in Los Angeles than it represented a US-American White experience in general. Her experience as a White woman in the South is different from my experience as a White woman in California.

More broadly, the optimistic sense of personal agency that is so characteristic of people from the United States (and which can be irritating to our brothers and sisters in other parts of the world!) is part of the gift we bring to the collective work of the people of God. For example, US-American missionaries, with all their human limitations, have been pioneers and founders of hospitals and schools and churches in many previously unreached parts of the world. The can-do spirit has led to addressing multiple social, cultural, and spiritual problems in the US and around the world.

The second question is about you specifically. What is your answer to the question, "If you could do anything for Jesus, what would you do?" Is there some element of deep awareness in the marrow of your bones? Yes, this has to be held with an open hand. Our deepest desires can be warped and distorted by our contexts and experiences. We all know examples of people who have interpreted their own wishes as being God's will. Yet God is at work in each one of us. In the depths of our born-again souls is the imprint of God's fingerprints. Answer the question without fear and hold the answer with open hands before God.

CALLING AS A MAJOR ROLE

The majority of writing and teaching about vocational discernment in the United States is focused on a person's occupation. We ask variations on the question, "What should I be when I grow up?" with that "be" almost always associated with a particular job. "I always knew I wanted to be a pastor," or "I wanted to be a teacher since I was a kid," or "Music has been my passion for my whole life" are typical of expected responses.

Consider how this view of occupation influences how we approach education. A common mental map of education is "get a degree to get a job." High school juniors are under a lot of pressure to know what career they want to pursue so they can identify what college degree and major they are going to pursue. College students are expected to name a major that leads to a job after college, with the assumption that the college degree will facilitate entry into a well-paid occupation.

What if, instead of viewing an occupation as a goal, we saw it as a context for living out our God-given purpose? The sense of purpose is the internal compass; an occupation or role is the particular path a person walks in a given season of life. The role and the purpose may be closely aligned in an occupation or a person might redefine a role or occupation in a way distinctive to their sense of purpose.

Consider Rob Dixon's occupation as a staff worker and then a supervisor as an example. He sensed a purpose early on toward developing leaders and narrates that, at one time, he would have said this was his calling. Many of us would see Dr. Dixon's original decision to join InterVarsity as a staff worker as him responding to God's calling. Yet the role itself was not so much Dr. Dixon's calling as it was the context through which he began to live out his sense of purpose.

Dr. Dixon's sense of purpose has developed over time, emerging from a variety of aims to a focus on developing leaders to an even more specific focus on developing women and men in ministry partnerships. His role, in the meantime, has shifted and developed as well. As his sense of purpose has focused more on flourishing partnerships, his role has needed to shift as well to better facilitate living into that purpose. Dr. Dixon's new role as a Senior Fellow for the InterVarsity Institute, for example, reflects his and the institution's joint sense that he has something unique to offer and the need for a role that facilitates that contribution.

Some individuals do enter a particular role and find that that role is the place of living out their calling for a lifetime. Think, for example, of pastors who enter the ministry in their twenties and continue for decades in that role. There are also individuals who enter an arena of work and shift their particular job within that area over the course of decades. This seems to be Rob Dixon's pattern. Still other people have a particular occupation and may only gradually begin to see that they are living out their purpose through that role. This was the case for Laura Gordon, the CPA we met in chapter three. With her pastor's help, she came to identify herself as a "marketplace minister," with her occupation being the context in which she could do this work.

Other individuals may shift from role to role for a long season of time, only settling into a major role—in which their distinctive capacities and sense of purpose match the specific needs of the role—in their fifties or sixties. David Douglas, whom we met in chapter five, might be an example of this. He'd had multiple occupations and jobs and, at the time I met him, was in the midst of another life transition. While he didn't have a focus on a single role, he did discern a thread throughout his various roles: engaging with people as what he called a "cultural apologeticist." Still other people may have an occupation that is not an expression of their calling but rather facilitates the functioning of their lives in such a way that they can live out their purpose. An example of this might be a person who works in a particular field to provide financial resources—food, shelter, and so forth—while their passion lies in an area in which they labor without pay.

Think back across your life. What occupations have you considered? Can you identify some aspect of those considerations that reflects the values of your family or of some element of your social location? Might your desire for a particular occupation reflect a sense of purpose? Or perhaps you do not have a clear sense of what would represent a major role for you. If so, you are not alone! How might you reframe your understanding of the very things you are doing now—even as they may not be what you will do for a lifetime—as the current context through which you live out your purpose and in which you are currently being formed for participation in God's work in the world?

CALLING AS MINISTRY COMPETENCIES

When a person is considering any occupation, it is normal to think about exemplars in that field. Architect Frank Gehry is known for a particular approach to buildings. Coco Chanel grew a couture empire on a distinctive stylistic approach. Actor Meryl Streep is known for her gift at inhabiting characters. Producer and director Ava DuVernay is known for telling stories in a distinct manner. Michael Jordan is one the best basketball players and Pelé perhaps the greatest football (or, as we say in the US, soccer) player of all time. William Carey opened the modern missionary movement from Europe, innovating the structure of the "missionary society," and J. Hudson Taylor inaugurated a new era of mission by leaving behind his fellow foreigners in the mission station and going into the interior of China. Similarly, Pete Scazzero is known for his emphasis on emotionally healthy spirituality and Beth Moore is known for her Bible teaching.

Each of these people became known for their distinctive methods and competencies. That methodology did not emerge fully formed and mature, however. Their capacities were developed across time and with much effort. And yet, as we've seen in these pages, in telling the stories of our heroes we tend to skip over the long, complicated, often painful process of developing the skills and values embodied in the work they do.

Consider Rob Dixon's story again. Embedded in his narrative is the history of developing skills. He had multiple experiences that shaped his views of women and men in ministry. One was the specific experience with the pastor who confronted him, which was a turning point, but being confronted about his practice and theology of women in ministry was not a one-time event. He mentioned that "every year someone would raise an objection about women in ministry." A longer conversation with Dr. Dixon would elicit more examples and details about these occurrences.[2] The recurring nature of the conflict was a context that continued to shape Dr. Dixon's sense of purpose and to provide the impetus for

---

[2]For further reflection on this point, see Rob Dixon, *Together in Ministry: Women and Men in Flourishing Partnerships* (Downers Grove, IL: InterVarsity Press, 2021).

continued learning and skill development. He studied and read and thought. He became practiced in articulating a theology of women in ministry. He also underwent personal formation in the midst of this learning; he notes specifically that he was challenged about his tone and attitude in the discussion with the pastor. He had to develop emotional intelligence competencies and continue in character formation.

Dr. Dixon followed up on these formational experiences by doing doctoral work investigating this area of leader development. He began to lead seminars on women and men in ministry partnership. He increased in relevant skills, such as facilitating hard discussions and framing learning experiences. He learned to speak to groups who were theologically committed to women's leadership as well as groups opposed to women in leadership. To watch Rob Dixon in action now is to see a skilled coach and facilitator; this developed over time and through his various roles and experiences.

What natural abilities and talents did God gift you with? What skills have you acquired over time and with experience? God may have formed certain areas of capacity in us through opportunities and life circumstances. Some of this is the redemptive work of God, taking what was intended for our destruction and using it for good. Some of this is the blessing of access to opportunities and open doors for the expression and development of our capacities.

Much of the popular literature from a Reformed-tradition perspective puts an emphasis on a person's gifts, passions, and personality. For example, Rick Warren's popular book *The Purpose Driven Life* emphasizes God's sovereign work in our lives.[3] The related text, *S.H.A.P.E.: Finding and Fulfilling Your Unique Purpose in Life*, specifically explores a person's spiritual gifts, "heart," aptitudes, passions, and experiences.[4] For some people, this approach may be a familiar aspect of their mental map of

---

[3]Rick Warren, *The Purpose Driven Life: What on Earth Am I Here For?*, 10th anniversary ed. (Grand Rapids, MI: Zondervan, 2013).

[4]Erik Rees, *S.H.A.P.E.: Finding and Fulfilling Your Unique Purpose for Life* (Grand Rapids, MI: Zondervan, 2006).

calling. Lean into the benefits of this reflection. While the list of your capacities is not the extent of calling formation, it is a fruitful area of consideration. If God is Creator, then how we are wired is part of God's purposeful equipping for life.

What is needed for people in the early stages of calling development is to experiment. Try things out. A piece of advice I give to young leaders—by *young* here, I mean people under thirty-five—is to make a choice to say yes to any request or opportunity that arises. When a person is young in vocational formation, the opportunities that present themselves are generally of a fairly short duration—a few hours to a few months in length. I've seen people perpetually say no, claiming, "That's not my ministry," and then be frustrated that no opportunities come along. Saying no repeatedly gains them a reputation of saying no rather than a reputation of being available. Say yes and give it a try. We discover what we're crafted for in the process of doing and then reflecting on that doing. Rarely do we know before we try. We develop mature, seasoned gifts and skills with a lot of practice.

There does come a time when the default answer should no longer be yes. When a default yes stops being a reflection of servant-hearted openness and becomes a people-pleasing failure to be faithful to the particularity of what God has given us to carry, it is crucial for us to accept that we cannot do everything. To attempt to meet everyone's needs and expectations is to get in the way of the people who *should* be doing the work. If we exhaust ourselves doing work that is not ours, we will have no energy left over to do what God has created, formed, and called us to do.

Sometimes I encounter people who don't see themselves as having any gifts or skills. Most of the time, when I have the opportunity to talk with these individuals in the context of a community, their community has a more accurate view of their capacities. A human characteristic is to assume that what is joyful and easy for us is just easy—as in, anyone could do it. A community sees the person's capacities for the gifts that they are, having been recipients of those gifts.

The community is also important in tempering our view of our gifts and skills. While some people default to focusing on their limitations, other people default to an inflated sense of competence. Being connected to a community helps us cultivate humility and service. Indeed, it is always for the common good that we are to steward our skills and competencies. Once we begin to build a little kingdom for ourselves, we have stepped out of the family business of God and heirs. The local body of Christ is a grace-gift of God to be the context of our formation and our contribution to God's work.

CALLING AS LEAVING A LEGACY

Think about the legacy left by people of faith—the blessing passed on to subsequent generations as an inheritance. Consider your heroes, those still on this earth and those who have gone on to be present with Jesus, who have inspired you. We see these women and men as people who have demonstrated what it means to live a faithful, godly life. We look at their lives as a model of what we hope to live out in our own.

The heroes of the faith who are most important to us are deeply reflective of our social locations. We think of the heroes who are heroes for our particular group and are often unaware of the heroes of another group. A few heroes are widely known between groups, but many heroes are the pillars of faith in a given community and are not known beyond their local context. The examples that follow draw from a variety of traditions and backgrounds, and their legacies fall into five categories: ministry, character, catalytic, ideation, and organization.[5] Consider, as you read, who the heroes in your context are in each category.

Legacies of ministry. For some people, the legacy they leave is the particular kind of ministry they do. Billy Graham (1918–2018) is a prime example of someone whose public ministry was both significant in its own right and formed a model that other people have followed. The Billy Graham Evangelistic Association's commitment to work with churches

---

[5]These categories are drawn from Clinton, *Strategic Concepts,* 41.

and to not ask for financial offerings at crusades, along with other organizational commitments, established something of a gold standard that
other evangelists and evangelistic ministries followed.

Jarena Lee (1783–1864) was the first woman preacher in the African
Methodist Episcopal Church. A self-taught woman, she was a leading
figure in the Second Great Awakening in the United States, preaching up
and down the mid-Atlantic states for twenty years during a time when
chattel slavery was legal and women of African descent could neither
vote nor own property. Lee's autobiography, the first biography of a Black
woman to be published in the United States, and her ministry blazed a
trail for women and Black leaders, and inspired many in her generation
and the following generations.

Another kind of ministry legacy is that of mentors. These are people
for whom the legacy they leave is the people they helped develop. Hen-
rietta Mears (1890–1963) is one example. As a teacher and longtime
Christian education director at Hollywood Presbyterian Church, she has
been cited as a significant influence on Bill and Vonette Bright (Campus
Crusade), Jim Rayburn (Young Life), and Billy Graham. Hundreds of
young people who came through her ministry went on to spend their
lives engaged in Christian ministry.

Assemblies of God (AG) pastor Jesse Miranda (1937–2019) founded
Alianza de Ministerios Evangélicos Nacionales (AMEN), a multidenomi-
national networking organization bringing together Latino/a Pente-
costals and evangelicals. Through his work as a denominational leader—
Miranda served as an AG presbyter for forty-one years—organizer, and
educator, he mentored and developed hundreds of Latino/a leaders, profoundly influencing Latino/a evangelicalism in the United States.

For some communities, the concept of calling is limited to this arena
of engagement; calling is God's appointment of a person to be involved
in a formal ministry role. Heroes of the faith are the women and men
who have planted and pastored churches, engaged as an evangelist or
missionary, or in some other way overtly engaged in a Christian ministry.
This is, indeed, one important category of legacy; it is not the only one.

The body of Christ needs a multiplicity of expression. God calls people to engage with God's work in a variety of ways, only some of which are formal ministry.

Legacies of character. The legacy some Christians leave is the model of their life. These people are not perfect but they live in such a way that other people are moved to emulate them. Mother Teresa (1910–1997) is one example whom many people cite. Her years of persistent service, her dedication to the poorest of the poor, and her deep commitment to the dignity of all people won her a hearing even from people who don't agree with her theology and beliefs. Watchman Nee (1903–1972) and Dietrich Bonhoeffer (1906–1945) are both examples of people whose faith in Jesus led them to stand in opposition to the ruling regimes of their countries.

A legacy of character can also be found in a person's children. Susanna Wesley (1669–1742) is one historical example of this kind of contribution. Her parenting played a very significant part in the Christian formation of Charles and John Wesley. In fact, her discipleship of her children was, in many ways, the model on which John Wesley's bands were founded. Many fathers and mothers, grandmothers, grandfathers, aunts, and uncles leave a deep and lasting impression in the lives of children they help to shape and shepherd. Other people are not biological family, but, as spiritual parents and friends, and sometimes coaches, pastors, or teachers, they deeply influence the formation of the lives of young people around them.

Prayer is a key spiritual disciple of those who leave a legacy of character. Brother Lawrence (1614–1691) is known for prayer without ceasing, or "practicing the presence of God," as articulated in the letters his colleague Joseph de Beaufort gathered and published.[6] Joon Gon Kim (1925–2009) was the founder of Korea Campus Crusade for Christ and was known for his regular habit of fasting and prayer. Barbara Williams-Skinner (1943–), along with being a public policy adviser and cofounder

---

[6]Brother Lawrence, *The Practice of the Presence of God: Being Conversations and Letters of Nicholas Herman of Lorraine (Brother Lawrence)* (Mansfield Center, CT: Martino Publishing, 2016).

of the Skinner Leadership Institute, is known for her passion for prayer.[7] And many a church community is blessed by the gray-haired (and not-so-gray-haired) prayer warriors whose practice of intercession forms a pillar of the community.

Many people whose legacies flow from their character and the intimacy of their relationship with Jesus will not be well known outside their circle of personal friends and acquaintances. The influence of their lives ripples outward from the lives they touched. The full extent of their impact will not be known this side of eternity.

Catalytic legacies. Some people leave a catalytic legacy in the change that they bring about in communities, societies, organizations, and countries. These individuals may be change agents who address injustices in society, churches, and organizations. Martin Luther King Jr. (1929–1968) is a well-known example of a person whose legacy is in the fight for social change. As a pastor and a community organizer, King sought to address what he saw as the three dominant issues confronting the people of the United States: racism, militarism, and poverty.[8] His legacy lives on both in the social changes he helped to foster and in the example he set of his faith motivating him to engage change.

There are many other examples of leaders whose faith motivated them to engage with and change some societal issue. Quaker Lucretia Mott (1793–1880) was an early abolitionist, women's rights activist, and social reformer who was an outspoken supporter of William Lloyd Garrison's American Anti-Slavery Society and who, together with Elizabeth Cady Stanton, called together the famous Seneca Falls Convention in New York in 1848, which was dedicated to women's suffrage. Toyohiko Kagawa (1888–1960), a Japanese Protestant minister and peace activist, was deeply committed to the poor, identifying with and

---

[7]"Barbara Williams-Skinner on Power and Prayer," interview by Mark Labberton, January 27, 2021, video, 44:52, https://youtu.be/HlgunCaHIwA.

[8]King gave many speeches beyond the most famous "I Have a Dream" speech. His speech "Beyond Vietnam: A Time to Break Silence" at Riverside Church in New York City on April 4, 1967, directly confronted militarism. On April 14, 1967, he spoke at Stanford University concerning race, poverty, and economic injustice in a speech titled "The Other America," which he also delivered to various audiences throughout 1967.

living among them for his lifetime.[9] Roman Catholic Archbishop Óscar Romero (1917–1980) courageously stood against a corrupt and vicious regime in his home of El Salvador and was martyred as a consequence. The Roman Catholic faith of César Chávez (1927–1993) inspired and sustained his lifelong work for justice for farm workers in the United States.[10]

Baseball legend Jackie Robinson (1919–1972) is perhaps best known for being the first African American to play in the Whites-only Major League Baseball, breaking the color barrier when he was signed by the Brooklyn Dodgers in 1947. Less known is the role Robinson's Christian faith played in influencing his life choices. It was his faith that prompted him to persevere as a trailblazer and catalyst for change in society beyond baseball, actively engaging in the civil rights movement of the 1950s and 1960s.[11]

Another arena of catalytic legacy is people who pioneer new means of ministry engagement or open new fields of endeavor. A number of notable pioneering educators fall into this category. For example, Robert Raikes (1736–1811) was an English philanthropist and Anglican layman who began what came to be known as the Sunday school movement. It started in the 1780s with four women who held weekly Bible classes in their homes for children, and by 1831 there were over a million children being educated for the first time in these schools during a period when there was no general education and most children worked six days a week.[12] Another educator, Booker T. Washington (1856–1915), was the founder of the Tuskegee Institute in Alabama, a teachers' college and trade school for newly freed persons of African descent. Washington

[9]Robert M. Fukada, "The Legacy of Toyohiko Kagawa," *International Bulletin of Missionary Research* 12, no. 1 (January 1988): 18-22.

[10]Roger Bruns, *Cesar Chavez: A Biography* (Santa Barbara, CA: Greenwood Publishing Group, 2005).

[11]For more on Jackie Robinson's Christian faith, see Michael G. Long and Chris Lamb, *Jackie Robinson: A Spiritual Biography: The Faith of a Boundary-Breaking Hero* (Louisville, KY: Westminster John Knox, 2017); and Ed Henry, *42 Faith: The Rest of the Jackie Robinson Story* (Nashville: Thomas Nelson, 2017).

[12]Ruth A. Tucker, *Daughters of the Church: Women and Ministry from New Testament Times to Present* (Grand Rapids, MI: Zondervan, 1987), 249-51.

believed economic and social prosperity would come through education and hard work.[13]

One more area of pioneering work—one that is perhaps more commonly referenced and certainly often honored in our churches—is that of missionaries working outside the United States. Adoniram (1788–1850) and Ann Judson (1789–1826) were among the first "foreign missionaries" sent from the United States, traveling first to India and then to Burma (present-day Myanmar) in 1813. Ann's translation of the Gospel of Matthew into Thai was the first portion of Scripture ever rendered in that language.[14] Adoniram spent thirty-seven years on the field, translating the Bible into Burmese and seeing the establishment of the church in a previously unreached people.[15]

Eliza Davis George (1879–1980) was born in Texas to formerly enslaved parents. Despite organizational and social opposition, she traveled to Africa, arriving in Liberia in 1914, to begin many long decades as an evangelist and church planter. When she was in her sixties, the Baptist mission that had supported her tried to forcibly retire George. She turned to supporters, who set up clubs to fund her return to Liberia, where she continued to trek from village to village until she was in her nineties. An entire denominational expression of the Christian church in Liberia has its roots in George's ministry.

Elizabeth "Betty" Greene (1920–1997) also pioneered new paths in missions. After learning to fly as a teenager, she served with the Women Airforce Service Pilots (WASP) during World War II, but her heart was for missions. Greene presented the vision for missionary aviation in an article in a Christian magazine, which led to a group of pilots contacting her and inviting her to join them in the founding of what became Mission Aviation Fellowship.

---

[13]For more on Washington's life and faith, see Booker T. Washington, *Up from Slavery: An Autobiography* (Auckland, NZ: Floating Press, 2009).

[14]Dana L. Robert, "Judson, Ann ('Nancy') (Hasseltine)," in *Biographical Dictionary of Christian Missions*, ed. Gerald H. Anderson (New York: Macmillan Reference, 1998), 346.

[15]William H. Brackney, "The Legacy of Adoniram Judson," *International Bulletin of Missionary Research* 22, no. 3 (July 1998): 122-27.

Catalytic legacies may also be left by artists whose creative break-throughs bring about innovation. Some artists use words as their primary medium. Fanny Crosby (1820–1915) was the author of more than nine thousand hymns and gospel songs, including "Blessed Assurance" and "To God Be the Glory." At a time when women were not allowed to preach or teach the Bible in a church service, her hymns offered sermons for the soul that continue to preach to this day. Guatemalan poet-theologian Julia Esquivel Velásquez (1930–2019) used her skill with words to craft powerful testimonies and challenges in her fight for indigenous peoples.[16] Spoken-word artists might be a contemporary example of a word-based artistic innovation.

Other artistic legacies include the work of visual artists working in a variety of mediums, such as Maximino Cerezo Barredo (1932–), who is referred to as a "painter of liberation" for the ways in which he reflects current events in his murals portraying biblical stories, or Kim Ki-Chang (1914–2001), a traditional ink painter whose work includes a series of paintings depicting scenes from the life of Jesus interpreted in the style of traditional Korean culture.

Legacies of ideas. Researchers, promoters, and writers contribute legacies around ideas. Researchers study issues and make sense of complex issues. Writers capture ideas and experiences, putting them into a form that influences the lives and thinking of people. Promoters are able to articulate ideas and strategies in ways that resonate with people and allow those ideas to be put into action.

The contributions of writers can live on after them for many years, even decades. Ecuadorian theologian and missiologist René Padilla (1930–2021) profoundly influenced mission in the Americas, coining the term *misión integral* (in English: "integral mission") to describe an approach to ministry that takes seriously the relationship between

---

[16]See, for example, Velásquez's books of poetry: Julia Esquivel Velásquez, *Threatened with Resurrection (Amenazado de Resurrección): Prayers and Poems from an Exiled Guatemalan* (Elgin, IL.: Brethren Press, 1982); and Julia Esquivel Velásquez, *The Certainty of Spring: Poems by a Guatemalan in Exile* (Washington, DC: Ecumenical Program on Central America and the Caribbean, 1993).

proclamation of the gospel and living out the gospel in justice.[17] American Baptist preacher and theologian Howard Thurman (1899– 1981) strongly influenced a generation of civil rights activists, including Martin Luther King Jr., with his deeply spiritual writing that articulates a theology of nonviolence.[18]

Phoebe Palmer (1807–1874) was a promoter who is sometimes re- ferred to as the "Mother of the Holiness Movement." Her informal Tuesday prayer meetings, conducted over the course of some twenty years, and her writing on holiness deeply influenced a generation of Methodist ministers. Historian Ruth Tucker notes of Palmer's ministry, "At the time of her death, she was credited with having brought some 25,000 people to Christ for salvation."[19]

Organizational legacies. Another arena of legacy-leaving is organiza- tional. Many of our heroes of the faith are people who have planted churches, started denominations, founded schools, and initiated new mission organizations. Martin Luther (1482–1546) and John Wesley (1703–1791) both began as ministers seeking renewal in their respective church settings and ended up founding movements. William (1829–1912) and Catherine Booth (1829–1890) founded the Salvation Army to work among the poor and addicted in the cities of Victorian England. Frus- trated at the resistance to abolition and the continued segregation in existing churches, Richard Allen (1760–1831) established the African Methodist Episcopal Church, the first predominantly Black church in the United States. A. B. Simpson (1843–1919), a Canadian preacher, founded the Christian and Missionary Alliance, a denomination emphasizing world evangelization. A fellow Canadian, Aimee Semple McPherson (1890–1944), was a well-known traveling evangelist in the early days of the Pentecostal movement in the United States before settling in Los

---

[17]For an articulation of a theology of mission, see C. René Padilla, *Mission Between the Times: Essays on the Kingdom*, rev. ed. (Carlisle, UK: Langham Publishing, 2010).

[18]Dr. King is supposed to have always traveled with a copy of Thurman's book *Jesus and the Dispos- sessed*. For a rendition of this story, see Henry Louis Gates Jr., *The Black Church: This Is Our Story, This Is Our Song* (New York: Penguin Press, 2021) or the second episode of the PBS documentary of the same name.

[19]Tucker, *Daughters of the Church*, 263.

Angeles, where she started a church—Angelus Temple—that grew into a denomination, the International Church of the Foursquare Gospel.

Mary McLeod Bethune (1875–1955), the child of formerly enslaved persons, desired to be a teaching missionary in Africa but was rejected by her denominational mission board based on their policy barring Black people from serving as missionaries. With this door closed to her, Bethune turned her prodigious capacities to addressing the inequities in educational opportunities for Black people in the United States, founding a school that is today Bethune-Cookman University. Ever an entrepreneur and activist, Bethune founded many organizations as well, including the National Council of Negro Women, for which she served as the founding president. Her activism and commitment to education and race relations brought her to national attention, and in 1936, President Franklin D. Roosevelt named her the director of Negro Affairs of the National Youth Administration, making Bethune the highest-ranking Black women in the United States government at that time. In 1940, Bethune became vice president of the National Association for the Advancement of Colored People, a position she held for the remainder of her life. Bethune's story is a model of a life motivated by faith and perseverance that turns from a closed door to seek other avenues for fruitful service.

COMMITTING TO LIFELONG DEVELOPMENT

Notice how the four elements of calling—life purpose, major role, competencies, and legacy—are all at work in Rob Dixon's life and ministry, and how these have developed across a lifetime with indications that further development is yet ahead. Dr. Dixon's life purpose centers around the development of leaders, particularly flourishing ministry partnerships between women and men. His major role within InterVarsity and his developing role with the InterVarsity Institute are a context for this work. The skills and concepts Dixon has developed through his scholarship and experience offer unique gifts for this work. He has begun leaving a legacy. What the ultimate legacy of his life will be can be guessed at but not yet known. Yet the fruit of his life's work can be seen in the people he has supervised and helped to develop according to God's purpose in their lives. He is in the midst of influencing multiple organizations who are seeking to foster healthy ministry partnerships among women and men; his ideas and strategies offer a way forward for these teams and organizations. His life to this point suggests his legacy will involve aspects of ministry, ideation, and organizational change.

Dr. Dixon is unique in his particular giftings and callings, and he, along with the other individuals who have contributed their calling stories to this book, are among the thousands and millions of followers of Jesus who seek to faithfully respond to God's invitation to participation in God's work in the world. Instead of focusing on fruitfulness, let us focus on faithfulness. Let us cultivate a mindset of lifelong development.

We do not know what legacy we are going to leave. Even at the end of our lives, we cannot fully or completely assess what our legacy will be. But here is a key: our job is not to leave a legacy! Our task is to be faithful. God is at work in the world. The mission of God is the ultimate legacy. Our small part is a meaningful contribution. We will not see our legacy with absolute clarity until we see from the perspective of eternity. We cannot even fully know the legacies of the well-known people whom I have named here. Yet we can see indications. We can seek to be faithful to steward what is ours to do.

QUESTIONS FOR REFLECTION AND DISCUSSION

1. What are the foundations of purpose in your own life? What early life experiences shaped your understanding of yourself and your understanding of God's work in the world?

2. How have your life experiences shaped in you a sense that God has God's hand on you for a particular purpose?

3. What, at this point in your Christian journey, do you see as the essence of that purpose?

EXPLORING A BIBLICAL NARRATIVE: PAUL

1. What do we know about Paul's early life? Read Acts 22:3 and Philippians 3:5. Consider Paul's childhood and adolescent years. How do you imagine these early experiences shaped and equipped him for the work God would call him to?

2. We know Paul grew up in Tarsus, a city that was a Roman colony. We know that he was a Roman citizen (Acts 16:37; 22:25; 23:27). We also know that this citizenship was not part of how Paul identified himself to the church in Philippi, although that city was also a Roman colony (see Philippians 3:5-6). How was Paul's Roman citizenship a resource given to him to facilitate the work God had called him to?

3. Read Acts 9:1-19. Look carefully at the passage for what was communicated to Paul as instructions. What did Paul know in that moment? Consider his retelling of this event (Acts 22:3-21 and Acts 26: 2-23). What do you see as Paul's understanding of God's revelation to him of his life purpose?

4. Read 2 Timothy 4:7-8. What was Paul's sense of fulfillment? What do you see as the fulfillment of Paul's God-given purpose? What legacy did he leave behind?

SUGGESTIONS FOR FURTHER READING

Bill, J. Brent. *Sacred Compass: The Way of Spiritual Discernment*. Brewster, MA: Paraclete Press, 2012.

Stoltzfus, Tony. *The Calling Journey: Mapping the Stages of a Leader's Life Call*. Redding, CA: Coach22 Bookstore, LLC, 2010.

CONCLUSION

Finish Well

Well done, good and faithful servant.

MATTHEW 25:23 NIV

I have fought the good fight, I have finished the race, I have kept the faith. From now on there is reserved for me the crown of righteousness, which the Lord, the righteous judge, will give me on that day, and not only to me but also to all who have longed for his appearing.

2 TIMOTHY 4:7-8

"BEGIN WITH THE END IN MIND," wrote author and leadership coach Stephen Covey as one of the principles of highly effective leaders.[1] As followers of Jesus, we have an end in mind: we want to finish well. We want to stand before God and hear, "Well done, good and faithful servant" (Matthew 25:23 NIV).

When I was in my twenties, I yearned to live a life that "mattered." I wanted to be like one of the heroes of the faith: people who had responded to God's calling and had, over the course of their lives,

---

[1]Stephen Covey, *Seven Habits of Highly Effective People* (New York: Fireside Book, 1990).

accomplished great things. I set off after college to be a missionary, expecting to change the world for Jesus! My early ministry experience was nothing like what I expected. Yes, I had some great learning experiences, and I have some entertaining stories to tell (having tea with the assistant to the Russian archbishop in Tomsk, finding myself in the middle of a riot in Belgrade, preaching for the first time on the streets of Bogotá). But I came away from those five years of full-time ministry with a sense of having accomplished very little. Certainly, I was not living the extraordinary life I yearned for.

A major turning point in my own development came as I was working on my master of divinity degree. I took a course looking at the lifelong development of leaders. Coming to understand calling as a lifelong process was an important step in my formation. I certainly wasn't happy in my ambitious twenties with the thought of waiting a lifetime for the kind of meaningful work I desired to do. I wanted to get busy changing the world *now*! The idea that God had formational work to do in me was frustrating. At the same time, beginning to see my development in lifelong perspective was also encouraging. I came to understand something that I went on to share with students for years: if there is a deep desire in your heart, it may be in your heart because God put it there with the intention of fulfilling it.

To finish well is to have lived a life of cooperating with the transformational work of the Spirit in our lives. Finishing well comes from a lifetime of attending to what God is doing in us and our community. It is not our responsibility to fulfill God's purpose on our own through our efforts; it is our responsibility to respond to God's invitation and to take the next faithful step.

Consider Nehemiah's wall as a metaphor for God's work in the world and God's invitation to participate in that work.

In the first chapter of the book of Nehemiah, certain men from Judah arrive in the Persian capital, Susa. Nehemiah asks them about the Jews who survived captivity and about Jerusalem. They answer, "The survivors there in the province who escaped captivity are in great trouble and shame; the wall of Jerusalem is broken down, and its gates have been destroyed by fire" (Nehemiah 1:3). Nehemiah's response to this news is deep grief.

Nehemiah then plans to travel to Jerusalem to do something about the shattered wall and the scattered people. In preparation for this task, he asks King Artaxerxes for a letter to the keeper of the king's forest allowing Nehemiah to acquire the timber he will need to rebuild the gates of the city (Nehemiah 2:8). There is no record of Nehemiah questioning the visitors from Judah, but we can infer from the specificity of the requests made that Nehemiah knew what resources would be present on site and what resources needed to be obtained elsewhere.

When Nehemiah arrives in Jerusalem and reveals his purpose to the people there, they respond with an enthusiastic, "Let us start building!" (Nehemiah 2:18). They were, says the text, committed to the common good. Other people were not. Nehemiah 2:19 reads, "But when Sanballat the Horonite and Tobiah the Ammonite official, and Geshem the Arab heard of it, they mocked and ridiculed us, saying, 'What is this that you are doing? Are you rebelling against the king?'" These three critics would continue to ridicule the project, attempting to halt the rebuilding of the walls by trickery and threat and force.

In Nehemiah 3, we have a record of the people and families who rebuilt the wall. From here to here, so-and-so built the wall. This family rebuilt the Sheep Gate. This other family rebuilt the Horse Gate. Another group repaired a different portion of the wall. This is a chapter we tend to skip when reading Nehemiah, as it seems, at first glance, to be an uninteresting list of workers. Yet the presence of this roll call is important to the narrative.

Think of Nehemiah's story as a representation of God's work in the world. God sees creation is in ruins. The image-bearers God created to flourish are "in great trouble and shame." The cultural systems God created to shelter societies are broken down. The gates where elders met to transact business and make decisions are destroyed.

God is actively engaged in the world. Unlike Nehemiah, God does not require the activity and resources of humanity. God is enough. Yet, like with Nehemiah, God draws people into active participation in the building. Each person and each *ethnē* is invited to an assigned place of building God's wall.

Archaeologists have identified what they believe to be Nehemiah's wall. It is a wall built of rubble. The people built with the materials available; those materials were the remains of the old wall. Likewise, God uses the materials that are available today: the people and cultures and resources present in a given context. God uses this content even when it is "rubble" left over from years of destruction. God doesn't reject the rubble as unfit for the building and instead bring in pristine, newly quarried stone. God is a God of redemption. God restores the broken places, as Isaiah said:

> Your ancient ruins shall be rebuilt;
>   you shall raise up the foundations of many generations;
> you shall be called the repairer of the breach,
>   the restorer of streets to live in. (Isaiah 58:12)

As well as using the available rubble, God supplies resources that are not present in our contexts. As Nehemiah had the foresight to procure timber, so God also provides what's required to build what is beyond our human capacity. The literal gates of a city was the place where elders met to conduct business and rule on matters of justice (see Genesis 23:8-11; Deuteronomy 25:7; Joshua 20:4; Ruth 4:1-12; Esther 3:1-3). Destroyed gates of the physical city parallel the destruction of social structures. Just as Nehemiah brought resources for the rebuilding of gates that gave protection and were the location of governance, so also today are social structures rebuilt with the grace-gifts of God.

In the midst of the building, we receive ridicule and threats as did the people building Nehemiah's wall. Individuals and groups who, like Sanballat, Tobiah, and Geshem, benefit from the status quo of human brokenness will resist the building of God's people. These powers will use the same means—accusations of treason to duly constituted systems of law (Nehemiah 2:19), jeering criticism of the "rubbish" that constitutes our lives and cultures (Nehemiah 4:2), and mocking assessments of the inadequacy of our building (Nehemiah 4:3). These powers will work to bring confusion (Nehemiah 4:8) and plot for our death (Nehemiah 4:11) to stop the work. And when our participation in God's work prospers, those same powers will attempt to co-opt us individually and as societies (Nehemiah 6:2).

Just as the people needed Nehemiah's wisdom in the process of the work, so we need the wisdom of the Holy Spirit to participate in God's work. God offers an invitation to a specific place of building. We are assigned to the work that has been identified as ours and for which we have been shaped (Ephesians 2:10).

While Nehemiah's wall was a physical barrier around a specific city, we are living stones, chosen by God and precious, being built into a spiritual house (1 Peter 2:4-5) and resting on the cornerstone: Jesus. We are both the builders with God and the building being constructed. We look toward that holy city, the new Jerusalem, whose gates will be eternally open and will welcome the peoples of every nation (Revelation 21:25-26).

As we walk the journey of a life seeking after God's purposes, we join a crowd of witnesses who have walked this way before us. "I lift my eyes up to the hills," the pilgrims sang on their way to Jerusalem (Psalm 121:1). "I lift my eyes up to the skyscrapers of the business district and the towers of government" say the pilgrim Jesus-followers. "I lift my eyes up to Stone Mountain and to Lookout Mountain," say the justice-seeking Jesus-followers, paraphrasing Dr. Martin Luther King Jr. "I lift my eyes up to the ivory tower of the academy," say the academic Jesus-followers. "From where will my help come?" (Psalm 121:1). Our help comes from the Lord, the maker of heaven and earth. We can say with Paul, "I am confident of this, that the one who began a good work among you will bring it to completion by the day of Jesus Christ" (Philippians 1:6).

This book has been an invitation to self-reflection in the midst of your journey. What do you see now that you had not seen before? Can you recognize God's fingerprints in the circumstances of your life? Is there an emerging sense of purpose? Do you have hints about roles and skills that you have begun to develop that might be the context for living out God's purposes in your life? My hope is that this text has offered a space for encounter with God. As we sit in the presence of the Spirit, God moves us to see and to realize. God continues to work transformation in our lives. We continue to develop and grow to be more fully human, more fully who we were created to be.

I conclude with this point I regularly suggest to my students. Hold your dreams and yearnings before God with an open hand. Being faithful now—particularly faithful in the "very little" (Luke 16:10)—is your investment in developing toward God's purpose for a lifetime. If the general pattern of your life is to get up in the morning and, to the best of your ability, be faithful to God, then you can't miss God. Sometimes "the best of my ability" is really terrible. I believe God is big enough to meet us in our worst as well as our best. God gives us light for the next faithful step. If you take that step, and keep taking that next faithful step, then, again, I don't think there's any way to miss God's purposes in your life.

Radical grace reached out to you and won you for Jesus in the midst of all the good and terrible circumstances of your life. Radical grace calls you to engage with God's work even though God does not need our inept efforts to accomplish the work. Radical grace sees you fully as who you are even when you do not see yourself. Radical grace gives you resources to participate in God's mission, some of which are your socially constructed, adopted, and assigned identities. The place of your contribution is exactly where you stand in all of your glory and shame. Radical grace welcomes you as you are. Radical grace says, "Before I formed you in the womb, I knew you" (Jeremiah 1:5). Radical grace says, "Here, join me in building. This spot is reserved for you." Radical grace pours out the power of the Spirit to build with the labor of human hands.

God calls you on the way. You are on a journey that began even before you were aware of God. This journey will not end in this life. We look for the day when we stand before God, bringing our lives as an offering. We look for the day we will hear, "Well done, good and faithful servant" (Matthew 25:21 NIV).

GENERAL INDEX

SCRIPTURE INDEX